Praise for *Among Tigers*

"**This is a tale of high adventure.** Capturing and then tracking tigers raises one's heart rate like nothing else. On foot in the forest, their presence is terrifying. Yet some of this book takes place in the corridors of power. There, politicians can help—or pose more of a threat than a poacher. Karanth is at home in both these worlds. He brings science to tiger conservation, confronts the managers and politicians alike, and never forgets the needs of the local people who must live with tigers."

—**Stuart L. Pimm**,
President, Saving Nature,
and author of *The Balance of Nature?*

"Ullas Karanth describes his evolution from scientist to conservationist and fills one with hope that science can show a way through the thicket of competing political and commercial interests and ultimately allow a way for wild tigers and people to coexist."

—**John Robinson**,
Joan L. Tweedy Chair in Conservation Strategy,
Wildlife Conservation Society

"There is no creature more magnificent than the tiger, and there is no scientist who knows it better than Ullas Karanth. In this richly observed and deeply felt book, **Karanth leads us through the joys of the forest and the perils of the forestry bureaucracy as his life has intertwined with the lives of great cats.** Despite all the factors piled against tiger survival, it will give you some hope."

—**David Quammen**,
author of *Monster of God* and *Spillover*

"This unique and vividly written book by one of world's finest wildlife biologists is a compelling read. *Among Tigers* is many things at once: a fascinating personal memoir from the man who spearheaded change in protecting tigers in Asia, particularly India; a wonderfully clear account of major issues in top-level conservation science; and a humane account of the wild tiger's precarious position at this moment of crisis for nature everywhere. Karanth makes a compelling case that humanity needs to save tigers for its own good."

—**Ruth Padel**,
Professor of Poetry, King's College, London,
and author of *Tigers in Red Weather* and *Darwin: A Life in Poems*

"In this remarkable story, Ullas Karanth shows how sound science and a deep compassion for wildlife and people can win an enduring place for tigers in the face of the gravest political obstacles and modernization."

—**David Western**,
former Director of Kenya Wildlife Service and author of *We Alone*

"**This book is a must-read for anyone interested in the science and conservation of wild tigers in the last five decades.** It also highlights ignorance of the new forest bureaucracies that now rule the land of the tiger without any vision whatsoever."

—**Valmik Thapar**,
conservationist and author of *Tiger Fire* and *Saving Wild India*

"In *Among Tigers*, Ullas Karanth walks the reader through his unique, lived experience—a fifty-year personal journey from reluctant engineer to farmer, biologist, and finally one of the world's foremost tiger conservationists. . . . **Karanth's singular, lucid account leaves us convinced there is hope for the tiger's future. This book is a must-read for tiger fans.**"

—**Mel Sunquist**,
coauthor of *Tiger Moon* (with Fiona Sunquist)

"Drawn to nature since childhood, Ullas Karanth became the first person in India to radio-track its fabled tigers. He continued studying them for decades, and **his book takes us with him down tropical forest paths to gain insights about Asia's most powerful carnivore—often at startlingly close range**. Yet what distinguishes *Among Tigers* is the way it also brings readers deep into the realities of conservation in a crowded, rapidly developing country."

—Douglas Chadwick,
author of *Four-Fifths a Grizzly* and *The Wolverine Way*

"Karanth takes us on a roller-coaster ride through the jungles of South India, alternatingly describing his detailed fieldwork and the life of tigers versus the messy world of tiger politics—regionally, nationally, and internationally. Mincing no words, **Karanth makes the case for science-based conservation of tigers and the need for hard, grind-it-out fieldwork, but also explains why science is not enough**. A great read and a great story by a person who dedicated his life to the tigers of India."

—Dale Miquelle,
Coordinator, Tiger Program
of Wildlife Conservation Society

"Ullas Karanth, world-renowned tiger expert, lays bare the hardscrabble struggles through his single-minded pursuit to save a majestic species. From the science of tiger tracking to the dirty politics of corrupt bureaucrats, you will almost feel like you are among tigers in the Nagarahole jungle. Karanth has no patience for urban idealistic tiger lovers or overfunded, underperforming, faraway organizations. Based on his decades of fighting for tigers, his prescriptions for conservation stem from the reality on the ground."

—Ruth DeFries,
Professor, Dennings Chair in Sustainable Development,
Columbia University, and author of *What Would Nature Do?*

"*Among Tigers* is one of the most engaging pieces of nonfiction I have ever read.** Good science and entertaining writing seldom come from the same person, but author Ullas Karanth is an exception, fascinating the reader with dramatic scenes that range from adventures capturing and filming wild tigers in Asian jungles to legal battles in Indian courtrooms and political influence and intrigue in the halls of government."

—James D. Nichols,
Emeritus Scientist, USGS Eastern Ecological Science Center

"In this autobiographical account, the world's foremost tiger conservationist explains that brilliant science alone won't save tigers. No less essential are political and media savvy, a skin tough enough to shed calumny of any kind, and a stubbornness before which even bureaucracies must yield. To all these qualities, Ullas Karanth adds one more: the ability to tell his own story—and that of the charismatic predator to which he has dedicated his life—with penetrating insight, clarity, and verve."

—William deBuys,
author of *The Last Unicorn* and *The Trail to Kanjiroba*

"One of India's 'midnight's children' who grew up in tiger country to become India's most acclaimed tiger ecologist, Ullas Karanth exquisitely captures the grandeur of the apex predator as it elegantly glides through the forest, as well as the abased political conflicts and struggles that have so often undermined this most magnificent species' salvation. With acute insights and elegant prose, Dr. Karanth's private experiences dealing with the dichotomy between conservation theory and conservation practice, and public debates ranging from landscape protection to tiger tourism, render *Among Tigers* to be **a must-read for everyone who cares deeply about the future of the world's most popular animal.**"

—Thomas S. Kaplan,
Cofounder of Panthera

AMONG TIGERS

FIGHTING TO BRING BACK
ASIA'S BIG CATS

K. ULLAS KARANTH

CHICAGO
REVIEW
PRESS

Published by Chicago Review Press Incorporated
814 North Franklin Street
Chicago, Illinois 60610
ISBN 978-1-64160-654-7

Library of Congress Control Number: 2022942658

Interior photos are from the author's collection unless otherwise noted.
Interior design: Nord Compo

Printed in the United States of America
5 4 3 2 1

To my wife Prathibha, who stood with me through it all,
And to my daughter Krithi, who made it all worthwhile.

CONTENTS

FOREWORD,
BY GEOFFREY C. WARD

I'VE BEEN LUCKY ENOUGH to know Ullas Karanth for more than three decades. I first met him in early February 1990, while on assignment for *National Geographic*. He was just beginning his pioneering work radio-tracking tigers and leopards in Nagarahole National Park in the Southwestern Indian state of Karnataka.

He had already shown that there was simply not enough prey in the Indian National Parks he studied to support anything like the numbers of tigers some of their directors claimed. And now, just within the last month, he had managed to immobilize, collar and release four tigers for radio tracking—the first Indian researcher ever to do so.

During that first visit he invited me to ride along with him in his battered green Suzuki as he drove first to one high point and then another, stopping to sweep his antenna above his head, hoping to locate one or another of his collared cats through his headphones.

He and I seemed to hit it off. Ullas was then, as he is now, utterly serious about science and uncompromising about conservation, but also mordantly amused by things within and beyond his chosen field.

He seemed to understand that accompanying a radio-tracker as he patiently listens for beeps only he can hear is not a spectator sport, and after I'd driven with him two or three mornings, he was kind enough one afternoon to climb with me up a lofty watchtower that overlooked a waterhole in the heart of the park.

Here are my notes of what I saw.

Four broad firelines had been cut through the gray-green jungle, and waiting there while the late afternoon shadows lengthened was something like attending an infinitely complex tennis match, my head swiveling back and forth from clearing to clearing as one by one the animals emerged for their evening drink. Each species had its own way of approaching the water. Sambar and chital clung to the tree line, ears twitching with anxiety. Barking deer, red-brown and little larger than cocker spaniels, undulated through the grass, heads down as if moving through waves. Three wild boar raced for the water, snorting as they went and scattering two peahens. A leopard appeared out of nowhere and disappeared as suddenly and silently as he came.

Larger animals came, too. A bull gaur materialized at the water's edge, his body a dark, daunting wall of muscle out of all proportion to his small head and tiny, stockinged feet. As he lowered his horns to drink, mynah birds flitted on and off his massive shoulder.

Then, just at dusk, a young bull elephant splashed into the water, drank his fill, somehow sensed my presence, whirled around and around in melodramatic fury, flapping his ears and trumpeting all the while, then crashed off through the brush.

I've never forgotten that afternoon, never failed to be grateful to Ullas for sharing it with me. No subsequent visit to any jungle anywhere in India has ever given me as vivid a sense of what her forests had once been like and what, if science and rational management were applied, they could one day be again.

As a teenager in the mid-1950s I had lived in New Delhi where my father worked for the Ford Foundation and where I'd done some amateurish hunting, fascinated by the jungle but blissfully unaware of how bleak the prospects for India's wildlife then seemed. I'd come back to India forty-odd years later as a writer, not a hunter, still fascinated by those forests but now drawn to tiger wallahs, the handful of men whose mission was to restore the tiger's world to something like what it once had been. And so, over the months and years that followed that first visit to Nagarahole, I kept track of Ullas. I visited Karnataka twice on assignment to report what he and the extraordinary band of volunteers he'd gathered around him were doing, and I met with him over single-malt whiskey at my New York home twice a year when he visited the

Bronx Zoo headquarters of the Wildlife Conservation Society whose India program he headed.

Among Tigers is his lively personal chronicle of the years during which he became what his mentor George Schaller has called him, "the best tiger biologist in the world." The ingenious methods of monitoring animal population densities he and his colleagues developed—incorporating camera traps, line transect sampling, and occupancy modeling, all clearly explained here—are now employed in tiger range countries throughout Asia. Simultaneously, Ullas also became one of India's most effective conservationists. He and his fellow citizens have used their constitutional rights to legally fight for the diversion of roads through protected areas, and closure of a vast strip mine that was ripping apart Kudremukh National Park in the heart of the biodiverse Western Ghats. They also developed a model voluntary resettlement plan which, without pressure or intimidation, has persuaded some two thousand families to leave prime tiger habitats and begin new and better lives beyond their borders.

The obstacles Ullas overcame accomplishing all this are nearly as extraordinary as the accomplishments themselves. A mob burned his Suzuki and destroyed his field camp in Nagarahole. He's been taken to court too many times to count.

Ullas, who has never suffered fools gladly, has sadly had to deal with more than his share of them: tabloid journalists willing to distort facts about his work to sell papers; forest ministers who knew nothing about the forests in their charge; venal local officials more interested in siphoning off funds than saving wildlife; Central Government officials who stubbornly refused to consider fresh approaches to long-standing problems; international organizations that lavish funds with little understanding of how they will be used—or misused; and living-room conservationists more interested in the fate of individual tigers—even if they have killed people—than in the survival of the species as a whole.

Through it all he has remained an optimist, committed to his cause, convinced that, if properly defended and managed, India's forests can potentially hold ten to fifteen thousand tigers, three to five times the current estimate of around three thousand.

When he and I first became friends all those years ago, neither of us had grandchildren. He now has two. I have four. If, in the distant future, our grandchildren's grandchildren are still able to see tigers in the wild, it will be in no small measure because Ullas Karanth never backed down from a fight, never stopped seeking to understand the beautiful, elusive animals he says he is "hardwired" to understand and defend.

Geoffrey C. Ward is an American historian and the writer of television documentaries including *The Civil War* and *The Vietnam War* and nineteen books, including (with his wife Diane Raines Ward) *Tiger Wallahs: Saving the Greatest of the Great Cats.*

PREFACE

I FIRST STARTED WORKING on an early version of this book in the year 2000, during a rare "sabbatical" at Columbia University provided by my employer, the Wildlife Conservation Society (WCS) in New York. However, soon after, my mandate to conduct wildlife research and real-world conservation—both at the same time—gave me no time to finish the manuscript. While the book was important, it never seemed as urgent as the crisis on hand. The manuscript languished in various forms until 2019, when my responsibilities to the WCS ceased.

Luckily, at that point in time, I met Jane Dystel, whose enthusiasm as a literary agent is exceeded only by her passion for tigers! Encouraged, I started working on the book in earnest. When Jane connected me to senior editor Jerome Pohlen at Chicago Review Press, I finally saw the light at the end of the tunnel.

This story is a cocktail of three spirits: the "hard science" of tiger ecology, the "dismal science" of real-world conservation, and my personal journey as a naturalist. Natural history has always coursed through my blood, even as my career meandered through engineering and then farming before coming home to my true passion: understanding tigers.

After gaining "freedom at midnight" from colonial mastery the year before I was born, my India also stumbled along, trying to seek prosperity and equity for its impoverished citizens. Although India covers just 2.4 percent of the earth's land, it is the world's most populous democracy and also its sixth largest economy—one that is growing rapidly.

Despite this massive transformation, somehow India has managed protect three-fourths of the world's wild tigers on just a quarter of the tiger habitat that remains. The big question now is whether India, one of the world's top nine mega-biodiversity nations, can hold on to its biological riches while also addressing difficult social transformations coming its way. Recovering wild tiger numbers from the present abysmally low three thousand to something more befitting the country's size and economic clout is a prime example of that challenge, which its top leaders are failing to even recognize.

In this account I have narrated my five decades of effort to understand and recover India's tigers. For me, writing about the natural history and the "hard science" around tigers was far easier than narrating the complexities of my interactions with humans involved. Among them are "seniors" who mentored me, "peers" who stood by me, and "students" I groomed. Because of the constraints of space here, not all of them appear in this narrative. I have used real names or initials for such individuals, including several public figures. There were a few others who, driven by incompetence, corruption, vanity, or other personal reasons have played adversarial roles. I have masked their names with pseudonyms to avoid distractions from the key conservation issues involved in these contestations.

The first seven chapters of this book are focused on my own experiences in southern India's spectacular Malenad landscape, when wild tigers came to the brink of extinction, followed by the near miracle of their sporadic recovery after the early 1970s. Unfortunately, after 2005, the global attention and flood of money directed at India's tigers have led to mission-drift, stalling that early promise.

In the last two chapters I have tried to synthesize my science and these experiences to propose a pragmatic framework for recovering wild tigers in the future, at a scale which is both necessary and possible. I plead for boldly leveraging the irreversible transformations which are already underway in diverse domains, such as land-use change, energy production, agriculture, nature tourism, and economic demography, to recharge tiger recovery. I cannot honestly share the dreams of many of my conservationist friends that wild nature can be saved only by traveling back in time to an imagined golden age of harmony between humans and tigers.

My overall view is that if—and that is a big *IF*—we do the right things now, tiger populations can rebound even more vigorously in the future. If I can convince my readers to reexamine the flawed approaches to tiger recovery currently being pursued by the well-meaning animal welfarists, social activists, academics, bureaucrats, and donors, I will have met my modest goal.

K. Ullas Karanth

1 | A DAY IN THE LIFE OF A TIGER

I RECALL EVERYTHING about the day January 29, 1990.

It was 0845 hours in the emerald jungle of Nagarahole in southwestern India [**MAP 1**]. The ten-meter-tall *Randia* tree I had carefully selected was 200 meters from the wild tiger resting near its kill. I climbed the rickety bamboo ladder gingerly and found just enough space to stand by squeezing my frame into a V-shaped fork in the tree. I held the loaded gun firmly.

Ten meters away, both to my left and right, teams of five men each were walking behind two riding elephants, goaded forward by mahouts sitting on their necks. Two other men sitting on the elephant's backs unrolled lengths of meter-wide white cloth steadily to the men following them on foot. The cascading fabric was deftly picked up and strung to bushes by these men. Soon, the two taughtly stretched waist-high cloth curtains diverged deeper into the forest trying to encircle the tiger. If it was still there.

The men worked in pin-drop silence, so that the tiger's acute ears would pick up only the normal sounds of the tropical jungle: two elephants lumbering along, noisily breaking off branches to feed, all the while emitting loud rumbles, squeaks, and growls. The cat would not suspect some trickery was afoot.

The elephants and men were soon out of sight. The "beat" for the tiger would soon begin. For centuries, such beats had been employed to hunt wild tigers to the verge of extinction. Now I was employing them to save the big cats. In the months and years to come, I hoped to track generations of wild tigers—from the time they were born, learned to hunt, roamed freely, dispersed, found one another, mated, raised cubs, and finally died—in the heart of the Indian jungle.

The stockade of beat cloth used to catch a tiger.

I practiced slowly moving the gun barrel—really just a tube of polished aluminium—in a gentle arc, concentrating on the foresight. I hoped the tiger would come down the jungle trail that cut through the *Chromolaena* shrubbery ahead.

I carefully tried to anticipate all possible scenarios. My feet, tightly wedged into the cleft, would be barely three meters above the shoulder of any tiger that came by. Even if I fidgeted slightly, the cat's razor-sharp eyes or ears could detect my presence. If that happened, the big cat could bound away, giving me no chance to shoot at it. Or, in a worst case, it could rear up ferociously and pull me down like a rag doll. The second unpleasant scenario was unlikely, unless the animal was a nervous tigress accompanied by small cubs. Fifteen years earlier, Nepali forester Kirti Tamang had been pulled down and severely mauled by a tigress when he climbed a tree to get a better look at her cubs.

The weapon in my hand was a flimsy compressed-air gun that could only shoot a single plastic syringe and inflict nothing stronger than a pinprick to the tiger. I contrasted my situation with the one faced by the American trophy hunter Jack Denton Scott. In his book *Forests of the Night*, Scott claimed to be in grave danger while waiting on a high *machan* (tree platform), out of reach for even the most athletic tiger. Furthermore, in those ebbing days of tiger hunts in India, Scott was armed with a powerful rifle. In the end, the lucky tiger did not turn up at all.

At 0900 hours sharp, the walkie-talkie in my breast pocket crackled briefly.

The tiger "beat" had begun. The teams of beaters, all the men now safely on elephant back, were approaching the tiger cautiously. The two elephants had to maintain the right spacing. They had to get close to the tiger, trying to gently "push" the tiger, without letting the wily cat sneak back past them unseen. Their goal was to quietly persuade the tiger to come my way. I was confident they could, because they were led by my old friend and extraordinary naturalist, Forest Ranger Chinnappa.

In Nagarahole, groups of tribesmen wandering in the jungle occassionally shooed away wild dogs, leopards, or even tigers off their kills to steal the meat. A wild tiger's natural instinct is to quietly sneak away before the foraging men found its kill, hoping to come back and consume it later. I wondered what this particular tiger would do.

At 0902 hours I heard a low growl, quickly followed by the alarmed cackle of a silver-hackled jungle fowl that rocketed off the ground to a safe perch. The tiger was on the move. But was it coming my way?

I waited for what seemed like an eternity, but my watch said it was only five minutes since the beat started. Suddenly, I saw a ghostly shadow move through the dense brush of *Randia* stems one hundred meters ahead. My heart was pounding, I feared, almost loud enough for the tiger to hear.

Then I saw it: a big male tiger, padding calmly, with its massive head held low, glancing from side to side. He was a picture of power and grace. The shade cast by *Randia* foliage painted harlequin patterns, black filigree on sunlit gold. The tiger turned left, changing direction to a trail leading away from me. Then he froze in surprise, his left forepaw lifted off the ground. The curtain of bright white fabric in striking contrast to the greenery, which barred his way, worried him. He turned around and followed another trail, this time heading in my direction.

I swung the gun around slowly, hoping I would not catch his eye. My best chance was a broadside shot, through an opening in the shrubbery seven meters ahead. I clicked off the safety catch, steadied the gun, and looked through the scope. I was now seeing the tiger like floating pieces of an orange-and-black jigsaw puzzle. I kept the barrel moving just ahead of the tiger's muzzle, and stopped. As his head, shoulder, flank, and, finally, thigh emerged in the cross-hairs, I squeezed the trigger ever so gently.

There was a soft pop of compressed air. The silvery syringe with its bright red tailpiece shot out, zipping furiously like a gigantic bee. I saw it sting the tiger's massive thigh. He jerked, cursed the dart with a loud growl, hopped a couple of steps, and stopped. I froze too, not even daring to breathe.

Finally deciding nothing was amiss, the tiger continued padding down the trail. I saw the rippling of his thigh muscles eject the syringe, which dropped to the forest floor. The muscle-bound big cat walked away with all the swagger of a bodybuilder. Soon he was out of sight.

I fished out my wireless handset. Choking with excitement, I whispered, "I got the tiger." The beaters at the other end instantly fell silent. I got down from the tree and examined the empty syringe. The tiger had got his full dose, eight hundred milligrams of the tranquilizer. Good!

Next came the second nerve-racking part of the hunt: I had to find the sedated tiger quickly. The sooner we found him, the safer he would be from any chance encounter with another tiger or a bull elephant.

By now the capture team reassembled around me. Ranger Chinnappa, standing at six feet, five inches tall, towered over everyone. He was from the local *Kodava* warrior caste, and was eight years older than I. Chinnappa had schooled me in jungle craft in the years since we first met two decades earlier. We found we shared a passion for saving wildlife, not hunting it, which was the social norm those days. Over the years, we developed a deep bond of friendship.

With us were two more men from the same warrior caste: forest guard Subbayya, a well-built, mustachioed former soldier in his forties, who was Chinnappa's able deputy; and the veterinarian Nanjappa, a professionally competent, compact man in his thirties.

The rest of the team was comprised of the two elephant *mahouts* (drivers) and a dozen trackers. All were skinny, unimpressive-looking men from the local *Jenu Kuruba* (honey gatherer) tribe. Their darker complexion, curly hair, and unique facial features indicated their earlier and stronger links to original migrants from Africa, the first humans to colonize the Indian subcontient seventy thousand years ago. These tribesmen were masters of jungle craft.

Our team of tiger catchers was all male, except for the two beautiful female elephants. Unlike the men, these stately ladies would not flinch even while facing a wild tiger at close range. They were really the linchpins of this tiger beat.

I had posted Raju, the best among the spoor-trackers, as a scout on a tall *Terminalia* tree about one hundred meters down the trail from where I had darted the tiger. From his much higher perch, Raju looked out for the tiger after it was darted, and picked up its spoor. The rest of us followed him, fanned out in a semicircle. Behind us came the elephants with their mahouts, also scanning the jungle ahead of us for the tiger.

In late January, the earth was parched and the dry leaves littered the forest floor. Untrained eyes could never detect tiger spoor here. But Chinnappa and these hawk-eyed tribesmen could pick up minute clues—overturned leaves, grass pressed down by the passage of a heavy animal, or the faintest impression of a single toe. Tracking tiger spoor is an art, rather than a science. I was pretty good at it, but no match for these true masters.

From my scientific training, I was aware that within a few minutes the sedative would begin to paralyze the cat's hindquarters. Thereafter, tracking its spoor as it dragged its hind feet would be easier. Within ten minutes, muscles of the tiger's forequarter would also become immobile, compelling it to lie down, reluctantly. How far the tiger was able to go depended on its weight, physical condition, and the amount of drug injected. The farther it moved, the harder it would be to find. Beyond a few hundred meters, finding spoor would be nearly impossible.

After fifteen nerve-racking minutes, an eerie yell ahead startled me: it was tracker Raju. My heart skipped a beat, and then his words sank in: "Huli sikthu, saar!" ("I have found the tiger, sir!") The English honorific "sir" phonetically degenerates into a *saar* as it rolls off the tongues of the Kannada speakers in southern India.

A great weight lifted off my shoulders as I raced forward.

Raju told me how he had seen the big male tiger cross the dirt road, barely fifty meters from where I darted it. Raju was now in full flow: "I leaped down from the tree like a langur monkey, Saar, to dash after the tiger. He was walking all wobbly, like a drunkard returning home from the arrack shop," and added, "I followed him sir, barely an arm's length behind, totally fearless. I know you have injected him with the most powerful drug in the world, and he would do me no harm." These seemed like the words of a brave man.

I cracked a smile, and reminded Raju and other tribesmen of the events that unfolded three weeks earlier, after I had darted my very first tiger, Mudka. That was the first tranquilized tiger these men had ever laid their eyes on. When we found it, it lay on its flank, its massive chest muscles heaving as it breathed. It occasionally twitched its ears, and, most ominously, its cruel yellow eyes were wide open.

Only four of us had approached the fallen tiger: Mel Sunquist (my collaborator at the Univeristy of Florida), Ranger Chinnappa, Guard Subbayya, and me. The trackers had stood twenty meters away, watching us in alarm. We of course knew the tiger was temporarily harmless because of the loss of muscle control induced by the sedative. To these jungle trackers, however, the tiger seemed menacingly awake, and our actions entirely suicidal.

After much coaxing, the tribesmen had, one by one, inched forward to gather around the tiger. They hesitantly joined me to assist in measuring the tiger's body dimensions with a tape.

Then the tiger moved its head head ever so slightly, and it was like throwing a firecracker at a flock of feeding pigeons. The tight cluster of tribesmen around me exploded. They dashed off helter-skelter, seeking the safety of any nearby tree. Five of them, led by Raju, clambered up a pole-sized sapling of *Phyllanthus* with the agility of langur monkeys. Unable to bear their combined weight, the sapling had bent earthward, forming a graceful arch. The terror-stricken men hung on for dear life, their feet just inches off the ground. With their glittering black eyes and skinny frames, the dimunitive men strung along the bough tightly looked like giant fruit bats clad in khaki shorts. My peals of laughter had not helped. It took much coaxing for them to resume work.

Now, I teased Raju about his bravery in the presence of *that* tiger. Everyone joined in the laughter. Finding *this* tiger had released our bottled-up tensions. Although we had a lot to do, my team was ready to work with clockwork precision.

Plotting the Hunt

Earlier that morning, when it was still dark, I had left my field camp in Nagarahole. I drove into the jungle along the dirt road to check the baits I had staked out to catch tigers. Raju sat huddled in the back of my little green Suzuki 4x4, wrapped in a blanket to ward off the morning chill.

Our first stop was a location labeled SKR 1.4 on my field map. The label meant the point was exactly 1.4 kilometers from my camp in Nagarahole, along the bumpy dirt road to Sunkadakatte in the southern part of Nagarahole Reserve [**MAP 2, Point 1**]. As I drove up to the location, my headlights lit up the bait: a fifty-kilogram water buffalo calf tethered by its front leg to a wooden peg driven into the ground. The calf was lying down, peacefully chewing cud. To its luck, no tiger had come its way the night before.

I was not happy about being compelled to use live bait. However, because wild prey animals were plentiful in Nagarahole, tigers were not as attracted to dead meat as they were in Southeast Asia. Nor did the tigers readily enter box traps set to catch them, as they do in areas where wild prey are scarce.

My buffalo calves came from among the millions of surplus cattle that wreak havoc on India's forests and pastures. Upper-caste Hindus who shun beef sold these calves to whip-wielding cattle traders. Herds of them were force-marched for miles, without any fodder, on their final pilgrimages to primitive slaughterhouses. The butchers, usually devout Muslims, had to follow their own religious diktats. They would slit the animals' throats with razors, reciting sacred texts to dispatch the animals heavenward painfully.

I had purchased a few such calves that were en route to a butchery. For the next few days, they fed on lush jungle grass during the day, then were staked out at dusk. I hoped that a passing tiger would notice them, creep up undetected, and swiftly deliver the killing neck bite. I was sure these animals suffered far less while serving the cause of my science than they would have to propitiate two great religions of the world. In any case, that logic was convenient to my agnostic mind.

Ten minutes later, as I drove up to the next bait site [**MAP 2, Point 4**], Raju stood up in the back of the car and yelled, "This buffalo is gone, Saar!" One end of the severed rope, however, was still attached to the wooden peg. This was a good sign. First, the buffalo had not simply slipped the rope off to irretrievably get lost in the forest. Second, a leopard could not have bitten through the thick rope; a tiger had taken this bait, and from the size of its paw prints, the killer was likely a big male.

The blood stains on the dew-soaked grass showed that the tiger had dragged its kill on an animal trail into a dense patch of secondary forest riddled with thorny *Lantana* bushes. The tufts of coarse gray buffalo hair plucked by these bushes indicated the path taken by the tiger. The drag mark headed down a shallow gulley running northward.

It would take painful ground tracking, at times crawling on all fours, to figure out where exactly the tiger was hiding its kill. Instead, I relied on technology. I had tied a small radio transmitter, commonly employed for tracking raccoons, to the stubby horns of the buffalo. The signals from the transmitter would tell me where the kill was. I hoped the killer would be close by, guarding it from potential thieves—other tigers, leopards, sloth bears, and even wild pigs—until he had his fill.

I quickly got out my telemetry gear: a receiver slung from my shoulder, into which an H-shaped Yagi antenna and earphones were plugged. Based on the direction from which the strongest signals were coming, the kill was at a compass bearing of thirty-four degrees to the north of the bait site. But how far away was it? To figure that out, I had to get more bearings to triangulate the kill's exact position.

Listening carefully, I walked 250 meters eastward along the dirt road to get a second fix. Then I walked roughly the same distance to the west and got a third fix. The carcass and—if all went well—the tiger would be at point where all three compass bearings converged. Plotted carefully on my field topographic map, I estimated the tiger was a couple of city blocks away from where I stood.

I could imagine the scene: the buffalo lying in a shallow gully fringed by dense culms of the stately *Aundinacea* bamboos. Its mouth would be agape, glassy eyes staring emptily at the killer lying down next to it. The tiger could be fastidiously licking its coat clean. Or it could be sleeping, belly bloated with twenty kilograms of raw beef it had bolted down in the first feeding frenzy. It might even be lying flat on its back waving its paws in the air like a giant kitten, swishing away the annoying swarms of dirty bluebottle flies with its meter-long tail. If this cat were to similarly relax in a motel room, it would need two king-sized beds placed end-to-end.

I could also imagine the tiger panting lightly, just to keep cool. Its four canine teeth, each the size of a man's middle finger, would be visible. A bite from these ivory daggers powered by its strong jaw muscles could easily cut through a man's torso and crack his backbone.

In contrast to these badges of brute strength, the tiger's coat sported delicate colors and patterns. Its orange-ocher face had two snow-white orbits circling a pair of blazing yellowish-green eyes, and at the tip of its muzzle was the dainty pink Rhinarium. The tiger's fascia was overlaid with a fine pattern of jet-black squiggles surrounded by a ruff of long white hair. No makeup wizard in Hollywood could have conjured up this splendid visage.

Now I had to plan, to the minutest detail, how to catch this tiger. The method I chose blended modern technology, acquired from my academic studies, with insights of ancient hunters, imbibed over the years from my companions, particularly Ranger Chinnappa.

In the early 1970s, Mel Sunquist, then a biologist at the Smithsonian Institution, had learned about the "beat method" of catching tigers from his Nepali shikaris (hunt assistants). These shikaris had modified a method originally developed to shoot tigers. I had added an innovation of my own in Nagarahole: fitting a small radio collar, commonly employed to track raccoons and bobcats, to the baited buffalo.

When the beat began that morning, the equipment and supplies necessary to catch this tiger were ready: an air-powered dart gun and its plastic syringe containing the precise quantity of the drug; a fist-sized very high frequency (VHF) radio transmitter fused to a flexible belt that would go around the tiger's massive neck; a radio receiver, with its antenna and earphones needed to track the radio signals; and the all-important "beat cloth" essential to hoodwink the tiger. It consisted of a meter-wide white cloth cut to lengths of eight meters, neatly stacked on the back of the two trained riding elephants.

Oddly, employing the beat method to shoot a wild tiger dead is far easier than safely catching the same tiger alive. In a traditional tiger hunt, beaters chase the animal toward one or more waiting hunters. They either shoot it dead, or more often, injure it with the first shot and finish off the disabled animal with follow-up shots. Generally, hunters would be safe from the tiger, sitting on high *machans* (tree platforms) or in *howdahs* (boxes) secured to the back of riding elephants, which formed a formidable phalanx of defense if the tiger attacked.

In contrast, my air-powered gun was a useless weapon against a tiger. The featherlight dart must hit the tiger with great precision to achieve effective sedation with a single shot. Even after that, it would take several minutes for the drug to kick in. Unlike a bullet, the dart could easily be deflected off course by any intervening leaf or twig. While the tiger hunt would be a noisy affair with dozens of yelling beaters, my capture team had to work in stealth to ensure the tiger would be totally unaware of what was going on, even after the dart hit it.

My success that day depended on predicting how this tiger would behave during the beat. I had to think like a tiger. After the tiger makes a kill, it usually stays close by and consumes most of the edible parts over three or four days. However, the chance of finding a tiger right next to its kill declines after the first couple of days. Which meant I had to act quickly after the tiger killed the bait.

The objective of the beat is to encircle the tiger in a "stockade" that is roughly triangular in shape, with a twenty-meter-wide gap left open at its apex. The tree I was on overlooked this opening. The two sides of the triangle are about 150 meters long. The stockade is really just a taut curtain made of strips of white cloth tied to bushes. The two arms of the triangle diverged away from the opening, trying to enclose and surround the tiger, without getting too close to it. When the beat starts, the tiger, one hopes, is still near the kill. The elephants, with men piled on them, then enter the stockade at the base and quietly head toward the tiger.

Why does the beat method work? Years ago, some unknown shikari had intuitively discovered that the white beat cloth was an effective psychological barrier. Strangely, a powerful beast like the tiger fears this flimsy cloth barrier, and prefers to dodge it rather than jump over it. Compelled to thread its way on one of the animal trails inside the stockade, the tiger finally exits through the opening at at its apex, where the hunters wait.

Tiger beats conducted by hunters did not always proceed as planned. Sometimes, a wounded tiger would turn back on the line of beaters on foot, mauling or even killing some helpless men in its path. Such deaths were mourned in passing, perhaps, over celebratory pegs of scotch around campfires later in the evening.

Biologists had to modify this hunting technique. First, the cat had to be "gently persuaded" to sneak off its kill, rather than bolt in panic as it does in any noisy beat. Second, the beaters sat on the backs of the elephants rather than scouring the bushes on foot. And the tiger they were pushing would never be a ferocious injured animal. Quite to the contrary, a sedated tiger becomes less dangerous by the minute. Truth be told, in this sort of tiger beat, the only person marginally at risk would be me.

I had estimated from the size of its tracks this animal weighed about two hundred kilograms. I used this information to decide the initial dosage of the drug I used, a cocktail of a dissociative anesthetic and a muscle relaxant. These were ordinary veterinary drugs, proven to be safe. Moreover, the tiger was sedated lightly, just enough to fit the radio collar. In contrast, a tiger undergoing surgery in a zoo would need much more of the same drugs.

However, I did worry about one thing: finding the darted animal quickly. It was theoretically possible for a drugged tiger to walk into a pond the size of a bathtub and drown. If the weather was warm, and the tiger lay exposed to the hot sun for long, its temperature could rise dangerously. So I made sure my bait site was far away from any pond. The forest in Nagarahole would be shady and cool at least until February, after which I planned a break in capture operations.

A Tiger Returns Home

So far, things had gone well when we found the sedated tiger in a perfectly safe condition. Biology, technology, and traditional field-craft had all played their roles to catch this tiger safely. I knelt down and examined the tiger, a well-proportioned handsome male cat. Chinnappa chose to name him Mara, the Kannada name for the god of love.

The handsome male tiger Mara, captured and radio-collared by Ullas Karanth.

Assisted by the men, I measured Mara: his total length was 289 centimeters, including a 100-centimeter-long tail; the girth of his chest was 127 centimeters; and he was 109 centimeters tall at the shoulder. There were other standard measurements of mammalogy to be noted in my data form.

Weighing Mara was a challenge. We dragged him onto a hammock made from a strong nylon fishing net. The hammock was strung from a 227-kilogram spring scale. The trackers quickly fashioned a stout pole by hacking a sapling with their machetes. Six tribesmen held the pole at its ends and pushed it through the steel ring of the weighing scale. Then, with a collective mighty heave, a dozen men were able to lift the massive tiger a few inches off the ground for a few seconds. I quickly noted Mara's weight: at 209 kilograms, Mara was big, a young tiger who would grow even bulkier as he aged.

The veterinarian Nanjappa gave him an additional dose of the drug to keep him down a bit longer. It would not help if Mara woke up halfway through the process I had to follow. Nanjappa also drew a sample of Mara's blood for my future studies of tiger genetics. I also carefully picked ticks and parasites from Mara's body for similar studies of disease.

I opened Mara's jaws. A wild tiger's teeth concisely reveal its life history. Animals younger than eleven months still possess milk teeth that are small and fragile. Later, the permanent teeth begin to erupt through the gums, displacing the milk teeth. By eighteen months of age, the young tiger is ready to kill large, tough prey animals using its robust permanent canines.

During the first few years of its adult life, a tiger's teeth are sharp. They appear clean and white, with a slight pinkish tinge. As the animal ages, its teeth undergo tremendous attrition: they wear out, get blunted, chip off, and occasionally break. This wear and tear occurs as the tiger hunts down large, tough prey animals, and during fights with other tigers. As the animal gets older, a thick coat of tartar turns the teeth to a dirty yellowish-brown hue. Finally, unable to kill its prey, the tiger starves to death at the end of its life.

Mara's teeth were white, sharp, and undamaged. I estimated him to be four to five years old. His neck had already attained its maximum girth of seventy-nine centimeters, requiring a full-sized collar. I quickly fitted a new collar, adjusting its length to ensure a comfortable snug fit, and tightening its locknuts to secure it. The radio transmitter was encased in a fist-sized metal locket, coated with plastic resin to render it waterproof, because when the weather turns hot, tigers love to cool off in ponds or streams.

I punched a black tattoo on the pink skin inside Mara's ears. It read T-04. Mara was the fourth tiger I had radio-collared in Nagarahole. Three other tigers—Mudka, Sundari, and Das—had preceded him. Even if anyone found Mara dead later, without his collar, this tattoo would identify him. I also took a few photos of Mara's stripe patterns, which would uniquely identify him as surely as fingerprints. I did not realize how useful these photos would prove to be not far in the future.

To save the charge in its lithium battery, I had switched off the transmiter by taping a small magnet to the casing. Mel Sunquist, who had been involved with animal radio-tracking technology for years, had warned me repeatedly, "Don't ever forget to take that damned magnet off before you let the animal go!" Many aspiring radio trackers, who had done everything right, had still lost their study animals because, in all their excitement, they had forgotten this key step.

I removed the magnet on Mara's collar, turned on the receiver, and set it to his unique radio frequency, 150.070 megahertz. A steady stream of beeps issued forth, sounding exactly like the call of the coppersmith barbet, ubiquitous in these jungles. Mel had laughed while mentioning that when he took his boss at the Smithsonian, the legendary ornithologist S. Dillon Ripley, to radio-track tigers in Nepal, the venerable scientist had trouble distinguishing between birdcalls and the signals from the tiger they were tracking.

Mara was in excellent shape. All the same, a sedated animal needs careful attention during the recovery. We made a rough and ready canopy from a large plastic sheet tied to nearby trees, which shielded Mara from the afternoon sun. To keep his body cool, we sprayed a steady mist of water on him using a pedal pump.

I monitored his body temperature every five minutes, inserting a digital thermometer coated with petroleum jelly into his rectum. Starting at 102.0 degrees Fahrenheit, Mara was cooling off nicely as time progressed: 101.9 degrees, 101.6 degrees, 101.5 degrees . . . I also applied liberal quantities of ophthalmic ointment to Mara's eyes and kept them covered by a piece of cloth. This prevented the tiger's eyes, staring unblinkingly because of the sedative, from drying. This blindfold also reduced visual stimulation. We all spoke in whispers. Mara was down, but he could see and hear everything going on around him. As he recovered, his stress levels had to be kept as low as possible.

The evening sun began sliding down the western sky. Yellow rays filtering at an angle through the jungle's leafy canopy turned Mara's coat to burnished copper. The upper part of his body was a rich, tawny ocher, in contrast to his white chest, belly, and inner limbs. Overlaid on this colorful pelage was his unique monogram of black stripe patterns.

In the bad old days of tiger hunting, native hunters in my region claimed tigers were of two distinct types, the "broad striped" and the "narrow striped." Mara instantly proved them wrong. He was asymetrically striped, with his left flank being "broad striped" and his right "narrow striped." Wisdom of the native often provides bad data, as I have realized over the years.

I could never for a moment have guessed how these unique markings on Mara's skin would not only advance tiger science, but also soon help save my own skin!

The elephants and trackers had already headed home. The animals would now be busy swallowing, one after another, fist-sized balls of boiled ragi millets, thrown dexterously into their cavernous pink mouths by their caretakers. The tribesmen would be getting into their cups of home-brewed liquor to celebrate the end the day. Only three of us—the ranger, the veterinarian, and the scientist—were left to keep vigil. This show was not over until the fat tiger walked.

Gradually, Mara began showing signs of a smooth, full recovery. His head moved, and his ears twitched. He began to swallow and yawn, sticking his long pink tongue out. He looked around, shaking his head a couple of times as he felt the new ornament around his neck. He would soon get used to it. Next, he stood up, wobbling unsteadily. The muscles of his hindquarters, first to go, would be the last to come back.

After a couple of tries, Mara rose to his feet and looked around. We watched in fascination, hidden in the thick shrubbery barely ten meters away from the huge tiger. Somehow sensing our presence, Mara began to walk away. He walked slowly but steadily until we lost sight of him at 1810 hours. I turned my radio receiver on and pointed the Yagi antenna in his direction. Mara was still walking away. Three of us stood up and shook hands all round, grinning. The tension that held us in its grip throughout the day was finally gone. Mel Sunquist had returned to the United States two weeks earlier; I had successfully captured, sedated, and radio-tracked a tiger today all on my own. I was exhausted, but felt strangely lighthearted.

I listened to Mara's beeps fade away. Soon there was only silence. I guessed that he had walked a kilometer by now. He was out of range for my receiver. Mara was a wild tiger once again, perfectly free to go wherever he wanted to, whenever he felt like it, just like his ancestors who had ruled these Asian jungles for over two million years.

The Land of the Tiger

Mara's ancestors had evolved in what is now central China about two million years ago. They gradually expanded their range, tracking populations of hoofed animal species such as deer, antelopes, pigs, and wild cattle, which had evolved earlier and radiated through Asia. These large ungulates, in turn, had spread in response to changing patterns of vegetation driven by climate change. Both genetic and climate data suggest tigers entered India from the east about twenty thousand years ago as the periodic sea-level changes broke up or reconnected the Southeast Asian landmasses.

Responding to evolutionary and ecological pressures, humans had also migrated out of Africa, reaching the Indian subcontinent about seventy thousand years ago. They had also spread rapidly across the rest of the world by applying their unique technological, social, and cultural tools. Soon humans were the dominant species wherever they reached. No other species could modify its own habitat to suit its own needs like humans could, even though humans only possessed simple tools at this point: fire, axe, and plow.

Yet the powerful striped cat, which arrived much later, was much feared by the early hunter-gatherers. Tigers preyed on them. And, after they turned to farming and herding, tigers also became a menace to their livestock. Humans fought back, for sure, with their primitive weapons. However, it wasn't until a mere five hundred years ago that humans finally got the upper hand in this contest. Tigers retreated in the face of newer technologies like steel and gunpowder. Modern genetic studies suggest that about five centuries ago half a million tigers may have roamed the jungles of the Indian subcontinent.

By the nineteenth century, better equipped than ever to confront the dreaded cat, native kings and their colonial overlords declared tigers to be royal game to be targeted by "sport hunting." Meanwhile, ordinary farmers and herders, encouraged by government bounties, probably killed even more tigers. In addition to shooting tigers like the elites, these subaltern social classes employed a variety of ingenious snares, traps, pits, deadfalls, and poisons to eliminate tigers. Historians estimate that sport and bounty hunting together led to the slaughter of over eighty thousand wild tigers between 1875 and 1924.

By the time India gained independence from colonial rule in 1947, only remnant numbers from those vast populations of wild tigers survived. Ironically, most of these were confined to a few "game reserves" of the erstwhile elite classes. Within these zones, hunters from the subaltern classes were barred from hunting tigers, as well as prey species. There is no denying that this colonial practice of social discrimination did help the dwindling tiger populations to cling on for a couple of decades. But the democratic power shift that followed the regime change in 1947 suddenly empowered the plebeian classes to hunt. Now everybody could hunt pretty much anything, anywhere, using any means. Tigers quickly disappeared from most forested landscapes of India. In the fully forested state of Nagaland in northeastern India, the native Naga tribe extirpated wild tigers within a decade of independence.

Tigers were slaughtered by the thousands during the colonial period.
Creative Commons

With the lifting of relatively strict controls over gun ownership, after independence "crop protection guns" proliferated among farmers as part of the state-sponsored "Grow More Food" campaign. While the last of India's wild tigers were being shot, trapped, snared, and poisoned, millions of farmers, herders, and tribesmen starved for protein also felt free to hunt the tiger's chief prey, such as deer, pigs, and wild cattle. At the same time, millions of semiferal cattle were literally eating the lunch of these wild ungulates. They also killed them off by passing on deadly anthrax and foot-and-mouth diseases. Given a free rein to fell forests to feed the hungry nation, Indian peasants cleared nearly ten million hectares of forested land between 1950 and 1970, ten times more than all the land that was lost to industrial and urban growth.

Free India was a huge country, despite the severance of Pakistan and present-day Bangladesh—it was a third the size of the United States. After the late nineteenth century, nearly a quarter of India's land was under the custody of forestry departments in different states. After 1947, India's avowedly socialist government resorted to massive state-sponsored logging in these Reserved Forests to fill its depleted coffers. India's foresters and villagers got the mandate to virtually mine these forests for valuable timber, wood fuel, and industrial raw materials.

As commerce grew, Reserved Forests began to be exploited for a bewildering variety of hitherto uneconomic forest products, such as bamboo, rattan, grasses, bark, leaves, roots, fruits, nuts, and seeds of jungle trees to meet the demands of rural, urban, and industrial consumers. Escalating collection of such "nontimber forest products" adversely impacted many wild animal species that depended on these myriad bounties of nature. This thoughtless, intense exploitation was hailed as "scientific production forestry" and later as "community-based forest conservation" in India's official policy documents.

There was also a cultural dimension to this change in forest management. Many colonial foresters were keenly interested in natural history. India's foresters, who took over their reins, came from the literate middle class. In that era, unlike today, this class had no interest in wildlife. It perceived wild animals as a danger to be eliminated, to keep people safe.

Born in 1948 to an upper middle-class family, I was one of India's "midnight's children." To my little boy's eyes, there appeared be no tomorrow for wild India. For an ancient society shedding its colonial yoke, filling hungry human bellies, growing the economy, and expanding social welfare were India's priorities. In the overall scheme of things, the fate of the tiger did not matter.

Enter the Tiger

I grew up in tiger country. The forests around my home in the small town of Puttur, Karnataka [**MAP 1**], were once ideal habitats for tigers and their prey species. This is Malenad—"hill country" in Kannada—a rugged landscape that straddles a spectacular mountain chain known as the Western Ghats. The Ghats run north to south, parallel to India's western coast. They are a part of the vast tiger range, which once extended across Asia, from Armenia in the northwest to Indonesia in the southeast, and from Iraq in the southwest to Siberia in the northeast.

The thirty-five thousand square kilometers of forested landscape in Malenad was riddled with villages, rice paddies, and plantations of coffee, tea, rubber, and a variety of fruit and spice crops. It was also inhabited by five million people, and even more numerous livestock. All around me I saw the intensifying competition between people and tigers. And the cats were clearly losing. When I finished high school in 1964, there were perhaps less than one hundred tigers left in that huge landscape.

India is a federated union of several states, each with its own language. The major administrative languages in the five southern states belong to the Dravidian group, which is quite distinct from the group of Indo-European languages linked to Sanskrit, spoken in northern India.

India's human population, we now know, is a wondrous seventy-thousand-year-old cocktail of varied genes, races, cultures, languages, religions, and castes. My cultural identity, if anything, was Dravidian, descended from the ancient Harappan civilization that followed earlier animist hunter-gatherers.

Rich lore about the tigers was infused deeply within my culture. Spectacular folk arts and rituals involving tigers shaped my boyhood. The tiger was the main deity worshipped as a *Bhoota* (spirit form) in many tiny, ancient shrines. The tiger was depicted as the vehicle of many Dravidian deities, as well as of the Sanskritic gods, of those pre-Uber days. Even ascetic sadhus meditated in the lotus position on tiger skins, presumably to draw on the carnivorous beast's energy to make up the protein deficiency of their vegan diets.

The most spectacular among such rituals was the *Huli Vesha* (tiger dance). During nine days of the Dasara Festival, a few otherwise ordinary men—carpenters, masons, and mechanics—took a vow to turn into tigers. Their nearly naked bodies were painted spectacularly to resemble a tiger's coat. Different teams consisting of three or four "tigers" wandered the streets of my town. They danced vigorously to pulsating drumbeats, imitating the sinuous grace and energy of the big cat. The lead dancer wore a fearsome tiger mask made of papier-mâché. He wore a belt from which a spring-loaded flexible tail stuck out, encased in real tiger skin, which swayed as he danced. In the minds of little boys like me, who followed these men around all day, the spectacle remains indelible.

Devout householders gave tiger men food and money. On the ninth and final night, all the tiger troupes went in a procession to the temple of goddess Durga, who is depicted riding a tiger. Having fulfilled their vows, they washed off the poisonous lead paint that covered their bodies. Overnight, the tiger men once again became recognizable, returning to whomever they had been.

The *Huli Vesha* tiger dancers of Malenad.

Despite being honored in rituals, wild tigers were facing a grim reality. Although I felt surrounded by tigers, I saw only dead ones. Tigers were being killed by the dozens in Malenad—shot or poisoned, their carcasses, magnificent even in death, paraded on streets.

A circus had come to town in the early 1950s. As a six-year-old kid, I had accompanied a servant to the back of the big tent where animals rested during the day. There I saw my first live tiger. It lay in a stinking, urine-soaked narrow cage. Its fiercely sad yellow eyes had bored into mine, and I was mesmerized forever.

The educated class into which I was born dominated most professions, except those involved laboring in factories or farms. Generally, this class had little interest in wildlife. A doctor, lawyer, engineer, teacher, or even forester could not identify a handful of local bird species. Even among those who lived off the land or hunted animals, the interest stopped at species that provided meat, hides, or horns.

My father, Shivarama Karanth, was a writer and polymath. He was born just as the twentieth century dawned. Although a college dropout in the cause of India's freedom, he later educated himself well in both the arts and sciences. His interest in natural history was unusual among men of his generation. As I avidly turned the pages of the *National Geographic* and *Life* magazines he brought home, natural history entered my bloodstream. I also avidly immersed myself in the rich repository of British tiger-hunting lore in India.

Finally, in 1965, after I read an article by the American field biologist George Schaller about his recent study of tigers in central India, I had a new dream: to explore the secret world of tigers, bearing the torch of science rather than a gun.

When I was nineteen, after my father gifted me a noisy 250-cc Czech motorcycle, three jungles in Malenad became my favored haunts: Nagarahole, Kudremukh, and Bhadra [MAP 1]. Nagarahole lay to the southeast, across the ridge of the Western Ghats. It was a five-hour motorbike ride from my college in Mangalore (now known as Mangaluru). Its rolling slopes supported productive deciduous forests of the Deccan Plateau, forming ideal habitats for tigers and prey. Even closer, just an hour's bike ride east, was Kudremukh, which straddled the towering ridge of the Ghats. Lashed seasonally by incessant monsoon rains, often reaching eight thousand millimeters a year, Kudremukh sported dense, tropical evergreen forests. It was home not only to tigers but also to other unique endemics, like lion-tailed macaques and great hornbills. The rich bamboo forests of Bhadra lay one hundred kilometers farther eastward from Kudremukh, nestling on the spectacular slopes and valleys of a crescent-shaped out-spur of the Ghats, called the Bababudan Mountains. These three jungles found a special place in my heart.

Despite miles of trekking through the jungles, watching for tigers, I only saw their fading pugmarks. I heard gunshots everywhere, and saw forests laid waste by encroaching farms or industrial-scale logging. Vast herds of emaciated cattle were chewing up the forests to oblivion. Wild tigers would soon be gone from Malenad, like elsewhere in India.

At the same time, India's economy stagnated at the "Hindu Rate" of growth: a mere 3 percent per year. When mass starvation loomed, worrying about the fate of the tiger was a luxury. My dream of becoming a wildlife biologist was not a viable career option. Facing the grim reality, I chose to study mechanical engineering.

But I was not interested in engineering at all. I escaped from the classroom to roam the jungles, desperate to see a wild tiger before the last one was shot. I had no idea of the conservation miracle about to unfold before my eyes. No scientific model could have predicted it.

Back from the Brink

In the early 1970s, India's politics changed radically. Prime Minister Indira Gandhi stormed to power, riding a tsunami of socialist populism. Unlike other Indian politicians, she genuinely appreciated the value of wildlife. India's beleaguered conservationists finally found a powerful ally. An autocratic one, no doubt, but as far as tigers were concerned, that turned out to be a good thing. The ironfisted prime minister began to turn the tide for the big cat.

Indira Gandhi's immense popularity with the poor masses enabled her to pass strong conservation laws without a challenge between 1972 and 1984. These laws virtually banned hunting across India. They also carved out several wildlife reserves in which livestock grazing and logging were curtailed. India's disciplined, military-style state forestry staff, hitherto preoccupied with logging, was directed to implement the new wildlife laws. In the next couple of decades, some of these dedicated wildlife rangers and officials achieved what, in hindsight, can only be called a miracle. My friend Ranger Chinnappa, whom

I met in Nagarahole in 1969, was one such wildlife warrior. Working closely with the new generation of local foresters defending wildlife, I too got involved in their protective skirmishes. Most memorable among such efforts was that of Lakshamana, a tough forest officer who managed Nagarahole. After he was attacked by politicians and the media for removing dozens of squatters and hundreds of feral cattle from the northern part of Nagarahole in the 1970s—literally saving the entire area—I publicly defended him, leading to a friendship that lasts to this day.

Protected from human hunters and invading livestock, populations of wild ungulates—deer, antelopes, wild cattle, and pigs—rebounded in some wildlife reserves. Tiger numbers also gradually began to rise as more tigresses raised cubs, which then survived and bred. After tracking tigers fruitlessly for fifteen years, I saw my first wild tiger in 1981.

During the critical decade of 1970 to 1980, I also doggedly tried to find meaning in my own life. I met and fell in love with Prathibha, a speech pathologist, whom I married in 1974. She steadfastly supported my struggles, as I switched from a stable career in engineering to an uncertain one as a farmer near Nagarahole, in order to spend more time watching wildlife. I kept meticulous field notes of what I watched, turning them into articles that established my credentials as a naturalist, enabling me to establish my own nonprofit, Centre for Wildlife Studies, in 1984.

Unknown to me, the stage was being set in faraway lands for the aspiring wildlife biologist in me. A decade-long (1973–1984) study of tigers in Chitwan Park, Nepal, which employed new animal radio-tracking technology, was making waves in the conservation world. A fortuitous meeting in 1983 with the American tiger scientists involved in that study, opened the door for me when I connected with Mel Sunquist. Impressed with my eagerness and experience, Mel offered to take me as his graduate student at the University of Florida. However, he wanted me to notch up a couple more credentials: get high scores in the Graduate Record Examination (GRE) and get some preliminary training at the Smithsonian Institution's conservation training at Front Royal, Virginia. The math skills I had reluctantly acquired as an engineer two decades earlier finally proved useful. Having obtained both these credentials, at the age of thirty-eight I began what I can only call my second life.

In 1988, a chance meeting with George Schaller, who was visiting the University of Florida, cemented my future. While appreciating the work I had done, George had questioned me whether, like most Indians of my generation, I too aspired to settle down comfortably in the United States. I had replied that my lifelong plan was to study tigers in India, adding somewhat cheekily, "and to write a better tiger book than *The Deer and the Tiger*."

George had simply said, "Good—then come and see me in New York."

Soon I presented my plan to George, and his boss, the patrician William Conway, at the New York Zoological Society, located in the Bronx Zoo. I had to pinch myself when they instantly hired me to do research on tigers in India. Finally, I was going to live my dream.

Since the 1960s I had greatly admired, and deeply envied, George Schaller. Like no one before him, George had single-mindedly walked the planet to study one rare animal after another: gorillas and lions in Africa, jaguars in Brazil, giant pandas in China, and mountain ungulates in the Himalayas. And of course, tigers in India when I was still at high school.

Therefore, I choked with emotion at something George casually said while dropping me off at LaGuardia Airport: "I envy you, Ullas. There is no finer wildlife experience in the world than watching a tiger move silently through tall grass in the Indian jungle." Here was George, the lifelong object of my envy, longing to switch places with *me*.

Now, just a year and half later, having radio-collared my fourth wild tiger in Nagarahole, I was driving back to camp. The curtain of dusk was descending, making the tropical jungle around me seem like the candlelit interior of a magnificent cathedral. A strange feeling welled up inside me. Upon some reflection, I realized it was a sense of nationalistic pride, at being the first man in my country to radio-track wild tigers. It was the pride of a Brown village boy from southern India, who was emulating the feats of the "great White scientists" who inspired him.

I had no idea of the consequences I would soon face.

2 | THE REAL KING OF THE JUNGLE

I RETURNED FROM THE UNIVERSITY OF FLORIDA in October 1988, finally a proud holder of a graduate degree in wildlife biology. I immediately went about laying the foundation for my long-term—and, if possible, lifelong—work among tigers. I planned to start my study in Nagarahole and expand outward. I had the federal government permits required to capture and radio-collar tigers, leopards, and dholes (Asian wild dogs). However, something critical was missing: my mentor and extraordinary naturalist Chinnappa was not in Nagarahole anymore. For years, we had dreamed of applying the magic of radiotelemetry to enter the secret world of predators.

When I was away in the United States, some local malcontents—a cabal of poachers and timber thieves—had foisted a false criminal case on Chinnappa. They had accused him of abetting a forest guard who had shot a local farmer during an altercation. Although Chinnappa was soon absolved of any wrongdoing, his bosses in the forestry department had posted him out of Nagarahole to dampen the local animosity.

The ranger who had replaced Chinnappa, GR, was a thoroughly incompetent man. Illegal hunting had ratcheted up alarmingly in Nagarahole.

I met Chinnappa and asked him to come back to Nagarahole to help my tiger research. Chinnappa agreed to return to Nagarahole, only on the condition that he be assigned his earlier position as the ranger in command. I was able to convince senior officials about the crumbling protection, and GR was transferred out to a different range.

Back in command, Chinnappa aggressively cracked down on the forest criminals who had been emboldened during his absence, because GR had cozied up to them to line his own pockets. Now, deeply angered at his removal, GR covertly joined forces with the same malcontents to get rid of both Chinnappa and me from Nagarahole.

Blissfully unaware of all this, I set about planning the capture and radio-collaring of as many tigers as possible before mid-February, when the summer heat made tranquilizations risky to the animals.

On December 10, 1989, Mel Sunquist and his nature-writer wife Fiona arrived in Nagarahole. They brought massive amounts of baggage: dart guns, drugs, radio collars, receivers, antennas, and much else.

I felt truly grateful to Mel, who taught me much about carnivore ecology. A tall, handsome, balding man of Scandinavian roots, Mel had been a student at the University of Minnesota in 1967, just after William Cochran invented animal radio-tracking. Mel was the best teacher in the animal radiotelemetry business. Fiona, bright, statuesque, and beautiful, was a nature photographer, with a wonderful Scottish sense of humor. They often hosted me at their lovely home on the shores of Lake Serena

Ullas Karanth flanked by Mel and Fiona Sunquist.

at Melrose, not far from the university. Over the years, we had become good friends.

Even before they arrived, I had already recruited my team of "tiger catchers" from among the local tribesmen. Raju, the best animal spoor-tracker under Chinnappa, was seconded to my team. I was puzzled by the fact that every tribesman sported the same initials, "JK": JK Raju, JK Kala, JK Putta, and so on, until I realized the letters were an abbreviation name of their entire tribe, Jenu Kuruba (honey gatherers). Every man had to be a JK! Traditionally the tribesmen hunted, scavenged meat from predator kills, or collected forest produce like honey, which they sold in local markets. The new conservation laws had forbidden these practices, and they switched to logging labor, sometimes becoming forest protection staff at the lowest rung.

I also hired the services of two trained riding elephants from the forest department. Each obeyed a dozen verbal commands, but only if issued by its own mahout (rider). Ordering the beast around in a quaint "elephant pidgin," he could make it kneel, stand up, lift its trunk, tug a rope, break a branch, move forward, move back, or just stop. Each animal magically morphed into a tractor, bulldozer, winch, or a crane as needed by this voice-activated jungle Alexa.

Mel, Chinnappa, and I began intensively training the team of trackers in the beat method of catching tigers. Although no one had ever employed the beat method to catch leopards, I wanted to give it a try. In the first two beats we conducted, the buffalo bait had been killed by a large leopard that managed to bite through tethering rope and drag it away. Mel and I had chosen to sit up in two separate trees, hoping to dart the leopard as it sneaked out of the cloth stockade.

In the first beat, conducted on December 18, 1989, a large, handsome male leopard with a paler than normal coat emerged. He trotted rather hurriedly, passing right under the tree Mel was in. As Mel fired, the leopard appeared to sense the movement above, and veered off. Mel missed the shot. He was using a powder-charged dart gun, which sounded like a shotgun. Bounding along, without hesitating, the leopard leaped over the beat cloth and disappeared into the jungle.

On December 20, 1989, another bait was killed at the same site [**MAP 2, Point 5**]. This time, the large male leopard walked slowly and directly toward my tree. I guessed from his pale coloration that he was the same leopard. Two days earlier, he had learned that the "gunshot" had come from above. Now,

The tiger-capture team heading into the jungle.

as he approached my tree, the leopard looked up. Spotting me, he wheeled around, zigzagged through the *Chromolaena* bushes, glided gracefully over the beat cloth, and was gone. Although I had no chance to take a shot, I heard a muted growl as he spotted me. He seemed to be saying, "How dumb do you think I am?"

I realized the white beat cloth held no terror to the leopards, as it did to the tigers. Leopards are simply smarter than tigers. It is not a wonder that the leopard's global range is twice that of the tigers, and spans both Asia and Africa.

I speculated on the reason. Leopards hunted in daytime, constantly looking for langur monkeys in the canopy above. After locating the langurs, they ferociously charged as high up the tree as they could go. The terrified langurs, particularly the inexperienced youngsters, sometimes jumped to the ground, hoping to escape—exactly what the crafty predator wanted.

Keeping an eye on the canopy was an instinctive behavior with leopards. Trying to catch them using the beat method was a waste of effort. After these failures, whenever a leopard took the bait, I just let the animal enjoy its meal in peace.

My First Tiger: Grand, Old, and Wounded

On December 22, 1989, we ran a beat for a tigress that took the bait we had staked out on the animal trail that connected Chikapala Pond to Bison Road *Hadlu* (grass-swamp) [**MAP 2, Point 2**]. She had three large cubs with her. During the beat, three tigers had come along the trail that passed close to the tree in which Mel waited. Because of the dense cover, I could not see him from my tree. When Mel took a shot at the first tiger, his dart was deflected by the shrubbery. The three tigers had dashed away.

On December 25, the tigress made another kill at the same site. However, this beat also came up empty. The wary tigress had heard our team's arrival on vehicles and moved quickly from the area even before the beat began. We conducted an opportunistic beat on December 30 after finding a sambar deer kill made by a tiger near the Mavinahalla Watch Tower-1 [**MAP 2, Point 15**]. Because the killer was not next to the carcass, the beat failed to encircle the tiger. After much effort, I had come up empty-handed, once again.

By January 1990, I was beginning to lose hope. I had not captured, tranquilized, and radio-collared a single tiger despite many attempts. Mel would be returning to United States in a couple of weeks, and I would lose the guidance of a true master in the art of capture and radio-tracking of large carnivores.

On January 7, 1990, however, fortune finally smiled. The bait at SKR 0.6 [**MAP 2, Point 1**] was taken by a tiger. From the quarter-plate-sized pugmarks, he appeared to be a real giant. Mel and I both took up our darting positions on adjacent trees. When the tiger emerged ten meters in front of me, broadside, it offered me a perfect shot. After I darted the mighty beast on his right thigh, he stopped and twisted around to look at the source of the annoying pinprick. As he padded away calmly, I noticed something that worried me: on his left shoulder, I caught a quick glimpse of a raw, pink wound that was rather large.

The ejected dart was empty: the tiger had received a full dose of the drug. We found the sedated animal 250 meters away, knocked out stone-cold. This tiger was a true giant, but very old. I had filled the syringe with a drug dose appropriate for his huge size. I nicknamed the tiger Mudka (the old man).

Mudka had a gaping wound, six inches across, on his left shoulder. It was turning gangrenous and was crawling with maggots. Because he was an old tiger, taking him to a zoo hospital was pointless; Mudka would never adapt to captivity. In any case, I was permitted by the federal government only to

The capture and radio-collaring of the tiger Mudka. *Courtesy Fiona Sunquist*

capture, radio-collar, and release the cats. My purpose was to document how tigers lived and died naturally, not to play God by meddling with their fates.

I marveled at Mudka's physique. He was 299 centimeters long, including a 107-centimeter-long tail. He also stood tall at 116 centimeters, while also sporting a massive chest girth of 129 centimeters. The trackers had a hard time heaving up a fishnet hammock to weigh him. The massive beast tipped across the limit of 227 kilograms on my spring scale. He was well over 230 kilograms for sure.

I was certain I had seen this giant tiger a year earlier. On the morning of February 13, 1989, while sitting on Watch Tower-2 overlooking Mavinahalla Pond [**MAP 2, Point 16**], I had heard the alarm calls of chital deer. Looking through my binoculars, I saw not one, but five tigers lounging around lazily three hundred meters away on the cleared grassy view-line!

There was an adult female with two leopard-sized cubs, another slightly slimmer adult tigress, and this huge male. The sambar kill they had obviously gorged on was hidden in the *Lantana* thickets nearby. They had all amicably shared the kill and polished it off. Now, the adult tigers were peacefully sunning themselves in the morning light. The two cubs were playing around with

Serious injuries found on the tiger Mudka.
Courtesy Fiona Sunquist

the carcass of a muntjac deer. The poor animal had just blundered into this conclave of tigers to become a plaything for these cubs. The cubs sometimes broke off from the play to go and nuzzle one of the adult tigers, including the big male.

Naturalists in India have occasionally recorded such "gatherings" of wild tigers. These typically occur when individual tigers are closely related. My guess was that the two adult tigresses were a mother and her adult daughter from an earlier litter. The two younger cubs were from her current litter. And the big male had sired these cubs. A year earlier, Mudka had been in splendid shape. Although he was still in good physical condition, with this serious wound his ability to hunt fleet-footed prey would soon be impaired. After starving for a few days, this massive tiger would rapidly lose muscle mass and weight. Death would come in matter of weeks.

Examining his teeth, I realized Mudka was truly old. His carnassial teeth were worn down to the gums, the canines were blunted, and a thick coat of tartar had turned his teeth yellowish-brown. I guessed he was at least ten to twelve years old. After a long and productive life, this tiger king was nearing the end of his territorial tenure. Soon a more vigorous rival would take over his territory, and with it, the priority right to mate with all the tigresses it held.

In fact, Mudka's injury could have resulted from a fight with another tiger a week or so earlier. When tigers fight seriously, they often attempt to bite the nape or back of their rivals, trying to puncture the spinal cord and paralyze the adversary instantly. Because Mudka's injury was not fresh, it was hard to guess what caused it. Chinnappa, who had seen many carcasses of animals shot by poachers, felt Mudka had been hit by a blast of pellets from a shotgun. Mel thought the wound could have resulted from a fight with another tiger.

With the help of a veterinarian, we tried to clean up the wound. As the veterinarian poked and probed at the infected tissue with gloved hands, he found a shotgun pellet. However, tigers do sometime carry old shotgun wounds and live for years. The doctor cleaned up and dressed Mudka's ugly wound, pumping him with antibiotics. However, we all knew this tiger's days were numbered.

I labeled him T-01, who broadcast signals on a frequency of 150.050 megahertz. Having fitted the radio collar, we began the vigil for his recovery. The seriousness of the tiger's wound and his old age meant Mudka's recovery from sedation could be slow. Although we were confident that he would eventually recover safely, a nagging worry would persist until he did.

As the night descended, a pair of tribesmen lit a campfire close to Mudka to chase away other animals that came too close. We moved two hundred meters away to listen to his radio signals. Mel, Fiona, and I took turns listening in once every five minutes. We were not far from my field camp in Nagarahole [MAP 2]. The Telonics collar I fitted had built-in motion sensors. If the animal was inactive for two minutes, the interval between beeps increased. When it turned active—even if the tiger just rolled over—the beeps would speed up. As the midnight hour passed, Mudka's signals never speeded up. I hoped he was sound asleep and not dead!

If Mudka died, it would be a catastrophe for my study. There were some well-known old-style conservationists and foresters in India who were opposed to the new animal research methods, such as chemical immobilizations and radiotelemetry. They believed their good old spoor tracking had already revealed whatever there was to know about tigers. The death of the very first animal I radio-collared, from whatever cause, could doom my project.

Although I was worried, Mel remained calm and confident. Around 0200 hours we decided to head back to the camp to catch some sleep. By 0600 hours we were up again. I wanted to rush back to the spot where Mudka had lain sedated. Mel said that was not good radio-tracking practice: "I am assuming the tiger has recovered and moved off. You will not get his signals from where he was yesterday. We must head straight to the best listening post and search for his signals all over the area to find him again."

Radio signals emanating in Nagarahole terrain could be picked up from long distances of three to four kilometers only from the two highest listening posts: Kuntur Hillock or Faith Hill [MAP 2]. On the dirt roads that ran at lower levels, intervening hillocks and dense jungle impeded signal transmission. There, I would have to get within a few hundred meters of Mudka to triangulate his precise location.

I climbed the nearly vertical thirty-meter-tall steel ladder to the top of the fire tower on Kuntur Hillock, feeling somewhat anxious. Tuning into Mudka's frequency, I instantly found he was now much farther away from where he was the previous night. The steady beat of active signals indicated that he was walking along. I breathed a sigh of relief. Mel flashed his "I told you so" smile at me.

My first wild tiger was now broadcasting his locations from Nagarahole, twenty-four hours a day. This old, wounded beast was unlikely to survive beyond a few weeks. However, even in that short window of time I hoped to learn the finer tricks of the trade in field radio-tracking from Mel before he left. Moreover, I could gather unique ecological data from Mudka: how a dominant male tiger's movements and home range would shrink as his condition worsened. My objective science had this ghoulish element, regardless of the sympathy I felt for this grand old animal.

A Beauty and the Beasts

After collaring Mudka, my luck at catching tigers turned decisively. Right from the beginning, my priority was to capture and collar as many territorial female tigers as I could. These tigresses had grown up and become strong enough to challenge an older tigress—usually their own mother, or a closely related animal—to take over her territory. After holding a territory, they had to defend it against other interloper tigresses over the next six to eight years.

The breeding tigresses come into estrus once every three weeks. While estrous, they attract dominant male tigers, which wander around seeking such opportunities for mating. The tiger mating spree typically lasts only three to four days but involves hundreds of couplings, each one lasting just thirty seconds. These couplings are interspersed with bouts of growling and rough playfighting. Despite all this effort, conception is not guaranteed. If it fails, the tigress will come into estrus again.

If the tigress conceives, after a gestation of 110 days, she gives birth to three or four cubs, sometimes more. For the next year and a half, the tigress does not ovulate. She focuses her energy on protecting, feeding, and training her cubs to be skilled hunters. Raising three or four cubs to independence is an exhausting mission that wears down the tigress. After she has raised three or four litters—about ten to fifteen cubs—during a territorial tenure of eight to ten years, the tigress fades away. A younger, more vigorous tigress will fight for her territory, and the story repeats itself.

These territorial females are cornerstones of the tiger society. Central to my study was observing their behaviors, recording movements, activities, and use of space. Therefore, I initially planned to capture as many as I could of the five tigresses that were operating in a hundred-square-kilometer area around my field camp. Packed densely with prey animals, this tract was the best piece of tiger turf in Nagarahole Reserve. This was also the place where I had witnessed the miraculous recovery of a tiger population in the previous two decades.

The buffalo baits were staked out at six places where I felt the bush cover, distance to water, and signs of tiger movement were optimal for conducting the beats. At these sites, I had the highest chance of catching tigers with fewest collateral risks.

I had prioritized the capture of a big, beautiful tigress, with a range that encompassed the productive Hadlu grasslands in the Kuntur, Kaithole, and Chikapala areas. Even tourists had seen this tigress and her three cubs over the previous year. Seven months earlier, the bold tigress had killed a huge bull gaur with the help of her cubs. Based on my sightings of this mother-cub association, I had estimated the cubs to be about eighteen to twenty months old. They were getting ready to disperse soon.

After they did, the tigress would give birth to her next litter. I hoped to learn how a real tiger mom like her raised her cubs. However, this tigress was a cunning animal. My two earlier beats had failed to capture her (or her cubs) at bait at BSR 1.4 [**MAP 2, Point 2**]. I had almost given up hope of radio-collaring her, but catching Mudka apparently broke the jinx!

On January 13, 1990, the tigress took the bait for a third time at the same site. By now we were fully aware of her wiles. We arrived in dead silence. After the previous failure, I had again reconnoitered the terrain around the site and reconfigured the layout of the beat. I selected an area with much thinner bush cover and better visibility.

This time the beat turned out to be picture-perfect. As three tigers emerged at the mouth of the funnel, two of them, both juvenile females, were skittish. They ran past Mel, giving him no chance to dart. Their much bulkier mother came up along a different trail, offering me a safe, ten-meter shot at her right flank. Using all my concentration, I pulled the trigger. The dart hit her muscular shoulder and popped out. She had received a full dose.

Before we found the tigress, she had moved about three hundred meters, giving us forty-six minutes of anxiety. Because she had got only three hundred milligrams of drug as the initial dosage, we gave her a further dose of three hundred milligrams. Finally, the tigress was out cold. I had outwitted the crafty Tiger Mom.

She was beautifully marked with broad, split stripes just like Mara, but on both flanks. Her measurements: total length, 169.7 centimeters, including the tail, which was 80.7 centimeters; chest girth, 114 centimeters; and height at the shoulder, 95 centimeters. Weighing in at 146 kilograms, she was a large tigress who truly earned her name, Sundari (beauty). Her ear tattoo read T-02, and her radio-collar frequency was set to 150.112 megahertz.

I was absolutely thrilled. Even if the male tiger Mudka died soon, as expected, Sundari was likely to hold her ground for five or more years. I hoped to observe her hunt, mate, produce cubs, and live the full life of a territorial tigress. Following her around would also be easy because her entire territory was covered by a dense network of dirt roads used for tourism, forestry, and patrolling.

Furthermore, when the transmitter batteries would run out in three years, I would not need a complicated beat to recapture and collar her. I could home in on her signals on elephant back and dart her easily. I could also observe other tigers—those without radio collars—that associated with Sundari to share kills or mate with her. In fact, in the next six years, as Sundari went on to live the truly charmed life of a strong, confident wild tigress, I did get some of those opportunities.

The problems that occurred along the way had more to do with my own life, rather than hers.

Big Tiger, Dainty Pugs

Suddenly I felt it was raining tigers in Nagarahole. Two days after catching Sundari, on January 15, 1990, a bait staked out at BGR 1.4 [**MAP 2, Point 3**] was taken by a tiger. This dirt road ran through a beautiful patch of unlogged natural forest of stately *Terminalia* and *Lagerstroemia* trees, with shrubbery on the ground dominated by Bodde (*Nicandra*) bushes with thick, plasticky green leaves. When their plumlike fruits ripened, local tribesmen avoided these patches, because sloth bears that loved these fruits lurked in them.

After examining the killer's hind-foot pugmark, we decided this animal was a tigress and loaded an appropriate dosage of 600 mg into both our dart guns.

This was an excellent place to conduct the tiger beat. Mel and I were able to stand on thick forks of two tall, gnarled *Ficus* trees that were close to each other. Instead of being cramped as usual, we stood comfortably leaning against broad boles. We could see each other and the ground in between us clearly, which was ideal for judging who had a better shot. Furthermore, even if this tigress was accompanied by small cubs, and decided to be aggressive, we were both safely out of her reach.

The beat proceeded smoothly, and soon a tiger emerged calmly padding along a trail, after being pushed off its kill. However, it was not the tigress we expected—but a large male. The tiger walked slowly but warily, then arrived between our two trees.

The dosage of 600 mg loaded into the dart guns was too low for this large male. He would go much farther before lying down and would require a second dose to knock him out. We both could dart him, but that would deliver far more sedative than necessary. These thoughts crossed my mind as the tiger stood still beneath Mel. We nodded at each other silently. I saw Mel look down, aim his gun, and fire!

The powder-charged gun made enough noise to scare the tiger. He let off a loud *Woof* and instantly took off.

We had to find the tiger quickly. The team fanned out and started following spoor. At 150 meters, we came across a strange sight: a freshly killed, partially consumed chital doe lay on the trail. Surely our tiger could not have killed her. Pugmarks around the deer and the distance between the canine punctures on its throat confirmed that the killer was a leopard. While the leopard was having his hard-earned breakfast, our darted tiger had come down the trail. By now the drug would have slowed his sprint to a drunkard's walk.

Normally, the tiger would instinctively attack the leopard and appropriate its kill. But in his groggy condition, the last thing this tiger would want was a chital for dessert after his buffalo steak.

The leopard, on the other hand, would be terrified and decisive. At the first sight of the tiger, it would have crouched down and scurried away, looking for a tall tree to climb up. The leopard would not know if the tiger heading its way was drugged and harmless or sober and lethal.

I had no time to follow the leopard's spoor. I had to find the tiger first, before he got too far. Fortunately, in the streambed where the chital lay, the soil was clayey, black, and moist. The tracks of the tiger clearly showed up. His forepaw prints were of normal size for a large male, whereas his hind pugmarks were only about the size of a tigress's prints. We had been fooled by his unusually dainty hind pugmarks. Following this clear spoor, we easily caught up with the tiger in the next hundred meters.

We had found the last two tigers, T-01 (Mudka) and T-02 (Sundari), lying flat on their sides, fully sedated. This tiger, T-03, was different. From about fifty meters we could see him lying down, but with his forequarters still propped up. He was scanning the jungle all round him, eyes menacingly wide-open. He needed an additional dose, delivered using my gun barrel as a blowpipe, to knock him out.

Although he was a big tiger, he was somewhat disproportionate and ungainly, with a big belly. I named him Das in honor of our camp cook, who possessed similar traits. The reaction of each individual tiger to the same drug can be different. Mudka, Sundari, and later Mara, had gone down peacefully, without trying to fight off the sedation. T-03 was trying hard to resist it. His measurements were: length, 305 centimeters, including a tail of 101 centimeters; chest girth, 127 centimeters; and height, 104 centimeters. We estimated his weight to be 220 kilograms on a full belly, in comparison to Mara, who had weighed 209 kilograms.

The capture team after the sedation of the tiger Das. *Courtesy Fiona Sunquist*

Before we could weigh him, Das partially recovered. We had to let him wobble a few meters and lie down. He was now in an open patch. The exposure to harsh sunlight could elevate his body temperature. But by now the capture team was fully trained. The trackers swiftly shaded him under a fabric tent propped up by four bamboo poles. After giving me some anxious moments, Das was now resting peacefully on his flanks. Despite receiving 900 mg of the drug, he recovered much sooner than other tigers had, and began to walk away slowly but steadily at 1545 hours. Das was broadcasting on a frequency of 150.012 megahertz.

Over the next two years, this tiger would provide me much interesting data, some extraordinary thrills, and at the end some real angst.

Lessons from a Master

After a sluggish start, I had caught four tigers in the last ten days!

Mel and Fiona were to leave in the next couple of days. I had learned a lot about the science and art of tiger tracking from them, but soon I would be on my own. I had to remind myself constantly that tiger telemetry, despite all its thrills, was not an adventure trip. It had to be a thoroughly solemn professional exercise. The safety of the big cats and of my team members was my responsibility. The sole purpose of using radiotelemetry was to collect ecological data that would otherwise be impossible to collect. I was sure that the purpose of tiger tracking should not be corrupted to seek publicity and glory, like a trophy hunter would.

During our lunch in the modest forest rest house in Nagarahole the day before he left, Mel gave me some final tips, not about tiger behavior or radio-tracking, but about human behavior under the spell of the tiger. He warned me not to invite any outside spectators to the tiger-capture operations. He feared I would come under pressure from local officials, politicians, and the media folks to do just that. He told me to stand firm and resist.

Mel told me how, because of distractions of managing such spectators in Chitwan, two sedated tigers had died during capture operations. An old tigress had died after overheating in the sun due to the delay in finding her. Another tiger, a huge male in its prime, had drowned in a pond the size of a bathtub, after he moved too far after darting. Both were hastily organized beats meant to show off tiger captures to visiting Nepali dignitaries.

It was for this reason, Mel reminded me, that we had wisely turned down a request from the local legislator CU from Hunsur, who wanted to witness the capture of Mudka. I had no idea how much the rejection of her request would come back later to haunt me.

Mel reiterated that I also had to avoid media men who wanted to photograph or film tiger-capture events. And to avoid those who would want to sensationalize my research as a tiger-show spectacle. Nagarahole was not Las Vegas: I could aspire to be neither Siegfried Fischbacher nor Roy Horn!

As we discussed all these issues, Chinnappa was standing outside. On the paved road a red compact car raced by. The driver saw Chinnappa, and braked to a halt. He walked up and greeted Chinnappa, who was somewhat of a local celebrity. The man, KG, was a journalist from Mysore (now known as Mysuru). The racy fare his popular tabloid, *Star Dirt*, served the readers had all fifty shades of yellow. A recent headline had screamed: TEENS ARRESTED BY POLICE, FOR MAKING LOVE IN AN AUTO-RICKSHAW.

As KG chatted with Chinnappa, he caught a glimpse of us through the window. Although I knew him slightly, I felt that encouraging him to report on me collaring wild tigers would not be a wise move. It was likely to turn out like "serving arrack to a macaque," as the local saying went. I chose not to introduce KG to my American visitors. Perhaps he felt slighted, for he soon drove off. I never for a moment thought how such a minor incident would play out over time.

A few weeks later, RR, one of India's best-known photojournalists, came down from Delhi. He was in the park to get pictures for an upcoming issue of *National Geographic*. When RR heard about my tiger telemetry project, he was keen to do a multipage photo spread on it for a major Indian newsmagazine. He told me he would make me famous nationally. I flatly—and in hindsight, rather tactlessly—turned down his offer. RR got angry and accused me of hiding my research from the public eye. He said he had powerful friends in Delhi who would not like such secrecy.

Obsessed with my own work, I had indeed turned into a grim, humorless scientist. I also had not developed the tact and political skill for managing the media around complex scientific and conservation issues. My frankness and naivete would soon prove extremely costly.

Yajamana: One That Got Away

After I had collared my fourth tiger, Mara, on January 29, 1990, my focus shifted to radio-collaring some tigresses that had territories adjacent to Sundari. I had roughly mapped out their expected home ranges and gave them nicknames of key localities in their ranges. To the east and north of Sundari were Mavinahalla Tigress and Doray Road Tigress. The first was an old animal that had raised at least two litters in the past. I sometimes saw her from the watchtower near the Mavinahalla Pond [**MAP 2, Point 15**]. The second tigress was Sundari's daughter, the one that we had failed to dart. She had dispersed afterward and acquired her own territory, much of which lay in the neighboring Kalhalla Forest Range [**MAP 2**]. The word *Doray* means the "white ruler." This dirt road was once an old bridle path on which colonial forest officers had ridden horseback to inspect teak plantations in Nagarahole, the oldest of which dated back to 1868. South of Sundari's range lay the territory of a shy tigress away from the tourist tracks. I had only seen her tracks, although later in this story she turns up under the label of NHT-105.

There was also another huge male tiger—much bigger than Das or Mara—who ranged over a wide area in the middle of the Nagarahole Reserve. Because of his bulk, I called him Yajamana (the boss). I guessed that he was the male tiger most likely to take over Mudka's territory. I had once photographed

Yajamana relaxing in broad daylight on the bund of Marappa Pond, which was at the western edge of his range.

I was keen to catch as many of these tigers as I could in my beats before mid-February, when the weather turned too hot to conduct captures. However, I had no success with three uncollared tigresses; the baits tied up in their ranges were killed by leopards. One poor buffalo calf had even been trampled to death by an irate bull elephant.

Finally, on February 10, 1990, the buffalo calf staked out just to the south of the Kuntur Hillock was killed by a tiger. This location was overlapped by the ranges of at least three tigers, Sundari, Mara, and Yajamana. The fact that radio signals from neither Sundari nor Mara were emanating from the kill site suggested Yajamana was the likely killer.

That morning the chief of wildlife of Karnataka, Appayya, was camping at Nagarahole. He was an old friend who genuinely encouraged my work over the years. I now had the uncomfortable task of telling him that he, and his entourage of junior officers, could not watch this tiger-capture operation. I patiently explained risks, citing instances Mel Sunquist had told me about.

My federal research permit was endorsed by Appayya. Most officials in his exalted position would have tried to pressure me. However, much to my relief, a gentleman to the core, Appayya agreed to wait in the forest rest house until the capture operations ended. I felt truly grateful to him.

Soon I was up on the fork of a *Cassia* tree, standing just five meters off the ground. With the advancing dry season, the trees and bushes around me were leafless. The bush cover at the exit from the beat cloth stockade around me was rather sparse. I anticipated the tiger would come along an animal trail, which passed right beneath me.

A few minutes after the beat started, the tiger did come along as anticipated, looking straight ahead. Because of the sparse ground cover, I could see the animal from sixty meters away. He was enormous. This was indeed Yajamana. The tiger padded briskly, heading directly my way. I held my gun steady, with the safety catch off. I could see the tiger's huge head with blazing yellow-green eyes in its scope. I hoped that as Yajamana got closer I would get a clear shot at his shoulder.

Suddenly I heard a rustle from the canopy of the *Cassia* tree above me. A fledgling emerald dove, brilliant metallic green above and pinkish-brown below, was fluttering down, after carelessly falling off its nest. The tiger also heard the noise and looked up at the dove careening down helplessly. The tiger was less than five meters away. I froze, hoping to blend with the foliage to avoid detection. But he spotted me in a trice. For a moment, his ears flattened, and his eyes narrowed. Then he took off.

The huge tiger bolted in great galloping bounds toward me. Although I aimed my barrel at him, because he was running full tilt, I could not be sure of getting a safe shot. Neither my ego nor the adrenaline surging through my veins could change that reality.

An ineptly placed dart could inject the drug subcutaneously—under the skin—instead of deep into the muscles. The slow absorption of the chemical by the tiger's body would delay the induction of anesthesia. Yajamana, who probably weighed around 240 kilograms, could go far, possibly too far for me to find him. The dry, gravelly soil below was not good for tracking spoor either. The weather was hot, and the leafless forest canopy offered no cool shade. I simply could not risk the tiger lying sedated in the hot sun for too long. I had to let Yajamana go, passing right under me.

I looked down. The fallen chick was still floundering around on the forest floor. It was lucky the tiger had not stepped on it as he raced ahead. However, this fledgling could never fly back up to the safety of its nest.

Bitterly disappointed, I tried to console myself. Although Yajamana had escaped on the last possible day of this capture season, I would get him in the next season. But unlike me, the ill-fated dove below had no ray of hope for its future. Its fate was to be a tasty morsel soon for a Shikra hawk or a mongoose that would come by. It was the way of the jungle.

In February 1990, I was running ragged trying to get daily radio fixes on my four tigers. My barely literate tribal assistants could not read compass bearings or triangulate and map the animal's locations, so I hired two sturdy Kodava boys from a village outside the park. Gini and Bopi, both in their early twenties, had passed high school. They quickly picked up radio-tracking skills.

Gradually my burden of daily tracking for all four tigers lightened. I could now turn my attention to leopards.

The Legend of Buddy Mackay and the Pigheaded Boar

A week after we had failed twice to dart the big male leopard in our beats, I had driven around the area with Chinnappa and Mel. Surprisingly, we had spotted the same leopard in broad daylight. He stared back at us insolently, before disappearing into the *Lantana* bushes. Chinnappa and I had sponta-neously muttered a Kannada curse word: "Buddy Maga!" Having caught our tenor, Mel too exhorted us to go "get that Buddy Mackay!" Our curse word had sounded to Mel like the name of a Florida congressman.

Later that evening, over sips of malt whiskey, I explained to the Sunquists the nuances of the rich vocabulary of curse words in Kannada, for instance, the tale of Buddy Maga. A married man had borrowed a big loan at a hefty interest from a bachelor friend. Unable to repay even the interest, the borrower had agreed that his friend could sleep with his wife until the principal was repaid. The son born from this union would constitute the interest payment. The boy would be called *Buddy* (interest on a loan) *Maga* (son). Henceforth, this pesky leopard would be called Buddy Mackay. (Mel promised not to share the joke with his congressman.)

Buddy Mackay, who had humiliatingly outwitted me twice, became my prime target.

As with tigers, catching leopards also was a fine art. I planned to catch leop-ards in box traps. With this method, higher summer temperature was not a con-cern. A leopard darted inside a trap could not wander off in a partially sedated condition and fry in the sun. Once trapped, it was also safe from other leopards, tigers, or wild dogs. Nor could it harm anyone in my capture team. All in all, cap-tures in traps were less dicey and more predictable than darting free-ranging cats.

I had two leopard traps built. The first one was a heavy wooden contrap-tion that required a farm tractor to take it around. The second trap, made of fiberglass, was not only strong but also light enough to be hauled around in my Suzuki.

Goats were the baits in these traps. The exterior of the trap was screened off by a dense mat of thorny *Acacia* twigs to make it blend in with its surround-ings. These thorns also deterred any leopard from using its delicate forepaws to squeeze the goat out between its bars. I had to persuade the wily cat to step into the trap only through its open door. If the cat's sensitive pad touched an unfamiliar surface, like wood or fiberglass, it would step back at lightning speed. The floor of the trap was covered with fine dust to encourage its next step, which would spring the trapdoor.

When the heavy trapdoor dropped, there had to be a gap for the leopard's tail to stick out. If not, the leopard was in danger of turning into a bobcat. However, during its frenzied escape attempts, the leopard would try to insert its forepaws through the same gap and lift the trapdoor open. Therefore, when the trapdoor slammed into position, two bolts slid in to lock it.

The leopard traps were kept off the dirt roads, hidden from forestry laborers who could get tempted by the prospect of a meal of goat curry. I stationed the leopard traps five kilometers apart, in the hope of catching different individuals.

The fiberglass trap was at BSR 1.4 [**MAP 2, Point 2**] on the trail, where I had captured Sundari. The wooden trap was stationed on SBR 1.2 [**MAP 2, Point 5**], close to where Buddy Mackay had thwarted our capture efforts. The goats were fed lush grass and water during the day and were ushered into the traps in late evening. Unlike the buffalo bait that stayed calm and chewed cud after its caretakers left, these goats bleated hysterically, inviting any cat within earshot to come and get them.

Examining the traps every morning, I noted that leopards, and even tigers, had circled around, inspecting them. However, no cat had been bold or hungry enough to enter the traps. These contraptions were, after all, strange objects in the jungle. With plenty of wild prey around, the cats were far too risk-averse to try them out. I realized it could be a long wait before I caught a leopard.

On one occasion, a leopard had managed to insert its paw through the bars of the fiberglass trap but failed to pull the goat out. However, that goat had died from its injuries. I left the goat's gamey cadaver as a dead bait, hoping the cat would come back to claim it. Meanwhile, I secured the sides of the trap with more swathes of vicious *Acacia* thorns.

The next morning, I walked to the trap site with Gini. As we approached the trap, we heard a tremendous commotion—a powerful animal was in the trap and battering it furiously. The fiberglass trap was strong. It was built to securely hold an adult tiger. But the racket we heard could not be from a tiger, leopard, or even a sloth bear. These carnivores would not recklessly ram the trap and hurt themselves.

Sprinting to the trap, with great curiosity, we had a surprise.

Looking mean and angry as hell in the trap was a giant wild boar that I guessed weighed at least a hundred kilograms. He was charging and ramming the trap with great ferocity. The badly bruised pugilist had no more interest in the stinking bait that had drawn him in. But if we did nothing, he would soon kill himself. Gini climbed on the trap and released its door. The boar shot out like a giant cannonball and disappeared into the forest, without even a word of thanks. I realized why the word *pigheaded* is in the human lexicon.

Gotcha! Sweet Revenge on Buddy Mackay

On February 13, 1990, my trackers Kala and Putta had gone to check the wooden trap set close to the field camp [**MAP 2, Point 5**]. They came back quickly, breathless with excitement. There was a big male leopard in trap! Gathering my gear, I hurriedly drove to the trap site.

A strange tableau was going on: the cat and the goat were engaged in a slow ballet. The leopard was going round and round in the trap, trying to find a way out. The goat was following about a foot *behind* it, trying instinctively to avoid being *ahead*. From the pale coloration of his coat, I recognized Buddy Mackay. The moment the trapdoor slammed down, the leopard forgot all about the goat. He had one mission: escaping from the trap to live another day. Even if the goat had stuck its head into his mouth, Buddy would not have been interested.

After watching this animal tableau for a minute, I got busy. I asked Putta and Kala to approach the trap and distract the cat. Seeing them, Buddy backed into the opposite corner, growling ferociously. I reduced the air pressure in the gun, pushed it between the bars, and darted Buddy's rump at point-blank range. The leopard turned back angrily and saw the goat. He swiped at it with his paw to punish the animal for the prick-prick on his rump. Meanwhile, the drug was inexorably circulating in his bloodstream.

All three of us withdrew out of the leopard's sight. The round-and-round ballet of the goat and the leopard soon resumed, with the goat's rump now bleeding profusely after being raked by the leopard's claws. However, the feisty animal was not giving up. As the drug kicked in, the leopard became visibly groggy. He stopped circling and sank down on his forelimbs. His pupils were now fully dilated. If left alone, Buddy would be out like a light. The feisty goat, however, had other ideas.

The leopard faced away from the goat and put his head down on his forepaws. The goat screwed up all its courage, darted in, headbutted the leopard's rump, and took a quick step back. No response. Emboldened, the goat charged and butted Buddy again, backing away to assess the damage before launching his next attack.

I could not believe what I was seeing. The leopard was sinking into a fully sedated state, but this crazy goat's antics could slow the process. I asked Kala to hold the trapdoor open, so Putta could gingerly pull the goat out. Sadly, the

The capture and collaring of the leopard Buddy Mackay.

goat was badly injured and unlikely to survive. Moreover, I had to take care of the leopard's recovery and radio-collaring. I asked Kala to take the goat home, leaving its fate in his hands.

I got to work, helped by other trackers who had now joined. We began to measure, weigh, and fit the radio collar on Buddy. His measurements were: total length, 218 centimeters, including a tail of 84 centimeters; chest girth, 80 centimeters; with a shoulder height of 70 centimeters. Buddy weighed 58 kilograms. He was a large, mature leopard in excellent condition. His teeth were yellowing, but still strong and unbroken. I assessed his age at six or seven years.

Buddy still had a few good years left in him. He could generate lots of interesting data. He was an established territorial male. Old scars on his body demonstrated he had fought his way up the leopard social ladder to attain this status. Leopards had been well-studied in Africa, but in Asia, very little data existed on leopard movements, activity patterns, home range sizes, and life history. I hoped Buddy would be the first Asian leopard to provide comparable data. I decided to forgive Buddy's earlier thwarting of my attempts to catch him!

Two More Leopards in My Bag

On the morning of February 24, 1990, I got a landline phone call (cell phones were yet to arrive) from Kushalappa, a senior forester and an old friend. He was a scholarly silviculturist who followed my research with genuine interest. His forest guards had captured a leopard. It had entered a coconut grove near

Nanjangud [**MAP 1**], not far from Mysore. He was not a jungle leopard, but one who hid in farmlands and survived by eating feral dogs that proliferate in every village. This "problem" leopard was being held in the zoo at Mysore. Kushalappa planned to release the cat in a forest area far away from the village. He inquired if I was interested in radio-collaring this leopard if he decided to release it in Nagarahole. I jumped at his offer.

Big cats were often trapped by forest officials after incidents of conflict with humans. They usually took them to a forested area to be released. However, there were no follow-up studies on the fate of these translocated cats. Yet most conservationists and forest managers believed these animals instantly adapted to their homes and lived happily ever after. After all, who had not heard of Elsa the lioness who had returned to the wilds, and was later made famous by the movie *Born Free*?

I now had the opportunity to collect real data on what really happens after such a translocation. Is the cat simply welcomed by others of its kind, like any new tenant of a hitherto vacant apartment? Even more fundamentally, was there even a vacant apartment?

I immediately drove to Mysore in my Suzuki. The leopard was an old male, but rather small in size. It was already sedated by the zoo veterinarian. Thanking everyone involved, I asked the zookeepers to load the sedated leopard onto the rear deck of my Suzuki. The zoo veterinarian jumped into the seat next to me with the tools of his trade. I sped away, while the large crew of men, equipped with a farm tractor-trailer and giant steel cage ready to return the leopard to the forest, watched our somewhat cavalier departure in awe.

The leopard appeared fully sedated. However, we had a two-and-a-half-hour drive through the city of Mysore, and several small towns and villages. I asked the veterinarian to inject the leopard with a small dose of the drug to make sure it stayed down all the way. If the cat stumbled to its feet and stepped out of my speeding car, I could have a crisis on my hands. I drove fast, without stopping even for a cup of coffee. If I had stopped, a few curious villagers would have crowded around the car to peek inside. Within minutes hundreds more would have gathered. There was no telling what could follow. If some busybody riled up the crowd, it could attack the leopard. On the other hand, if the crowd decided to celebrate its departure from farmland to the jungle where it belonged, it could even cheer me on. It all depended on the local leader of the crowd. I did not want to test those waters.

The only dangerous moment during the trip came when, as I was driving fast through a small village, a little girl suddenly decided to dart across the road at the last possible moment. The fender of my car missed her by a leopard's whisker. I refuse to speculate on what could have happened if it had not. Angry local mobs in India are unpredictable and dangerous.

I breathed easy only after I entered the limits of the Nagarahole Reserve. I felt much safer among the predictably familiar wild animals. On reaching the Nagarahole, I drove to the exact spot where I had trapped Buddy Mackay eleven days earlier [**MAP 2, Point 5**]. This is where I would release the translocated cat.

Because this leopard had been unusually quiet so far, I named him Mooga (the mute one). I was perhaps unconsciously following a local tradition. Parents often deliberately chose derogatory names for a newborn child, such as "the lame one," "the mad one," or "the mute one." This was to deceive evil spirits, which otherwise would kill a healthy child in the form of some pox or peril. Although I had given a derogatory moniker to the leopard L-02, unfortunately it did not inoculate him against evil spirits, as I realized later.

I weighed and measured Mooga and fitted him with a radio collar, operating on a frequency of 150.132 megahertz. He was truly a runt compared with Buddy. His body dimensions were: total length, 205 centimeters, with a tail of 82 centimeters; chest girth, 68 centimeters; and shoulder height, 67 centimeters. Mooga weighed only 43 kilograms but was a fully grown leopard, slightly older than Buddy at seven to eight years, based on the wear and discoloration of his teeth.

In the past, White hunters in India claimed that leopards like Mooga that lived in farmlands were smaller and had paler coats, when compared with forest leopards that were bigger and richly colored. They called the village species "leopard" and the forest one "panther." Mooga was certainly much smaller than Buddy. However, his pelage was darker, challenging this long-held belief.

To keep Mooga safe from other wild tigers and leopards, and to avoid exposure to the hot sun, I decided to keep him in the wooden leopard trap. We kept vigil around Mooga late into the evening. As the sun was setting, Mooga gradually recovered. We hid and watched him stagger out of the trap, move about fifty meters into the dense bushes, and lie down to sleep safely. I periodically checked his signals from the campus, until I dozed off at midnight. It had been an exhausting day. I was pleased to be conducting an interesting experiment on how well translocated big cats adapted to their new homes. And how the resident leopards would respond to this interloper amidst them.

I woke up at dawn and drove to the spot where Mooga was released. I held out my antenna and put on my earphones. His signals were coming from the east, somewhere along the banks of the Nagarahole rivulet. I could not get any closer to him in my car because of the terrain, so I decided to walk, with Kala watching out for wild elephants. I was trying to home in on him and get a look if possible.

When I had similarly tried to walk and home in on Buddy or my tigers, I never got close enough to see them. When I reached the spot they had been at minutes earlier, their signals would be receding away. Because of their acute hearing, the cats always sensed my approach and managed to sneak away.

However, Mooga was behaving differently. Even as I got closer, signals from his collar got steadily louder. The active mode of the signals meant Mooga was up and alert, but staying exactly at the same spot. Soon, I was fifty . . . thirty . . . twenty . . . ten . . . *barely five meters* from him. Still no leopard in sight.

As soon as I took my next step, I jumped back in alarm. A pile of dry leaves a little more than an arm's length from me suddenly rose in a swirl, and morphed into a leopard! A few more paces and I would have stepped on Mooga. He scurried away, dashed down the embankment into some thick sedges on its banks of the rivulet, and clambered up the other side. A few seconds later I saw him disappearing into the thick forest beyond. All this happened in the blink of an eye.

Mooga had lived in a densely populated farm landscape of grain crops and coconut plantations. He probably hid throughout the day in total silence, venturing out at night to grab a feral dog whose disappearance would bother no one. Mooga would occasionally snatch a goat or a sheep from a poorly secured livestock pen. Sometimes he would feed off a dead cow left to rot in an open field after being flayed.

If Mooga dashed off every time a villager walked close to where he was hiding during the day, he would soon be hunted down by the farmers. Often, these villagers never realized they had leopards as neighbors. Mooga had responded to my approach exactly as he would have to a farmer walking past him, totally unaware. Instead, I had headed straight at Mooga, almost stepping on him, before he thought it was time to move. Although witnessing the metamorphosis of a pile of dry leaves into a leopard had almost given me a heart attack, I had learned something new about leopard survival skills in human-dominated landscapes.

Modern genetic research shows these village leopards are not distinct from the ones in the jungles. However, after understanding their radically distinct behaviors, I could sympathize with the old hunters who thought they were different species.

While tracking Buddy Mackay, I noticed he rarely crossed to the west of the paved road from Hunsur to Kutta [MAP 2]. I also regularly found the tracks of a large male leopard in that area, when I was out looking for Sundari or Mara, whose domain this space was.

The trail not far from Buddy's range boundary was a regular patrol route used by several big cats, as indicated by a profusion of scent marks they left on the trees on either side. It was also the boundary between the territories of Buddy and this unknown male leopard.

On the morning of March 8, 1990, walking up the trail to check the fiber-glass trap, [MAP 2, Point 2] I heard growls. In the trap was a beautiful, richly colored leopard, as well as the black goat staked out as bait that had perished in the initial melee. As with Buddy, this leopard had also lost all interest in the goat after the trapdoor slammed shut.

I quickly tranquilized the leopard by darting his haunch while my assistants distracted him. His body measurements were: total length, 198 centimeters, with a tail of 65 centimeters; a chest girth of 74 centimeters; with a shoulder height of 70.5 centimeters. He was slightly longer than Buddy Mackay but weighed only 50 kilograms. I named him Monda (Shorty), because he had a shorter tail. Labeled L-03, Monda would broadcast signals on a frequency of 150.210 megahertz.

The wear and discoloration on Monda's teeth suggested he was about eight to nine years old. My guess was he could retain his dominant status a couple of more years. A younger rival was bound to evict him from his territory as his physical condition declined. Now, however, Monda was strong enough to repulse even Buddy Mackay's incursions into his space.

A Passion Turns into an Obsession

By now my daily routine was set. I was up at 5:30 each morning, driving to the top of Kuntur Hillock [MAP 2]. Climbing the steep ladder of the steel tower, I stood on its two-meter square platform. Sharing the splendid solitude as the sun rose was my usual companion: a beautifully arrogant peregrine falcon perched at the top of a dying teak tree. Like mine, her day also began by scanning the panorama below. She was trying to spot a flock of green pigeons flying across the forest canopy to launch her deadly dive at 300 km per hour.

At this elevation of 903 meters, my receiver picked up signals from the cats as far away as three or four kilometers, sometimes even farther. The jungles of Nagarahole stretched away in all directions, as if my green topographic map sheet had come to life. Across the canopy matrix, I could discriminate patches of the natural forests from the man-made teak plantations. I could pick up familiar geographic features such as smaller hillocks, dirt roads, and tourism roads that were labeled on my map. I could visually trace the major ponds in the hollows and shallow valleys through which streams and rivulets meandered. The view, and signal detections, were even better on Faith Hill at a 1,087-meter elevation.

Based on the direction and strength of the signal I picked up from each cat, I guessed where it might be profitable to search more intensively for the cats during the rest of the day. Such daily locations involved triangulation from my Suzuki at closer distances. Sometimes I tried homing in on the signal

Ullas Karanth radio-tracking big cats from the top of Faith Hill. *Courtesy Fiona Sunquist*

by walking, if the terrain was unsuitable for driving. I also had the option to stay with a collared cat for longer periods, during the entire day, or through the night, trying to watch its behavior, a method called continuous tracking.

After the initial direction to each cat was established, I returned to camp for a quick breakfast. During the rest of the day, Gini and Bopi would go out to locate each different cat and precisely plot its locations for the day. This was hard work, because the signals did not carry far in the densely forested, undulating terrain at lower levels. The advantage of a clear line of sight was lost once we descended from the Kuntur Hillock or Faith Hill.

The big cats were less active during the day, depending on whether they were resting or out hunting, looking for mates, or patrolling their territories. However, they could still be moving around a lot, making it difficult to plot each location precisely.

Although many natural history buffs imagine on-the-ground radio-tracking of big cats to be all adventure, fun, and games, it really is not. Most of the time I heard only the radio beeps because my earphones blocked out the myriad lovely sounds of the jungle. My reward was in sightings of other animals which abounded: herds of dainty, spotted chital; elk-sized solitary sambar; herds of statuesque gaur; or groups of giant elephants. More uncommonly, I saw sloth bears digging for termites, packs of wild dogs chasing deer, sneaky leopards trying to stalk langurs, and even tigers cooling off in ponds. The greatest reward, of course, was getting a look at my own collared cats.

At the end of the day, I returned to my spartan field camp, took a shower, and poured myself a whiskey before eating the rudimentary meal served by the cook, Das. When I did not have a nightlong tracking session, I went out to sit outside the camp, under the starlit sky, listening to the jungle come alive with wondrous voices of creatures of the night, just as the human cacophony in Nagarahole was shutting down: the hysterical calls of the large herds of chital that "yarded" around the campus seeking safety from predators and poachers; the "sawing" roar of a leopard, calling in frustration after failing to pick off a fawn from the herds; the series of loud *Dhanks*, the sambar's alarm as the deer relayed the movement of a tiger patrolling the trail that stretched all the way to the Kaithole Pond. Finally, above all, was the most unforgettable sound of the Indian jungle, a tiger's roar! A series of booming *Aaan-Ooongh, Aaan-Ooongh*s . . . gradually fading, far, far away until I could hear them no more. This roar had haunted me ever since I heard it first, right here in Nagarahole a quarter century earlier. Now, at age forty-two, I was living the dream inspired by that roar.

My passion had now turned into an obsession. I went home only once or twice a month, although the drive was only a couple of hours. My wife, Prathibha, tolerated my absence with much fortitude. I realized what I had accomplished would have been almost impossible without her support. Yet, even for her sake, I could not let go of my magnificent obsession. The triumphs and tragedies in the lives of my collared cats consumed me to a degree that is impossible to understand.

Obsessed with what my cats were doing, I was also paying no attention to what was going on in the local society. This was extremely unwise, because the attitudes of the people around me eventually impacted my work seriously.

Meanwhile, the pre-monsoon storm clouds were beginning to scud across the starlit sky above. Unknown to me, they were harbingers of storm of a different kind that would soon engulf me.

3 | DEFAMED, EXILED, UNDETERRED

IN CHITWAN, Nepal, the scientists of the Smithsonian had radio-tracked their tigers from elephant back, because there were few dirt roads in the park. Occasionally they used a Piper aircraft, which enabled homing in on wide-ranging transient tigers over much longer distances.

In contrast, the network of dirt roads in Nagarahole [**MAP 2**] helped me to move around rapidly, instead of relying on the painfully slow elephants. Among my collared tigers, Sundari was the easiest to locate from my perch at the Kuntur Hillock. I could then quickly drive around and triangulate her location precisely from a closer range.

However, the two transient male tigers, Mara and Das, moved over long distances to cover their large home ranges. My two assistants and I had our work cut out tracking them. On some days we simply could not locate the cats. That's when I wished I had the deep pockets of the Smithsonian Institution, which could have flown me up to find them.

The monotony of routine radio-tracking was occasionally relieved by exciting, dangerous, and even amusing incidents. Because watching the collared cats generated a lot more data on the nuances of tiger and leopard behaviors, I did my best to observe my cats in addition to plotting their locations on a map.

Before I could watch my big cats, they had to be habituated to my Suzuki. The network of dirt roads in Nagarahole sometimes allowed me to anticipate the direction in which the cats were heading. I could sometimes go ahead and wait for them. Using this technique, within three months, two of the tigers, Sundari and Das, and the leopard Buddy Mackay, all of whom lived in areas with denser road networks, became quite habituated to my car. They began to perceive my green Suzuki as a clumsy but harmless animal, which followed them around for no reason. However, the moment I stepped out, the cats instantly slunk away, as they would from any other human being. I could not fantasize about any special emotional bond with my cats.

Tigers have a flat-footed walk, with both the forelegs and hind legs on the same flank moving simultaneously (unlike dogs and hoofed animals). This gives an impression of languorous grace to their walk: no two-legged model sashaying on the "catwalk" can attain that grace. But the slowness of the tiger's walk is an illusion; the cat's lengthy strides can propel it forward quite rapidly.

I once tried to follow a walking tiger while remaining out of its sight. I saw Sundari cross the HGR tourism road [MAP 2, Point 11] heading toward Kaithole Pond. I got out of the car and followed radio-tracking on foot from one hundred meters behind. To save me from accidentally blundering into elephants, my tracker Kala walked behind me. I hoped Kala would at least alert me about any proximate elephant, before he clambered up the nearest tree with the agility of a langur. Experienced Jenu Kuruba tribesmen like him are truly gifted at sensing the proximity of elephants. Dodging elephants in the dense jungle had been an essential survival skill for thousands of years.

We walked determinedly for about four hundred meters, following Sundari's radio signals. I was getting ripped by every thorny plant species ever recorded by botanists in Nagarahole. Sundari, however, was moving so quickly that her signals became steadily fainter. Before I reached the Kaithole Pond [MAP 2, Point 24], I had lost her signals entirely. Only after climbing a tree to one of my tracking machans [MAP 2, Point 13], located on a nearby hillock, could I find her signals again. In less than half an hour Sundari had effortlessly walked over a three-kilometer distance, through all those thorny thickets that had ripped off pieces of my skin. My skin was also crawling with hundreds of pinhead-sized burrowing ticks. This horrible itching would last for several days. I wished I had Sundari's eighteen-centimeter-long, sandpaper-rough tongue to lick the bloody ticks off. If there was one animal species that I dread while walking in Malenad jungle, even more than a bull elephant, it is this tiny insect with an ugly name: *Hyloaedea*.

Besides the monotony of listening to radio signals, I had other distinctly unglamorous routines. One such chore was examining the carcasses of animals killed by tigers, leopards, and wild dogs. These kills were literally gold mines of data. How much a tiger eats at one go; what proportion of a kill it consumes; and what is the species, age, sex, physical condition, and health status of the prey animal it killed could all be answered by studying rotting carcasses. The kills also told me how exactly the predators subdued and killed their prey, and the habitats and time of the day when they hunted down their prey. I also identified the predator involved, how far the kill was dragged, and how it was hidden from pesky scavengers.

Leopards are adaptable predators that hunt a wide variety of prey. *Courtesy Diinesh Kumble*

Asian wild dogs (dhole) are skilled hunters of deer species. *Courtesy Giri Cavale*

I could collect data on whether the predator shared its kill with others of its kind, how long it had stayed with the kill, and who else had scavenged off the carcass after the predator left. This ecological data complemented my direct observations from radio-tracking to complete a picture of predatory behavior.

I also preserved the skull, lower jaw, and other biological samples from each kill. More detailed studies of such specimens helped me to determine the sex and the age of each prey animal. For example, I could study the sequence in which their permanent teeth erupted and wore out and observe through a microscope the tree-ring-like patterns on cross-sections of their teeth, to accurately fix the age of the ungulate prey animal. In the first three years, my trackers and I ended up collecting 154 kills made by tigers, which included 16 chital, 44 sambar, 22 wild pigs, 69 gaur, and even 2 elephant calves. I also collected 83 leopard kills and 100 kills made by wild dogs.

As the collection of skulls grew large, the forest department built a bamboo shed with a thatched roof next to the range office to store the specimens. The collection had some fine heads of gaur, sambar, and chital, which sported trophy-sized horns or antlers. My collection of skulls became quite a draw for

Ullas Karanth with the study collection of skulls of animals killed by predators.
Courtesy Fiona Sunquist

the tourists who thronged to the park. The tribal people referred to me as the *Moole* (bones) Ranger!

However, poking around these rotting carcasses of prey animals crawling with maggots and bombarded by buzzing swarms of blue-bottle flies was not exactly a pleasant experience. Many senior forest officials and conservationists who wanted to see research in action did so standing as far away as possible, covering their noses with handkerchiefs.

Furthermore, this "kill data" did not yield an estimate of the numbers and proportions of different ungulate prey species killed by each predator species. My detection of predator kills was heavily biased in favor of larger carcasses. Additionally, tigers, leopards, and wild dogs killed their prey in slightly different types of cover. They also cached them in different ways. All these factors biased my collection of sample kills.

The tracks, scrape marks, and scent signs left by the predator also helped me to identify the predator. But to get an accurate idea of the diets of predators, I had to collect samples of their scats (droppings). I stooped even lower in search of authentic knowledge. Examining predator scats is an even more odious chore than examining their rotting kills. For one thing, the scats smelled worse than rotting meat. They had to be washed and sieved using tea strainers of fine mesh to separate out the hair and bone fragments of the prey animals consumed by the predator. Based on the strained-out hairs' color, thickness, length, and other characteristics, I could accurately identify the prey eaten.

Initially, the nitpicky Brahmin project accountant in Mysore had objected to me buying dozens of tea strainers. He had snidely hinted I was padding my project accounts, saying, "After all, you are not running a tea shop for tigers." I explained the application of tea strainers in tiger research in graphic detail to the fastidious man—who likely bathed thrice a day—and he never questioned my accounting practices again!

The most important part of this research method was the fact that scat collection was not biased by the type of species consumed; it provided an accurate profile of the proportion of different prey in the diet of tigers, leopards, and wild dogs. My labor of love ultimately yielded 1,329 scats (490 from tigers, 535 from leopards, and 304 from wild dogs). It was a valuable data set for studying the relationship between predators and prey in Nagarahole, and years later it was published in some fine scientific journals, making me recall the Kannada proverb: "Only by dirtying your hands can you fill your belly with yogurt."

Shockingly, one of the leopard scats I examined contained a shriveled-up human toe! Around the toe was a ring traditionally worn by married women. However, no one in Nagarahole had been reported missing in the previous weeks. I concluded the leopard must have dug up one of the shallow graves on the edge of the forest and fed off the woman's cadaver. The fact that the ring was made of aluminum rather than gold suggested she was a poor woman.

Raising My Army of Citizen Scientists

Tigers are obligate predators that can survive only by hunting down large, hoofed prey animals. Virtually everything about tiger ecology and behavior depends on that "prey base." How many prey animals there are, and where they are in Nagarahole, were questions central to my research.

In 1986, when I began my work, I had focused on the challenge of accurately estimating the numbers of prey species taken by tigers, leopards, and wild dogs. To estimate these numbers, I had to figure out how to estimate their population densities: on average, how many animals of each species occupy a square kilometer of the forest? Such ungulate prey—"wild hoof-stock"—in Nagarahole included three species of deer: muntjac, chital, and sambar; the wild pig; gaur; and the elusive and rare four-horned antelope. Tigers also occasionally preyed on elephant calves.

I found that the official counts of these animals, generated by forestry departments across India, had practically no statistical foundation. The animal "census" that produced the numbers was more of an annual ritual than a true scientific count. It involved thousands of forest staff swarming across India's jungles to do the impossible: count all the animals out there. The numbers reported year after year were practically worthless.

I had to do better by choosing a proven method with strong roots in both statistics and species biology. Indeed, such a method, called "line transect sampling," did exist. Fortunately, I had been exposed to it during my stint at the University of Florida.

The line transect method was suited for counting the prey species in Nagarahole. It did not demand that I identify each individual animal or count all the animals out there. Instead, the method required me to walk silently along narrow trails to sample the forest. My objective would be to detect and count animals of every prey species I encountered on either side of the trail. Starting in June 1986, I repeatedly walked my transect lines in Nagarahole accompanied by a tracker.

Chital deer are preyed upon by tigers, leopards, and wild dogs.

Sambar deer are the preferred prey of tigers.

My transect lines were narrow, straight foot trails, each about 3.2 kilometers long, carefully cut following a survey designed well beforehand. I could comfortably walk this distance within a couple of hours without losing concentration or tiring. I had transect lines spanning Nagarahole Range to representatively sample different types of habitats used by the prey species: moist forests, dry forests, logged secondary forests, teak plantations, and grassy swamps known as Hadlu, which together formed a diverse mosaic of vegetation.

I sampled the transects during early mornings and late afternoons to detect, count, and record all the prey animals I saw, before they fled away. In effect, in each survey I was sampling a strip of forest that was 3.2 kilometers long.

Even massive adult gaur bulls are sometimes killed by tigers.

A herd of elephants in the grassy swamp known as Hadlu.

To cover my study area in Nagarahole, I had to walk 465 kilometers, spread out over 150 days.

From these data I was able to generate rigorous estimates of the population densities of each prey species. On average, in each square kilometer area of Nagarahole, there were 49.1 chital, 3.4 sambar, 5.6 gaur, 3.4 wild pigs, 4.3 muntjac, 3.3 elephants, and 25 langur monkeys. No one before had derived similarly rigorous estimates of prey abundance in Asian forests.

These transect walks involved quietly sneaking past potentially dangerous elephants, gaur, and sloth bears, sometimes from as close as ten meters. They provided some of the most thrilling experiences on foot, without the safety offered by a vehicle or machan. I was confident enough in my field-craft to be able to survive these walks, but most senior forest officials walked in these forests only when accompanied by armed forest guards. When I invited them to walk the transects with me without taking along firearms, less than a handful had accepted.

The line transect method was arduous and manpower intensive. If I wanted to extend it all over Nagarahole Reserve, and to areas beyond, I needed many more trained field workers. My team of tribal trackers could spot animals and even count them, but they lacked the ability to measure and record the distance and angle data necessary for the final analyses.

After I began my research in 1986, several young men, all keen naturalists, had come to me to seeking to know more about tiger research. In the summer of 1989, after I returned from Florida, I had the germ of an idea. If I could train these volunteer naturalists in line transect surveys, I could collect high-quality data on the numbers of prey animals in Nagarahole and beyond.

This idea worked out brilliantly. Over the years, I was able to attract and train dozens of young men (and a few women) to create my voluntary reserve army of "citizen scientists" spread across India. Their backgrounds varied: volunteers included students, teachers, engineers, doctors, journalists, planters, farmers, stockbrokers, and businessmen. Their common traits included physical fitness, a knowledge of natural history, and the ability to use instruments that recorded data. And, of course, the grit to withstand the hardships of my line transect camps.

I used these training camps to separate the grain from chaff from among the dozens of volunteers who clamored to join them. These boot camps soon became infamous. A vast majority of the enthusiastic new entrants failed to make the final grade. They often departed quickly, unable to tolerate the stress of hair-raising close encounters with the wild beasts, the infernal tick bites, and the spartan camp conditions.

The recruits who survived, however, acquired the necessary skills, and typically spent one or two weeks each year collecting data for me. Over the years, the number of such hard-core citizen scientists swelled. Through a process that resembled the training model in the *Star Wars* movies, some of my seasoned volunteers qualified as Jedi line transect trainers! A handful of them, smitten by the wildlife bug, refashioned their own careers to eventually join my tiger conservation efforts.

Ullas Karanth (ahead) and Samba Kumar conducting line transect counts of prey species.

Most prominently, Samba, a tall, sinewy business graduate who worked in India's space agency ISRO, changed his career to wildlife research. He became my first PhD student and was my capable deputy for the next twenty-two years. Savvy engineers Krishna and Prasad, advertising executive Praveen, and coffee planter Girish became dependable allies in my conservation advocacy.

How Tigers Talk, Walk, and Run

The tigers that I was tracking generally slept eighteen hours in a day, occasionally waking up to lick themselves clean. They often stayed close to their kills for three or four days, snacking on the carcass, until they could stuff themselves no more. With their bellies full, over the next three or four days they patrolled their home ranges, padding along forest trails and dirt roads.

Male tigers sought females in estrus, cubs followed their mothers, and owners of territories warned off unwelcome intruders. The wandering transients dodged the resident breeders, waiting until they were strong enough to challenge them. All this was possible because of a sophisticated tiger communication system that evolved long before we humans did. As a trained engineer, I was humbled by the technological marvels of Mother Nature.

As tigers walk, they deposit piles of scats, which they keep enticingly fresh and smelly by pawing some dust and grass over before moving on. Tigers also continually stop, lift their tails, and spray a jet of urine mixed with scent on the trees and bushes en route. The spray is a scent signature unique to each individual tiger. As they walk, the cats stop at some trees they pass and leave deep scratch marks with their powerful fore claws. Furthermore, they vocalize using varied growls, grunts, and deep roars, which carry three kilometers in the stillness of the night.

Such a sophisticated system of individual identification and communication—across time and space—enables tigers (and other big cats) to easily find or avoid each other, as the situation warrants. Imagine a dozen New Yorkers spread out over the same area as Nagarahole, functioning as a cohesive society, unaided by any modern system of transportation or communication. You get the picture.

I soon realized that each of my cats had some favorite resting spots within its home range, like a hammock in the back garden. When not watching over their kills, tigers used such locations for daylong siestas.

The pond at Mavinahalla, which could be observed from two different watchtowers, was such a spot for the tiger Das [**MAP 2, Points 15 and 16**]. If his signals indicated he was nearby, I usually spent the day on one of these towers waiting for him to turn up.

On one such afternoon, Das had been lounging neck-deep in a pond, shaded by the leafy *Pongamia* trees on its edge. A couple of hours later, at 1600 hours, a family of elephants approached the pond: a matriarchal female and her adult daughter, each with a young calf. They wanted to drink and frolic in the water. During the summer, I often watched parades of elephant families having fun in the pond and departing.

When the elephants were fifty meters from the pond, they lifted their trunks and picked up the tiger's scent. The mothers maneuvered the calves, now squealing in fear, jammed between them. They continued to march down the slope, toward the water. They were tired, the water was tempting, and the next pond was a kilometer away.

Hearing them approach, Das became alert and stood up. The elephants were now twenty-five meters from the pond. Das shook the water off his body like a dog after a bath. With a bloodcurdling growl, he charged up the cleared grassy strip, straight for the elephants. Barely was he out of the pond before the elephants turned tail and fled back, trumpeting in terror. Das turned and padded back to relax in the tranquil pond again.

The adult bull elephant is truly the king of the Asian jungles.

A couple of weeks later, I saw the incident almost repeat itself. However, this time the intruder coming down the trail was a huge solitary bull elephant. He was in *musth*—a condition like the rut in stags—during which tuskers are at their aggressive best. After hearing his approach, Das had stood up in the middle of the pond, thinking of repeating his earlier performance, I imagined. The tusker spotted the tiger in the pool, and without a moment's hesitation, curled up and rolled his trunk into his mouth, flattened his ears, and, screaming what I assumed to be choice obscenities at the impudent cat, charged down at full tilt.

Das wasted no time. I saw him furiously pedal backward in the water, turn his tail fully, leap out of the pond, and run bounding up the opposite slope. The pond was empty when the tusker waded into the water like an amphibious landing craft in a war movie. Das did not stop to look back.

Playing Chess with Leopards

One morning, I went out radio-tracking Buddy Mackay along Chikapala tourist road [**MAP 2, Point 21**]. When my Suzuki was two hundred meters from Buddy's signals, I realized he was not alone. The frequent, interspersed growls of two different leopards told me Buddy was in an amorous mating session with one of his consorts. However, both the leopards were invisible in this patch of moist-deciduous forest.

Hoping to get a look, I got out of the car and started tracking on foot with Kala following. When I got within forty meters, I saw the leopardess up on a tall, partially dead *Terminalia* tree that forked out into several leafless branches. She scrambled down from the fork the instant she spotted me. As we approached, I heard the leopards scurry away through the brush.

I could now hear the piteous squeals of a baby langur monkey above. It was huddled, way up in the thinnest leafy branches. Unlike the adult langurs that have silvery-gray coats and naked, jet-black faces, the babies have chocolate-brown coats and cute pink faces. This baby should have been securely in the arms of its mother, not alone at the treetop. The baby was looking down, screaming in terror. On a closer look, I saw the mother. She was wedged between two branches, obviously dead. Her mouth was open in a grimace of terror, with a thin trickle of blood oozing out.

I quickly surmised what had transpired. The mother langur had scrambled up the tree with the baby in her arms, when she spotted the frolicking leopards. The female leopard had charged up the tree at lightning speed and caught up, delivering a swift nape bite that instantly killed the monkey. Somehow, in the melee, the mother langur had let go of the baby just in time. The terrified baby's antipredator response had kicked in, making it clamber up all the way to the top where no leopard could reach. Our arrival had disrupted the hunt, making the leopardess abandon the kill and join her mate below.

If this baby langur kept squealing to wake up its dead mama, it would soon attract the crested hawk eagle that soared over the tree canopy. But even if the little monkey dodged the eagle's talons today, after dark the fearsome forest eagle owl would find it. If the baby survived them, it was too young to have developed the complex stomach chemistry necessary to digest the toxic leaves of tropical trees that its mother consumed. Without her milk, this baby was doomed. This was the way of the jungle.

With a heavy heart, I walked away. That night at camp, I woke up, hearing the baby langur's cries in my dream.

Radio-tracking data showed Buddy Mackay was a breeding male, holding a large territory of 31.3 square kilometers. It stretched between Kalhalla and Nagarahole along the east of the paved road [MAP 3]. Although I had not yet radio-collared a female leopard, I had seen Buddy associate with at least three of them in different parts of his range. He had priority mating rights over these leopardesses. The patterns of space use and land tenures of leopards in Nagarahole were similar to what researchers reported from African leopards.

The spot where I had released Mooga was on the southern boundary of Buddy's territory. It separated Buddy from another big male leopard whose range extended farther south. Both these dominant males intensively patrolled and scent marked the boundary, keeping each other at bay. Both were forest leopards that weighed over 50 kilograms, and preyed on the plentiful chital, sambar, and langurs. In contrast, Mooga grew up on farmlands of Nanjangud hunting much smaller prey, such as the black-naped hare, as well as the dogs, cats, goats, and chickens he stole from villagers. He was a lightweight runt who had no chance of surviving an encounter with his powerful new neighbors.

After Mooga had recovered from sedation, he had explored his home. From the scent marks he encountered, he would know the area was intensively patrolled by the two big males, not to mention the tigers. Released into this strange land, bereft of his usual prey, it would be impossible for Mooga to become a successful forest predator of fleet-footed deer. If either of his rivals caught him trying, they would hunt him down.

The male leopard Buddy Mackay boldly crossing a paved road in daytime.

As I radio-tracked Mooga's signals, I noticed that for nearly two weeks he stayed close to the release site, moving up and down for a kilometer along the Nagarahole rivulet. He was easy to track, because I got his signals loud and clear, right from the Nagarahole campus. However, I did not experiment again with tracking him on foot.

Then, on March 12, 1990, Mooga's radio signals suddenly vanished.

Failing to find his signals even from the Kuntur Hillock, I drove up to Faith Hill. At 1,087 meters in elevation, this was the highest point between Nagarahole and the towering 1,500-meter ridge of the Western Ghats [MAP 2]. The Ghats harbored even more dense, perpetually moist, tropical rain forests, like the ones I had hiked in Kudremukh as a teenager.

From the Faith Peak, I swept the Yagi antenna in a circular arc, starting with the interior forests of Nagarahole Reserve that stretched to my north, south, and east. No signals. As I turned westward, holding the antenna high facing the blue ridge of the Ghats, Mooga's signals suddenly thumped my eardrums—loud, clear, and quite nearby.

I triangulated Mooga's present position. He was well outside the Nagarahole Park, hiding in a landscape mosaic of deep-green coffee plantations and yellowing rice paddies that stretched all the way to the Ghats. This was an entirely human-dominated landscape. It harbored the prey familiar to Mooga—village dogs, cats, and goats, with an occasional wild muntjac for variety. Furthermore, unlike the dry farmlands he grew up in, these wooded coffee plantations, thickets, and rocky outcrops gave him plenty of hiding space in daytime. Moreover, his new home range supported very few leopards. Mooga's risky long-distance move of ten kilometers to Kutta village [MAP 2, Inset] had paid off: fortune had favored this brave runt, at least for now.

I kept tracking Mooga's location a couple of times a week. He stayed well clear of the forest, comfortably settling down in his new home range. A coffee planter friend of mine even reported seeing a leopard with a collar in the headlights of his car while driving home.

This incident clearly showed that moving "problem" leopards from farmlands to unfamiliar forests occupied by others of their kind was unlikely to work. Such a strategy would not solve the "problem" of livestock depredations, because another transient village leopard in search of a territory would fill the vacated space. In Mooga's case, the forest department had only succeeded in shifting the "problem" from one village to another.

The tactic of moving big cats around wide landscapes like pawns on a chessboard would not overcome their survival strategies honed by evolution. The "Born Free" model, while rather cute and appealing to city-bred animal lovers, has little practical use in big cat conservation.

The Jigsaw Puzzle of Tiger Territories

Gradually, the locations of the tigers that I plotted on a map clarified how they were carving up the space in this part of Nagarahole. Sundari was a resident breeding tigress. The subadult cubs that she had with her when I caught her soon dispersed away. Mara and Das, both transients and about the same age, had large, spread-out ranges, over a hundred square kilometers, showing a small overlap in the area around Chikapala Pond [MAP 3].

One weekend when I was on a trip home, Gini, who was tracking Sundari in my absence, saw something astonishing. Sundari had been on the move, moaning continuously, even after the sun was up and the day got hotter. When Gini saw her in the open Hadlu, near Chikapala [MAP 2, Point 17], he detected signals from Das, who was heading toward her. The two tigers soon met and mated, noisily and frequently. Around noon, Gini had also picked up the signal from Mara, who soon arrived. Thereafter, Das retreated, and Mara had taken over the mating spree with Sundari. A tigress mating with two different males during the same estrus had not been reported in the wild before. I was sorry I had missed this rare interaction.

There appeared to be a hierarchy among male tigers, with the holder of the territory having a priority, but with extra-pair copulations opportunistically occurring with other males. Evolutionary biologist Tim Clutton-Brock had theorized about opportunistic copulations in deer and other species, rather formally labeling the participants involved as "sneaky fuckers."

While I could locate and radio-track Sundari almost every day, Das and Mara proved harder to pin down. They behaved like young adults who had left their mother's range about two years earlier, and were wandering widely trying to find and settle into territories of their own. The competition for tiger territories was fierce in Nagarahole; these two transients had to challenge some weaker resident males and take over their territories.

If I failed to get the initial directions to Mara, Das, or Mudka from Kuntur tower or Faith Hill in the morning, I faced a challenge finding them later in the day. I had to then depend on random sweeps for their signals by driving along the network of dirt roads in accessible areas. Sometimes I had to climb one of the flimsy bamboo machans [**MAP 2, Points 13 and 14**] I had built on trees standing atop smaller hillocks to improve signal reception.

Among the three male cats, the home ranges of Das and Mara overlapped partially in the zone with a network of dirt roads for showing tourists around. After I darted Mudka, he had stayed entirely outside the tourism area, although I had seen him with his "extended" family a year earlier near Mavinahalla Pond [**MAP 2, Point 16**] in the tourism zone. Mudka's movements had now shrunk to a smaller area of 34.8 square kilometers on the west side of Nagarahole, which had poor road access. He appeared to be avoiding the areas frequented by the three younger tigers, Das, Mara, and Yajamana [**MAP 3**].

At times I felt like a kid assembling a jigsaw puzzle that had many missing pieces. I had four collared tigers. But clearly there were other tigers I had not yet collared. The elephant in the drawing room was a tiger: the big male Yajamana, the one who got away on the last date of the capture season. He seemed as big as Mudka but was much younger and vigorous. I guessed from Mudka's wounds that he had suffered them early in January 1990. There were now at least three other robust males busy carving up his former range. Being the biggest and the strongest, Yajamana had probably taken over much of Mudka's old range. Das and Mara were still wandering widely, trying to nibble away at other pieces of prime tiger turf.

By late February 1990, I was witnessing an amazingly fluid situation in the land tenures of tigers in Nagarahole. I had some inkling of how things could unfold, based on earlier studies by Mel Sunquist and, later on, by David Smith in Chitwan. I presumed that the next couple of years would showcase a violent, turbulent period in the tiger society of Nagarahole. If I wanted to get the full picture of what was going on, I had to radio collar and track more tigers after the monsoon ended: I was rearing to go.

Long Live the Tiger King!

We were now in March, and temperatures soared. I was trying to assiduously track Mudka. I had once tried to home in on him on foot, triangulating to pinpoint his location to a cool and shady spot on the bank of the Nagarahole rivulet not far from my camp. Mudka had heard me approaching and moved away unseen. I had missed seeing him by a few seconds. Moisture was still oozing into the tracks he left.

When I got to the exact spot, I saw not only his giant footprints but also the imprint of his whole body in the moist sand. He appeared to have been writhing in pain, lying in the moist bed of sand. More ominously, there was a foul stench from his gangrenous wound mixed with a whiff of the antiseptic potions we had applied after his capture. *How long would his agony endure,* I wondered. The detached scientist in me wanted to document his decline in meticulous detail, but the animal lover in me wanted him to die painlessly and soon.

On March 12, 1990, I got a call from Nanjappa, the manager of the Faith Coffee Estate. He was a friendly man whom I knew from my frequent trips to the top of Faith Hill to find radio signals for my cats. Nanjappa was agitated that a huge but very emaciated tiger had just been seen by laborers as it moved through the coffee bushes in broad daylight. The tiger had a collar belt around its neck.

This was the peak of the harvest season. Dozens of women picking coffee berries by hand had panicked. They refused to work until someone took the monster away. This was not like a normal tiger, which would scurry away at the sight of any human being. This tiger had walked slowly and silently, apparently in a daze, not bothered by the dozens of hysterical women screaming their heads off. If the tiger accidentally bumped into a worker among the dense coffee bushes, the consequences could be disastrous.

I drove at a furious speed to the Faith Peak and started searching for Mudka. I immediately picked up his signals. He was half a kilometer downhill, on a steep rocky slope clothed in stunted coffee bushes. The ridge I was on sloped down all the way to the boundary of the Nagarahole Reserve near Nanachi [MAP 2]. Mudka was moving downhill, and was within half a kilometer of the jungle. I tracked his signals until I judged Mudka was about to cross the cleared fire line that marked the park boundary. The succulent green grass sprouting on that open strip usually attracted herds of chital. They would confirm my speculation.

The shrill alarm screams of the chital soon told me Mudka had crossed the grassy strip and was now back home. No one had been hurt, and the immediate crisis was over. But it was also clear the days of Mudka being able to catch the fleet-footed deer were over.

Twelve days later, on March 22, 1990, I was searching for signals, driving along the dirt road called Bulldozer Road [**MAP 2, BZR**], which was regularly used by forest staff to patrol, surprise, and ambush poachers. The road skirted the western boundary of Nagarahole Reserve but was inside. This was an area that both Mudka and Das still frequented.

Around 1500 hours I picked up signals from Mudka. They were at their loudest as I got close to the Santhapura Hadlu grass swamp [**MAP 2, Point 7**]. They emerged from three hundred meters to my right in a shallow valley. I quickly triangulated Mudka's location. Surprisingly, he seemed to be right out in the open grass swamp, even in this broad daylight. A tiger as sick as he was usually is not so brazen.

I decided to investigate on foot. With my trackers Kala and Putta following, I clamped on my earphones and walked down the hillock following a well-worn elephant trail. The signals in my earphones were loud and clear, and ominously inactive. The grassy swamp was wide open before me, but the tiger was nowhere in sight. Mudka was in a deep rainwater gully that cut across the swamp, exactly where my triangulation predicted he would be. He had been dead at least for two or three days. Because the deep gully he had crawled into had blocked his radio signals, I had not picked them up from the Kuntur Hillock.

I was stunned by the sight of Mudka. In just nine weeks, the 230-kilogram giant of a tiger had turned into a mere bag of bones wrapped in faded tiger skin. I remembered Chinnappa had dumped a chital roadkill on Stream Belt Road [**MAP 2, Point 5**] four weeks earlier, after I located Mudka's signals close by. At night Mudka had scavenged off that carcass. That was likely the last big meal he consumed. As his festering wounds worsened, too feeble to move any further, Mudka had finally crawled into this gulley and breathed his last. The "Tiger King" who had lorded over a huge territory and maintained a harem of beautiful tigresses had finally starved to death, slowly and painfully.

I was sad. Mudka was the first wild tiger I had caught and radio-tracked. I consoled myself with the scientific reasoning that every wild tiger had to die a similar painful death, unless it was killed swiftly by a rival tiger or a human shooter. The death aspired to by every pious Hindu is a peaceful one. The king closes his eyes one final time, after drinking a few drops of the sacred water from the river Ganga, surrounded by his mourning family. That could never be the fate of any real tiger king.

I returned to camp to inform the forest officials in Bangalore (now known as Bengaluru) and Delhi. I speculated on the implications of Mudka's death. Yajamana now occupied much of his former territory. However, Mara and Das were also wandering through it, trying to nibble off pieces for themselves to settle down and breed. Sundari was mating with both Mara and Das. She had firm control over her own prey-rich territory [**MAP 3**].

However, raising her next litter would be a real challenge for Sundari. Her territory was sandwiched among ranges of three contending males: Mara, Das, and Yajamana. Studies of tigers in Chitwan had discovered that, like all cats, tigers practiced infanticide. When a male cat who sired a litter of cubs dies, the new male who takes over his range seeks out and kills the cubs of his predecessor.

Evolutionary biologists explained why infanticide evolved and persists. So long as her cubs are with her, a tigress will not come into estrus. The new dominant male will not be able to sire his own progeny. On the other hand, if her cubs are lost for any reason, the tigress immediately becomes estrous and mates with the new male. Infanticidal behavior has persisted among tigers—and many other mammals—because only the males that practiced it have propagated their genes into future generations.

Infanticide has been a successful evolutionary strategy. It has nothing to do with individual tigers being good guys or bad guys according to a human yardstick of morality. As a consequence, whenever contests for male territories become more intense, breeding males in the population turn over more quickly, and the number of surviving cubs drops. As the number of transient subadult competitors drops, the turnover among dominant males slows down and cub survival rebounds, only for the cycle to repeat itself.

Typically, the tenure of breeding male tigers is about three to four years, and five to eight years for females. A male tiger can sire only one or two litters from each of the females in his range. The tigress holding a prey-rich territory can raise three to four litters of two to five cubs during her tenure. A successful breeding tigress can potentially produce ten to fifteen cubs in her entire lifetime, thus replacing herself many times, despite these periodic bouts of infanticide.

Sundari's first litter of cubs had dispersed soon after I radio-collared her in January 1990. One cub, blinded in one eye by a porcupine quill, disappeared, as did the male cub. However, a fit subadult cub (later labeled NHT-116) seized and settled down in a territory to the north of Sundari's range [**MAP 3**].

After Mudka, a dominant male for years, declined and died, his death was likely to set off a turbulent period with a rapid turnover of male territories. I worried Sundari would not be able to successfully raise more cubs for a few years, despite ruling over a bountiful territory packed with food like a supermarket. I was, however, confident that I would catch and track more tigresses across the park. In the long run, they would help me realize my dream of understanding every nuance of maternal tiger behavior.

At least that was my plan in the long run. I was unwise to ignore the wisdom of the great economist John Maynard Keynes, who had cautioned, "In the long run we will all be dead anyway."

The Mystery of Tiger Deaths

On March 6, 1990, forest guards found a dead tiger in the Veeranahosahalli Forest Range. This area was on the northeastern edge of the reserve, thirty kilometers from my field camp [**MAP 2, Inset**]. The autopsy report said the tiger, a large male, died after eating the carcass of a cow it had killed. Before the tiger returned for a second meal, someone had poisoned it with a potent but easily available agricultural pesticide. Not only the tiger but also several crows and vultures that scavenged on the dead cow had also succumbed.

This part of Nagarahole Reserve was not as strictly patrolled as the central area I worked in. I also assumed that some local cattle herder had poisoned the carcass. Little did I know at that time, an entirely new threat to tigers from faraway China had reached the boundaries of Nagarahole.

That tiger had been poisoned twenty days before I found Mudka's carcass. If not for his radio signals, Mudka's death would have gone entirely undetected. Most tigers that die in the forests are never found. The chance of anyone randomly finding a dead tiger is extremely low because of the vast area of the forest and low densities in which big cats live. Human activities, such as logging, forest product collection, and livestock grazing, had been drastically curtailed in Nagarahole, reducing the chance of detecting dead tigers. People who entered the forest illegally for any reason would not report tiger deaths, of course.

Furthermore, animal carcasses decomposed rapidly in the hot, humid climate. Even as it decayed, any carcass would be swiftly consumed by the myriad scavenging animals: other big cats, sloth bears, jackals, wild pigs, vultures, and crows. The millions of maggots—larvae of flies that lay their eggs on the carcass—finish off whatever is left. Within three or four days, the stench that could lead someone to the carcass vanishes.

Dead tigers were found rarely, and only when forest guards on patrol smelled the stench and chose to brave the vicious thorns and ticks to mount a search. This poisoned tiger had been accidentally found while guards were clearing bushes to create a firebreak.

The next dead tiger, reported on April 2, 1990, was also found by guards because it lay in an open clearing in Kalhalla Range, along a paved road running through the park to Karmadu [MAP 2]. This tigress was about two years old, the age at which she would have dispersed away from her mother's territory. The tigress had a puncture wound on her shoulder and claw marks on her body, indicating she had fought with another tiger.

Intact skins from dead tigers were considered prize trophies for display in the offices of senior forest officials. They were sent posthaste to be mounted by the best taxidermist in India, who happened to live in Mysore. Jubert Van Ingen was a spry, dapper man in his eighties, the last one of several generations of fabled taxidermists. They had originally come to India in the 1700s as soldiers of the British Empire. Jubert was a Boer of South African descent, who still retained that South African lilt in his English accent. Although I was forty years younger, we had become good friends because of our shared interest in wildlife.

I had visited Jubert a few times to watch him guide his workers, who deftly skinned dead tigers and leopards. Having skinned and curated hundreds of animal trophies for decades, Jubert was a virtual encyclopedia on the anatomy of wild animals. I had spent hours at his "workshop" during my days as an amateur naturalist, absorbing as much as I could, while he delved into explanations about injuries and other features of animal anatomy.

After the precious pelt of this young tigress was skillfully peeled off, I watched Jubert probe deeper into the puncture wound on her shoulder. Buried deep inside, we found the broken-off canine tooth of another tiger! It had penetrated deeply, killing her before breaking off.

From the size of the killer's canine tooth, it appeared he was a male tiger. It was likely the tigress had intruded into his territory. I would never know why this male tiger had killed her, but instances of such killings had been recorded in the past. I was sure she would have been welcomed had she been in estrus—the male tiger would have courted and mated with her. Perhaps not being estrous, she may have resisted his advances. Or he may have taken over a kill she made, leading to an unequal fight. She was the third dead tiger in a row in Nagarahole.

The surprising series of tiger deaths continued. On April 28, 1990, the tough and competent ranger, Devaraju of Kalhalla, sent me a wireless message. He was a young man who slogged away weeks on end in Nagarahole fighting forest fires and catching poachers, while his pretty wife, a doctor, lived in Mysore. Devaraju was torn between his work and family just as I was!

A gravely wounded tiger was lying down on the shore of Manchalli Pond in the Kalhalla Range [**MAP 2, Point 27**]. I rushed posthaste. It was a young male tiger who was three to four years old. The tiger was lying flat on his flanks, fully exposed to the blazing hot afternoon sun. He was growling in much pain, unable to move away, even when he saw us approaching. He had become encased in a coating of thick mud as he rolled on the edge of the pond trying to ease his agony. I could barely see his stripes. He bore numerous wounds, the most visible one on his left forepaw. All the skin and muscle had been stripped off his paw, exposing the raw tissue and bones below. The tiger was also emaciated, suggesting he had starved for a week or more.

I tried to guess how he could have been injured so grievously, particularly that injury on his paw. There were tribesmen in India who were traditionally skilled in the art of trapping and killing tigers without using any firearms. Typically, these master trackers staked out concealed steel jaw traps along forest trails. After a tiger's forepaw was caught in the jaws of the spring-loaded trap, the agonized roars of the animal alerted the poachers hiding not too far away. One of them, possessed of great courage, no doubt, would skillfully ram a long steel spear into the tiger's open mouth, while other men bludgeoned it to death with wooden clubs. The sole objective was to kill the tiger without ruining its precious skin. An intact tiger skin earned top dollars in illegal markets.

These professional hunters were not forest-dwellers like the Jenu Kurubas of Nagarahole. They were mostly nomadic and traveled across the country. They made their living by selling body parts of mammals and birds, big and small, which they hunted. This has been their way of life for centuries. However, in the new age of wildlife conservation, their traditional profession had become a criminal enterprise.

I could imagine the fury of a trapped tiger as it fought for its life. If I withheld judgment, I could even say these tiger poachers were extraordinarily skilled and courageous hunters. There were instances when a tiger managed to free itself from the jaws of the trap—by sacrificing most of the skin and flesh on its paws—and turned on the men attacking it. Many poachers met their end this way; their clubs and spears were no match against the ferocity of a wounded tiger once it freed itself.

I wondered if the male tiger lying before me had freed itself from such a jaw trap, losing most of its forepaw. Whatever had happened to the poachers, the tiger could only wander around in agony, unable to hunt, and gradually starve to death. His fate was sealed. Even as I reflected on such issues, life ebbed out of the young male tiger. We measured him; he weighed 174 kilograms.

Although I could not be sure how this tiger's horrific injuries had come about, the government veterinarian decided he was injured in a fight with another tiger. There were no reports of the presence of any professional tiger hunters operating in the area. I had no basis to question his verdict.

My worry about the possibility of organized tiger poaching by criminals deepened, however. On May 4, 1990, a juvenile tigress of about ten months, with injuries in her body, had wandered into the fringes of a village on the southeastern end of the park. The villagers had gathered in a violent mob that mercilessly stoned her to death. She was 212 centimeters long with a 75-centimeter tail and weighed only 80 kilograms. This juvenile tigress was slightly larger than a male leopard.

The reality was that, unusually, four wild tigers had been found dead in different corners of Nagarahole in the previous two months. There was a fifth one too, Mudka, whom I found only because of my radio-tracking.

These facts were enough to get the rumor mills around the jungles grinding.

When Tigers Die, Rumors Fly

Speculation and gossip about the tiger deaths was soon rife in the jungle grapevine, which interconnected the many arrack vends, toddy shops, and bars in the villages on the fringes of Nagarahole Park. Tribesmen, poachers, timber thieves, and illicit collectors of forest produce gathered at these places to drink and trade stories. On the sly, some off-duty forest guards joined them, too. Deals were struck, bribes changed hands, and stories were retold. A rumor casually planted by a forest guard at these conclaves carried the additional stamp of official authority.

By the end of April 1990, one specific story had gained currency: the deaths of these five tigers were linked to my research project, specifically, to the tranquilizations that preceded the radio-collaring of tigers. This rumor flew in the face of facts, because four of the five dead tigers had never been radio-collared. Even Mudka, the only collared tiger to die, had fully recovered from the tranquilization six weeks earlier. He had been radio-tracked by me and seen by others several times before he had died as predicted.

I suspected this rumor was floated by the aggrieved ranger GR. However, with corruption and secrecy being rampant, a word-of-mouth rumor can take wings and soar like black eagles over the Malenad landscape. And this one did.

Soon the rumor became breaking news in cold print. KG's tabloid *Star Dirt* "scooped" the ridiculous rumor as a sensational fact: tigers were being secretly caught, tranquilized with a dangerous drug, and fitted with radio collars. These poor animals were dying, one after another. The perpetrator was a well-connected researcher with unlimited amounts of money. Corrupt forest officials colluded with the researcher to run this international criminal enterprise.

The scoop was soon picked up by other local tabloids and, eventually, state-level newspapers in Bangalore. Because of its sensational originality and news value, even the national press picked up the news. A major national paper ran the story under the headline "Blood on the Collar." As far as media coverage was concerned, I was toast. "Karanth's tiger scandal" was the flavor of the month during May 1990.

The minister for forestry in Karnataka State, BB, was a powerful politician. He had risen from the ranks of the oppressed *Dalit* class: India's former "untouchables." He had fought long and hard for their upliftment, boldly challenging the social hegemony of the upper castes. His bête noirs were the Brahmins, who traditionally claimed superiority over all other castes.

It was true my father was born a Brahmin. However, he had turned a rationalist in his late teens, thrown away his sacred thread, and some years later married my mother from a warrior caste, setting off a social storm in the 1930s. That made a me a blue-blooded half-caste, I thought. A colleague in Wildlife Conservation Society (WCS) had once introduced me by saying, "You have all heard of Boston Brahmins, but here is the real McCoy." Now, my Brahminical surname Karanth became the bull's-eye for the minister's target practice.

Many local people around Nagarahole, not just the forest criminals, resented the strict enforcement of conservation laws that barred their earlier hunting, forest extractions, and encroachments. They bore a particular grudge against Chinnappa for being a tough enforcer, unlike GR, who had given them a free rein. Because I had played a role in Chinnappa's return, I was also on their blacklist.

All these social forces were being forged into a formidable vendetta by the wild rumormongering in the media. Soon these hostile forces converged under the leadership of the legislator CU from Hunsur. She had felt humiliated when I did not accede to her request to witness the capture of Mudka. She now canvassed hard with Minister BB to get rid of me from Nagarahole.

BB bluntly asked Appayya and Alva, two senior officials who had helped with my research permit, "Of what use is this tiger research?" Apparently, their defense of science did not satisfy him. His next question was why a free-spirited wild animal like the tiger should be burdened with a heavy collar around its neck. The officials explained the collar weighed less than half a percent of the tiger's weight and did not hinder its activities. They pointed out even smaller animals like birds and bats were being routinely radio-tagged in advanced countries.

BB was furious at what he saw as defiance by these officials. He shouted at them, saying, "If the radio collar is not a burden at all, I will order all of you to wear them to work every day. At least I will get to know what you guys are up to behind my back." A crestfallen Alva, a good friend of many years, called to tell me he could not protect me from the minister's fury.

Soon I got an official letter ending my five-year research permit, lock, stock, and barrel. I was stunned. Although I tried to plead my cause with a few journalists, I was coming too late into the news cycle. The sensational "Karanth tiger scandal" was steadily driving up their readership.

However, the most senior forester in the state, Paramesh, was a feisty, well-informed man. He called his boss, Minister BB, to bluntly tell him what he was doing was wrong. In defiance of official protocols, Paramesh even went on television to publicly disagree with the minister. Appayya, Lakshmana, and Alva, who understood what I was going through, were sympathetic but helpless. I felt truly grateful for the moral support from these senior officials.

Somewhat belatedly, I started meeting influential politicians to explain the facts. The Federal Environment Minister Maneka Gandhi, Indira Gandhi's second daughter-in-law, was (and is) an animal lover. She tried to convince BB to let me continue my work. While BB lauded her late mother-in-law profusely, he dodged her specific request. A former chief minister, Gundu Rao, also tried his hand but failed. He told me plainly, "Karanth, no one can change this stubborn man's mind. Your only option is to challenge this termination in the High Court of Karnataka."

My next stop was the law office of Udaya Holla, a rising star among Bangalore's lawyers. A few years younger than I was, Holla and I shared the same roots in coastal Karnataka. He admired my father greatly. However, I was aware his fees were high and he was busy fighting cases for rich corporate clients.

Holla invited me in; he was on the phone talking to someone named "Craig Bolt" in Airbus Industries in Paris. One of their planes had crashed on landing at Bangalore few days earlier. Holla was their attorney. I had a sinking feeling he would have no time for me.

After getting off the phone, Holla heard me patiently. I could see he was getting interested. My case was entirely novel and very different from his usual ones. I was fighting for my academic freedom guaranteed by the Indian constitution; it was my right as a citizen to study tigers. After a couple of minutes Holla stopped me, saying, "Karanth, I will fight your case." Before I could bring up the matter of his legal fees, he added, "and I will do so pro bono." I choked with emotion. Thanking Holla, I left his office.

I convened a meeting of the small "crisis management" group that spontaneously emerged as the "scandal" unfolded. It consisted of a handful of passionate friends who had participated in my research project as volunteers—Krishna, Prasad, and Praveen, and a wealthy coffee planter named Nachaiya, who was a friend and admirer of Chinnappa.

A week later, Holla stood up and pleaded our plaint in the halls of justice, the impressive red-brick building of the High Court of Karnataka in Bangalore. The judge hearing the case was a stickler for rules. After hearing Holla briefly, the judge termed the order terminating my project arbitrary because it gave no reason and violated "natural justice." The judge issued a stay order—legalese for holding the termination in abeyance. I was free to resume my research until the case was decided. Being rather naive, I was elated!

I was back in Nagarahole on June 29, 1990, trying to track my three tigers and three leopards. On the next day, while clearing a firebreak around Mavinahalla [**MAP 2, Point 16**], forest guards found the scattered remains of some animals. I went there to investigate, hoping to find a carcass of some prey animal killed by a predator. However, on seeing the scattered scraps of meat and skin, I was stunned. They were remains of two tiger cubs. The killer had almost entirely consumed them. A few scattered bones and two dog-sized skulls was all the evidence he left behind.

I had seen these two cubs with their mother, the Mavinahalla tigress, a couple of times before. She usually brought them to the pond late in the evenings to drink and play, after they had fed on some prey animal the tigress had caught nearby. For the first two months, the tigress had nursed these cubs with her milk, as well as meat she regurgitated. When they were three months old, she started taking them directly to feed off her kills. When the killer cut their lives short the previous night, they were about six months old.

I did some quick calculations. Given the typical 110-day gestation, these cubs were produced by their mother mating sometime in October 1989. The male that sired them was most likely Mudka, who at that time was lording over this area.

Based on my radio-tracking data, I could also guess who the killer was. The previous evening, I had located Das in the area. He had probably detected the tigress and her cubs on a kill she made that night, and his infanticidal instinct had kicked in. The mother tigress stood no chance of protecting her cubs against the huge, 220-kilogram male tiger in a murderous mood.

This event showed Das was claiming at least this part of Mudka's former range. As a transient male, Das had wandered over a seventy-seven square kilometer area. It looked as though he had finally succeeded in carving out a territory for himself. Although I felt sad for the two cubs, I knew their mother would soon come into estrus, mate again, and have new cubs.

The dynamic of tiger land tenures in Nagarahole was becoming more interesting by the day. Mudka's fatal injury and his subsequent death had triggered a period of social turbulence. I wondered if the next litter of cubs of the Mavinahalla tigress would grow up to be adults. It depended on their father being able to hold on to this territory for an additional two or three years. If Das was lucky, his infanticidal behavior would pay off.

When the Big Guns Fire

My study of tiger behavior was back on track again. Or so I thought. Minister BB was furious at the court's order, which gave back my freedom to track tigers. However, he craftily withdrew the earlier order barring my research, thus legally ending my case.

BB apparently liked the wide publicity he was getting for trying to stop the "Karanth tiger scandal." However, when a sharp reporter told him radiotelemetry was widely used in advanced countries, BB lost his cool. He retorted that fighting the Brahminical monopoly on knowledge generation in India was the real issue. It seemed the fact that I was not killing tigers was a minor issue in his grand scheme of things.

By now, the statewide news media was no longer blindly attacking me, and began providing a more balanced picture. However, the local tabloids led by KG's *Star Dirt* intensified their attacks. The death of the tiger cubs, soon after I got back to Nagarahole, gave their rumor mills new grist to grind.

BB was convinced it was a case of simple avarice on my part: my research permit was a cover to deliberately overdose tigers with drugs in order to clandestinely smuggle their skins abroad. Did I not get thousands of dollars from the Americans for my research? Did I not travel to United States once or twice a year? He believed senior forest officials provided cover to rangers on the ground, like Chinnappa and Devaraju, who were partners in my crimes. The minister plotted his next move craftily, issuing another order on July 15, 1990, terminating my research project again. Unlike the earlier order, the new order provided the rationale for stopping my research. It read, "The research on tigers has raised alarm among lovers of the forests and animals, and after due consideration, the Government has decided that it is dangerous and unnecessary to conduct research on wild animals in the thick forest."

He also summarily transferred rangers Chinnappa and Devaraju out of Nagarahole to remote hardship postings in the northern part of the state. For good measure, GR was posted back as the ranger in Nagarahole again. The plot he had hatched had paid off.

In response, Holla filed a second petition in the High Court. However, this time around, the judge who heard the case was somewhat in tune with the social theories that BB held dear. He asked the government to clarify why it was dangerous to conduct research on tigers. Holla argued I was losing valuable radio-tracking data every day, and that I should at least be permitted to track the animals I had already radio-collared. He also demanded that the court direct the government to appoint a committee of technical experts to study the issue of tiger deaths and the conduct of my research.

The judge asked the government attorney to respond within a month. This suited BB because a time-tested tactic in the Indian legal system for a litigant to delay any case is to repeatedly seek adjournments. If the government was the litigant and represented by its highest-ranking lawyer, the advocate general, such adjournments were usually granted. The court was clogged with thousands of pending cases, and the advocate general was a busy man. Delays were inevitable; after all, my case was a minor issue of academic freedom for a wildlife biologist.

Holla filed repeated pleas to hasten the hearings. But I was losing precious radio-tracking data, day after day. My six big cats in Nagarahole were diligently broadcasting signals, but there was no one listening.

All this was unfamiliar terrain for me—the frustrating legal process, the inquisitive and sometimes hostile media, and the need for convincing politicians and the public about the importance of tiger research. All I could do was to wait, wringing my hands.

After about four months of this charade, the exasperated judge finally issued an interim order that permitted me to radio-track my six cats, without catching any new ones, until the case was decided. He also directed the government to form a committee of experts as demanded by me, expeditiously. However, I still had to get a fresh operational order from the forest department before I could enter the forest again to track my cats.

I realized that even senior officials sympathetic to me were unwilling to sign off on the necessary paperwork unless the much-feared BB agreed. Forest Secretary PP, the senior-most bureaucrat in the chain of command, blandly told me that "the minister would soon take a view" on the court's order. I felt I was sitting across the table from Henry Appleby, the bureaucrat in the hit show *Yes Minister*.

The doors had closed on me. One option was to wait for BB to "take a view" even while I lost precious data every day. The other was to file a case of criminal contempt of the High Court against the government. The second option was risky because all the senior politicians in the ruling Congress Party would rally in support of their government. Even the officials who had been sympathetic to my cause would start to avoid me like the plague. Finally, if the High Court indicted BB of contempt, the minister could be forced to step down by the raucous opposition parties. In that process, I would become a football in a bigger game between the ruling party and the opposition.

I was in a no-win situation.

However, because of the nationwide media coverage of my case, a few individual champions of the tigers' cause in the upper crust of Delhi society had begun to appreciate the value of what I was doing. I was able to meet one of them, Brijendra Singh, a member of the erstwhile royalty of India. I explained my tiger research and its nuances using videos and slides. Brijendra, a true tiger aficionado, was sufficiently moved and promised to help. He was a school buddy and friend of former Prime Minister Rajiv Gandhi (Indira's older son). Although out of power in Delhi at that time, Rajiv Gandhi was still the president of the Congress Party that ruled Karnataka. Because of his powerful electoral sway, Gandhi really decided who among the elected legislators would be ministers in the state.

Meanwhile, the aging chief minister VP in Karnataka was in political trouble. Dissidents within his own party were shaking his throne. Rajiv Gandhi had decided it was time for a change in leadership. VP, who was from a powerful upper caste, was suddenly replaced by SB, a rising political star from a backward caste. SB would form a new cabinet of his own ministers.

The day before Rajiv Gandhi met the new chief minister to guide him on the formation of his cabinet, Brijendra talked to Gandhi about my stalled tiger research. Late the next night, when the new state cabinet was announced, BB was not the forest minister anymore! He had been shunted aside to a relatively minor position. SB had smartly used the opportunity to reward the coveted forest portfolio to a man from his own community: a first-time legislator named ET from the treeless barrens in the eastern part of the state.

As soon as BB had been moved out, officials who had worried about the government's open defiance of the High Court order heaved a sigh of relief. If I had filed a case of contempt against the government, they too would have been in deep trouble.

I picked up the necessary paperwork from my friend Appayya, who finally wore a broad smile. I could now go back and track my collared animals while the court continued hearing my case. I was in a daze, wondering how quickly the sluggish Indian bureaucracy could really move when the political wheels turned.

The more I absorbed the lessons from my experiences, the more I realized that "conservation theory" preached from academic ivory towers was not of much use to the practice of conservation in the real world. Conservation was indeed a science, but a dismal one—just like economics—where human interests and values played a critical role in shaping reality. Every step toward being an effective conservationist made it harder for me to pursue my science.

4 | THE LONESOME TIGER

AT LAST, ON JANUARY 7, 1991, my court-mandated research permit in hand, I drove back to Nagarahole. Entering the park at dawn, with the rays of the rising sun piercing the dense fog, I switched on my receiver, listening hopefully for the beeps from my cats. For twenty-four kilometers along the paved road, I heard only the chatter of radio static. Points of brilliant sunlight reflected off the wet green forest foliage, a dancing mirage that concealed my big cats.

Rounding a bend, just 6.6 kilometers from my camp, I saw a tiger cautiously step out of the thicket on the left, its eyes widening as it spotted my car. The tiger bounded across the road and up the gentle slope on my right, disappearing into the dense shrubbery.

I had a fleeting but clear look. The tiger was a big male, and it wore a radio collar! From his broad, mirrorlike stripes I recognized Mara. I had also noticed the odd fact that his collar belt, which should have fitted snugly around his bulky neck, was hanging loosely. I got out of the Suzuki with my radio-tracking gear and ran up the slope after Mara, trying to get higher to track his signals. The hysterical screams of a herd of chital signaled he was passing by them one hundred meters downhill on my right. I connected the antenna to the receiver and tuned in to his frequency.

Strange: no beeps. My heart sank. Was a steep gully temporarily blocking his signals? Or had Mara's transmitter failed? If that was the case, I could not count on finding him by sheer chance, as I just had. After thirty minutes of radio silence, I drove to the Nagarahole campus in a somber mood. Why had

Mara's transmitter, which still had two more years of battery life in it, failed? The mystery would be solved a couple of weeks later.

I was soon back at my regular listening post on the fire-watch tower on Kuntur Hillock, sweeping the sky for radio signals. I quickly picked up signals from the tigers, Sundari and Das, as well as the leopards, Buddy and Monda. They were all emitting active signals within their usual home ranges. So far, so good. But I still needed to find the leopard Mooga, who had escaped from Nagarahole's protective boundary nearly ten months earlier, and settled down in the coffee plantations near Kutta [**MAP 2, Inset**].

In the afternoon, I drove out to the top of Faith Hill, the best place to find his signals. Disappointingly, there were no signals at all from Mooga. Anxious to locate him, I climbed four other adjacent peaks on the same ridge, scanning for radio signals from the southern and eastern parts of the reserve, just in case Mooga had chosen to return to the forest during my absence. Still no signals. Roasted by the blazing afternoon sun, soaked in sweat, I was dog-tired. As dusk descended, I returned to camp, worried about Mooga's fate.

If Mooga had died from any natural cause, I should still be hearing signals from his transmitter. But that obviously wasn't the case. I reflected on what I knew about this animal. Mooga was a village leopard well-adapted to preying on stray dogs, cats, and occasional livestock. Unlike in his original home, where not many farmers had firearms, in this landscape where gun culture was strong, Mooga was constantly at risk of being shot by some trigger-happy planter. Or he could have accidentally choked in one of the wire snares that migrant farmworkers concealed in hedgerows of coffee plantations to poach wild pigs. Even worse, Mooga could have bitten into a village poacher's "bomb"—an explosive cunningly concealed within a chunk of gamey raw meat. That homemade bomb could blow off the leopard's jaws.

Under any of these scenarios, if the killer of Mooga found a radio-collared leopard, he would panic. Arrest could mean years in jail. Locals were aware that the "Bones Ranger," with his magic devices, could locate his collared cats wherever they were, dead or alive. The safest option for the killer would be to smash the transmitter to pieces as quickly as possible.

Ironically, forest officials had asked me to translocate Mooga from a distant village to Nagarahole's protective wilderness to save him from exactly such a fate. Although I continued my daily radio-tracking routine, I never got Mooga's signals again. Not only was he dead, but his transmitter was, too.

After a couple of weeks passed, one mystery was solved. Forest guards on patrol along Karmadu dirt road found Mara's radio collar. His collar belt, which I had noticed to be hanging loose, had finally come apart and off. When I examined the radio collar, the belting appeared chewed up. The tough metal transmitter casing had deep bite marks on it. I surmised these bites were inflicted when Mara had fought another tiger. His adversary's fifty-eight-millimeter-long canines had punctured the casing and ended the transmitter's life. But that casing had probably saved Mara's life.

Indeed, when I'd seen Mara two weeks earlier, he was in fine fettle. Perhaps he had even decisively won that fight, establishing himself as another dominant breeding male. Had I been allowed to radio-track Mara, as the court had ordered six months earlier, I could possibly have witnessed this king-making battle. I felt frustrated and angry at the pointless stupidity of it all.

In a typical bureaucratic response, forest officials took custody of the fallen collar as "evidence." Of what, I was not sure. My nuisance value to the officialdom was increasing.

I was now down to two tigers and two leopards. Until the court finally decided the case in my favor, I had no hope of radio-collaring more animals. I intensified my radio-tracking efforts, with my assistant, Gini. The location data I obtained daily told me where each cat was. To generate a detailed picture of how these cats lived and died, I needed to track them continuously for hours on end, sometimes all day and all night.

I was curious to know how the two male leopards, Monda and Buddy, interacted. Monda was an older animal, clearly on his way downhill. Buddy, on the other hand, was still in his prime. He had a large territory of 31.3 square kilometers. Monda had a 25.1-square-kilometer territory. Their territories were roughly separated by the stretch of paved road between Nagarahole and Kalhalla [MAP 3].

Before my tracking was interrupted, both cats had been intensively patrolling this boundary. But now, six months later, I found that Monda had been pushed out of the southern half of his territory. I suspected a stronger rival male leopard had encroached into that area. Because Buddy had not occupied the area vacated by Monda, I surmised that a third male was now ascendent. I lamented that I could not radio-collar this new warrior in the fray and follow the battles that were unfolding. As with the tigers, leopard society was also in flux.

The male leopard Monda photographed at night.

On January 31, 1991, I was eating lunch at camp after tracking down the day's location for Sundari. Gini returned from a similar tracking effort with Monda along Doray Road. Gini had scoured the entire known range of Monda until finally, around noon, he had detected the cat's signals. From triangulation, my assistant determined that the leopard was in a patch of bamboo just half a kilometer from the rice paddies of the densely populated Karmadu village [MAP 2, Point 10].

Gini had listened for half an hour but detected only inactive signals, meaning Monda was not moving. This was not unusual: big cats, like house cats, stretch out and sleep for hours on end, especially during hot weather. However, after all the anxiety caused by Mooga's disappearance, I had become a true worrywart.

I decided to personally track Monda the next morning. Driving close to the bamboo patch, I listened. Monda was still there, and his signals were still inactive. I sat in my car for an hour, hoping he would roll over and emit an active signal. With each passing minute, my worry about his inactivity grew, especially on such a cool morning. He should have been out looking for a langur monkey or chital deer for breakfast. Finally, I could stand the tension no longer. I stepped out of the car and walked into the forest, trying to home in on Monda's signals. Any leopard in his right mind would sneak off as soon as it sensed my approach. Monda did not.

Ten minutes later, I found Monda. He was dead, and had been for at least two days, by the looks of things. An autopsy confirmed that he had been badly mauled in a fight with another feline. Monda, mortally injured, had slinked away to this quiet, shady spot to lick his wounds, and had steadily bled to death. I took the opportunity to examine Monda's teeth. In the ten months since I had radio-collared him, they had worn down significantly, and one more canine had broken off. Although he looked emaciated, Monda's coat still retained its unusually rich, deep ocher hue.

I felt sad for Monda, but this was how nature worked. As long as I studied big cats, I was fated to record these deaths again and again. I guessed the new male leopard would now expand his rule over Monda's entire territory. However, I would never be sure, because I had no radio collar on him.

For the tabloids, however, Monda's death was a long-awaited call to arms. They were frustrated that I was back in Nagarahole tracking my cats. The old Kannada saying "If you rejoice at locking the devil out of your front door, he will announce his return through the ventilator" would be foremost in their minds.

The day after Monda died, the tabloid *Star Dirt* proclaimed yet another cat had fallen prey to me. Later that afternoon, playing the role of "animal lovers," the tabloid reporters organized a "mass rally" against me in Hunsur. The local legislator CU took to the podium and thundered, "In the name of research, Karanth is killing government's tigers and leopards with brazen impunity!" She added that I should purchase a tiger of my own and conduct my lethal experiments in my own backyard. The rally provided fresh fodder for the next day's tabloid news.

Although I knew it was futile, I sent out a press release explaining the ecological factors underlying Monda's death. The state press was by now covering both the fevered stories on big cat deaths peddled by the tabloids, as well as my more prosaic explanations. Then something unexpected happened.

A New Theory Is Put to the Test

On January 28, 1991, a posse of hard-bitten reporters in Bangalore ambushed the novice forest minister, ET, seeking details of the "mystery behind the big cat deaths" in Nagarahole. ET, a small-time contractor from the treeless plains of the state, knew nothing about big cats. His being pitchforked into this exalted position was just an unintended consequence of the wheels I had set in motion in Delhi earlier.

Cornered by the reporters, ET speculated that my collared tigers could hear the radio signals emitted by the transmitters around their necks, and that the incessant beeps drove them to injure themselves fatally while trying to claw away their collars. ET thought his novel theory explained all the data on hand—the injuries on the dead cats and the months of delay between the dates of their tranquilizations and their deaths. The animals, after all, needed enough time to be driven mad by the signals.

There was just one problem: the very high frequency radio signals emitted by the collars could only be heard through a receiver tuned to the right frequency. While I did use such receivers to listen to the signals, my collared cats did not possess the receivers. Following this foray into the realm of wireless technology, ET became the butt of jokes in the press.

Rather than retreat in the face of ridicule, ET decided to personally investigate the big cat deaths in Nagarahole. On February 7, 1991, a pilot jeep flashing a red beacon, followed by the forest minister's limousine sporting the national flag, cruised into Nagarahole. ET stepped out of the limo. He was a nondescript man dressed in the regulation starched white bush shirt and pants favored by rising politicians in his party.

ET immediately established his authority over the bevy of officials by abruptly demanding a pack of imported cigarettes. The rundown little shop in Nagarahole, with its clientele of poor tribal folk, had never ever stocked the pricey Benson & Hedges he wanted. Rather than settle for something a bit more modest, officials diverted a patrol jeep to race a hundred kilometers to Mysore for a pack of cigarettes. I thought officials felt grateful to ET because he had not asked them to bring some other symbol of power and authority—say, a zebra-tail fly-whisk from Kenya, or a hornbill hat from Borneo.

With his underlings now scurrying around showing a satisfactory level of servility, ET finally turned to me. He rudely demanded that I show him my "stuff." We marched to my field camp, followed by officials of varied ranks who came in different shapes and sizes. In the grimy interiors of the shack that served as my field camp, I solemnly handed over a brand-new radio collar to ET.

There was pin-drop silence as ET tried the superhuman feat of listening with naked ears to VHF radio signals. He cupped his ear and puckered his face, holding the collar at arms' length. He then pulled the collar closer, jamming the transmitter to his left ear and then to his right. Still no signals. ET scowled harder, looking both puzzled and angry.

The expressions on the official faces around us resembled those on the faces of the grim subjects portrayed in Grant Wood's famous painting *American Gothic*. Someone invisible in the back rows began to cough, overcompensating for a suppressed titter. I desperately tried to keep a solemn face befitting a scientist seriously assisting a critical experiment.

Next, ET asked me to turn on the telemetry receiver slung from my shoulder. With the flip of a switch, a steady stream of beeps issued forth from the receiver. Annoyed, ET asked me to switch it off. His hypothesis on what caused the big cat deaths was growing shakier with every beep. His grim countenance made it clear he did not like the results that this experiment produced. He abruptly turned around and walked away to the forest rest house without even a word of thanks. Officials followed in his wake, in wavelets dictated by rank and seniority.

My radio collars were turning into a real pain in the neck, not for the dead cats, but personally to ET. I realized that, but for the court's restraint, ET would stop my work instantly just as his predecessor BB had.

Following ET's visit, the government's lawyer continued to delay and stonewall my case by repeatedly seeking repeated adjournments. I worried how long I could survive this rising tide of hostility that threatened to drown my science. To keep a low profile, and mitigate my tensions and stress, I tried to spend more weekends at home with Prathibha. In her arms I found solace. However, all too often I felt I was imposing my emotional burdens on her.

If God Said It, That Settles It!

On one such weekend furlough in Mysore on March 3, 1991, I received a call from Nairobi, Kenya. George Schaller had remembered my invitation of three years earlier, to visit my project. He politely asked, given all my problems, if I still wanted to host him. I was overwhelmed. Here was the legendary biologist who had inspired my dream—an idol to hundreds like me the world over—seeking my permission for his visit. Without a moment's hesitation, I said yes. A visit from Schaller was just the shot of adrenaline I desperately needed to revive my own sagging spirit.

The ten days George spent with me were unforgettable. Everything about him struck me as extraordinary—his superb physical fitness, monk-like austerity, and deep passion for watching animals. George missed nothing in the field, making quick notes in a small pocket notebook. Later, in the evening, he wrote everything down in his richly detailed journals. No computers, databases, or spreadsheets for old George. His encyclopedic mind and years of experience helped him effortlessly extract and synthesize disparate strands of observations. His magisterial books on gorillas, lions, giant pandas, and other wonders of the natural world were a testimony.

George was the first wildlife biologist to study tigers in the early 1960s, when India's forests were being ravaged. In his magnum opus, *The Deer and the Tiger*, George suggested prospects for India's wildlife were bleak. He had not been back since then, however, and had not witnessed the sporadic yet spectacular recovery of India's wildlife that unfolded later in places like Nagarahole.

As we drove to Nagarahole at dawn on March 8, 1991, George—his craggy face set in a stern expression—reminded me of my rather rash promise to show him wild tigers if he visited me. Although I sometimes saw my collared cats during the hours spent tracking them, if they wanted to be stealthy or wandered off into parts of their ranges where I could not radio-track them from my car, days could pass before I saw them.

Among my tigers, Sundari was the most predictable. She had a small territory of just 18.1 square kilometers, with good road access that enabled me to watch her more intensively. On March 10, 1991, I had triangulated Sundari's location to a cleared teak plantation, now swallowed up by dense bamboo. On a hot summer day like this, I hoped Sundari would come out for a drink at the Kaithole Pond at the edge of the plantation [**MAP 2, Point 24**].

George and I sat on the ground at the foot of a giant *Terminalia* tree. To conceal ourselves, we blended our profiles against a termite mound at the foot of the tree. Twenty meters in front of us was a salt lick meant to attract and supplement the diets of wild herbivores that congregated. We had a commanding view of the pond that glittered in the sunlight. Beyond a strip of sand on the opposite shore, about 150 meters away, lay the expanse of dense bamboo thickets. Sundari's radio signals indicated she was resting within, not far from the pond.

Knowing her ways, I guessed that when it got a bit cooler, Sundari might come down an animal trail to the sandy shore. She would hunch down and drink deeply for as long as two or three minutes. Sometimes, if fancy took her, Sundari would turn around and ease herself into the pond, in reverse gear so to speak. After cooling off wholly submerged below her neck, Sundari would head back into thickets. My hope was Sundari would perform for Schaller today.

At 1606 hours that afternoon, Sundari's quickening signals indicated she was up and moving. Soon, she appeared on the trail—and then delivered her full performance exactly as I had hoped. However, after her ablutions were completed, instead of disappearing back into the thicket, Sundari decided to skirt around the pond and cross over to our side. What next? Would she continue straight and disappear into the deep woods to our left, or would she turn right along the deer trail to the salt lick right in front of us? As she turned, I muttered under my breath to George, "She is coming our way!"

Sundari walked along the deer trail, frequently stopping to sniff the bushes on either side. She disappeared briefly into a tall clump of *Saccharum* grass, and emerged down the trail, getting closer. Soon, she was broadside to us. Her golden pelt, still dripping water, was brilliantly set off by the bright sunlight. Her jet-black stripes stood out like Chinese calligraphy.

We sat spellbound on the ground, barely twenty meters away, watching the wild tigress at eye level. Our cameras clicked incessantly. Sundari pricked up her ears and looked in our direction. Her gleaming orange eyes, surrounded by beautiful patches of white fur, stared at us. However, she failed to spot us, either because of our effective camouflage or because she wanted to ignore us like a celebrity disdaining paparazzi.

Having passed the salt lick, Sundari walked up to a leaning tree stump and rubbed her head and cheeks against it. She was checking for chemical messages from other tigers. Apparently learning what she needed to from the messages, Sundari turned around, lifted her tail, and sprayed a fine jet of scent-laden urine on the tree's bark to leave her own reply.

Sundari's belly was full, which meant she was not out hunting in any serious sense. She moved slowly, making no attempt at concealment. Soon, she was out of sight. Frenzied alarm calls from a chital herd and a pair of muntjacs continued to herald her passage through the forest.

The excitement of the close encounter left us both speechless. The normally taciturn George patted my shoulder and quietly whispered, "Ullas, you know your job." I was overwhelmed. At home, I was being reviled by my own people, while the world's most famous field biologist thought I was doing a fine job. With a smile, I suddenly recalled a huge billboard I'd once spotted outside a Baptist church in Florida: "If God said it, that settles it!" Indeed.

George spent a week with me in Nagarahole. I was also able to show him the male tiger, Das, and the leopard, Buddy MacKay. George invited me on a trip to his old tiger study site of Kanha in central India, where we saw even more tigers.

George's visit was just the emotional balm I needed. It boosted my morale and hardened my resolve. George left, the hot summer passed, and the monsoon showers arrived, turning Nagarahole green again.

The Big Cat Versus a Bigger Cow

On June 20, 1991, I began radio-tracking Das early in the morning. With me was a tall, gangly youth from Mysore named Madhu. Recognizing his aptitude for natural history, I had encouraged him to come with me to the field.

By 0800 hours, Das had stopped moving and seemed to have settled down for the day. With three good radio fixes, I triangulated the tiger's position. He was about 180 meters downslope from my car [**MAP 2, Point 21**]. I wanted to show Madhu how to directly home in on a radio-collared animal, instead of triangulating its location from afar. Walking stealthily, I thought we could get to within fifty meters of the resting tiger.

We got out of the car. Das was somewhere near a small, grassy glade, which was transected by a firebreak. These fire lines were thirty-meter-wide strips along which forest vegetation had been cleared. They helped stop summer forest fires from spreading to areas beyond. As I walked along the fire line, my headphones blocked out the delightful symphony of birdcalls or the joyful whoops of langurs around me. Only the steady beeps from Das's transmitter rang in my ears.

I normally would have brought a tribesman skilled at detecting the sound of an elephant's ears flapping—or even the rumbles from its belly. I hoped Madhu was up to this task of watching out.

When we got closer to Das, the signals indicated he was on the other side of the glade, hidden in dense *Cipadessa* bushes wrapped under a tangle of wickedly thorny *Ziziphus* vines. The inactive radio signal suggested he was likely resting. As we stepped out into the open glade, we saw a gaur cow standing fifty meters away broadside to us. She was staring intently at the cover that hid the tiger. She was so preoccupied that our arrival had not caught her attention.

The gaur appeared very jittery, stamping her feet and flailing her tail. Her behavior was unusual. When gaur sense a lurking tiger, normally they sneeze in alarm and bolt. Why was this cow standing alone, separated from the herd? I handed over the antenna to Madhu and looked through my binoculars.

The gaur cow was in no shape to run. A few minutes before we had arrived, the tiger had attacked her. Her rump was raked badly by the cat's fearsome claws. Blood streamed from a deep bite wound on her muzzle. The bite had torn off her nose, leaving a gaping wound. Yet the fact that she was still on her feet showed the severely injured gaur had still managed to beat back the tiger's initial assault. Weighing six hundred kilograms, all nearly solid muscle—three times as heavy as her assailant—the feisty cow was no pushover.

Failing to quickly bring her down and strangle her to death, the tiger had retreated behind the thorny bushes. At this very moment, his baleful yellow eyes were likely watching her every move. If the cow turned around to run, he would launch his second attack and pull her down. Making her last stand in the open glade, the brave gaur was trying to face down her attacker. Even with her terrible injuries, she was a formidable adversary. If the attacker made the slightest error, she could push him to the ground and rip his belly open with her wickedly curved horns.

This was raw jungle drama—predator and prey locked in mortal combat. We watched, transfixed, as minutes passed by. The tension of anticipation was unbearable, even for us. So, I could hardly believe my ears when the tiger's radio signals switched back to inactive mode. Had he gone to sleep? Or had he also been seriously injured in the first skirmish? I knew that Das was an experienced hunter of gaur. He had killed a young bull gaur, roughly the size of this cow, a couple of months before. With the initial element of surprise lost, he would not risk a second attack in this open meadow. Das was biding his time, aware that the injured cow, without the protection of her herd, was ultimately at his mercy.

Because of the copious bleeding, the cow was weakening by the minute. Soon, she could no longer remain standing and sank down to her knees. In the waist-high, parrot-green *Themeda* grass, we could not see her anymore. I moved a couple of steps closer, trying to get a better look.

Suddenly, the tiger's radio signals turned active. Had the tiger spotted me? Whatever the reason, the tiger's movement enraged the gaur. She sprang back to her feet and swung around, glowering, with murder in her eyes. Noticing me for the first time, confused and furious, she wheeled around, snorted, and charged.

I whipped around and raced up the fire line. I yelled at Madhu to run—unnecessarily, as it turned out. With his longer legs and youthful stride, he had streaked past me. Miraculously, despite the tangle of antennas, cables, receivers, and binoculars we carried, we managed to get away. A hundred meters on, breathless and panting, we stopped to look back. The cow had given up the chase. She must have suddenly remembered the bigger danger lurking behind her. Although I wondered what the tiger had thought of this strange spectacle, I was not going back to ask him.

I decided to follow up on Das the next day, because I had still had the locations of Sundari and Buddy to account for. The following morning, I found the carcass of the gaur cow where the fire line intersected my Line Transect-2. She had managed to walk about a kilometer from the site of our last encounter. The tiger must have stalked her patiently all afternoon and attacked when darkness descended. He would have had the advantage of his superior night vision and a weakened adversary. Yet for all his troubles, Das had consumed only about ten kilograms of meat before moving on.

An hour later, I located his oddly undersized tracks imprinted on soft soil about one kilometer away. His signals were receding farther and farther. Das must have abandoned his kill because something more enticing had beckoned him—the seductive moan of a tigress in estrus, perhaps, or the roar of a male intruder trying to encroach on his territory.

Finally, the Three Wise Men

Meanwhile, a different drama was unfolding in the courtroom in Bangalore. My attorney Holla had managed to cleverly and patiently corner his adversary, the advocate general. Hearing both sides, the judge ordered the government to immediately appoint a committee of experts to investigate the tiger deaths in Nagarahole. The government was compelled to issue an order on July 15, 1991, to abide by the court's command.

It was not easy, however, to find genuine experts who could assess the complex technical issues involved. These involved the behavior and population biology of big cats and methods of chemical capture and radio-tracking, as well as issues of veterinary forensics. I was concerned that the government would appoint some garden-variety senior officials lacking the necessary specialized knowledge. This practice was not uncommon in India. Therefore, I was somewhat relieved when I heard the names of the three men who would judge my work.

The committee was headed by Hemendra Panwar, a senior forester with years of experience leading Project Tiger. Although not a trained biologist, Panwar had plenty of field experience with tigers in Kanha Reserve. The committee also included Jacob Cheeran, a pharmacologist who had pioneered the use of chemical capture for wild animals in India, and Gopal Thopsie, a senior veterinarian who specialized in animal pathology. These men could comprehend the technical intricacies involved in my case.

The experts arrived in Nagarahole on August 28, 1991. They spent several days poring over the autopsy reports of the dead cats and interviewed the local veterinarians who had conducted them. They also interviewed veterinarians and forest staff, elephant mahouts, and tribesmen who took part in my big cat capture operations. I showed them videos or photos proving that all the seven cats I had collared—including the wounded old male, Mudka—had successfully recovered from sedation and walked away. I also shared with them images of the tigers that had died, showing the nature of the serious injuries or starvation that had led to their deaths.

One fact was obvious: there were time lags of weeks and even months that separated the dates of my captures of Mudka, Monda, and Mooga from the respective dates of their deaths. Thus, conclusively there was no causal link between the two sets of events. As to the other four dead tigers, they had not been radio-collared by me at all.

My position was clear-cut: all the cats, both collared and uncollared, had died either from natural causes such as injuries suffered in fights or from injuries inflicted by humans. There was no surprise. These kinds of cat mortalities had been reported from other tiger reserves across the country, where no one was tranquilizing the animals.

I took this opportunity to tell the committee how unique my study was. It was the first major study of tigers and leopards ever conducted in India. Its results would be vital to big cat conservation across the country in the future. I pleaded that my work should be encouraged by the government rather than unfairly hounded. Critically, the expert's report would set a precedent for how seriously the government would treat wildlife research in the future.

Finally, on September 28, 1991, the experts submitted their report, which was clear and categorical: the big cat deaths in Nagarahole were a part of the natural population dynamics of these cat species; I had carried out my capture and radio-tracking activities with skill and competence; and there was absolutely no basis for attributing the cat deaths to my research. Going a step further, the experts said the government was not at all justified in capriciously stopping my work. By doing so, it had caused the loss of valuable radio-tracking data.

They concluded that my work was crucial for tiger conservation in India and deserved active encouragement rather than unreasonable obstruction.

The more balanced state and national press endorsed the experts' findings. A couple of editorials even criticized the government for harassing me. The tabloids, however, were furious. My old nemesis, KG of *Star Dirt*, led the pack. He derided the experts as "carpetbaggers." He attributed their favorable findings to underhanded deals with me. KG seemed to believe that no one was immune to my guile . . . except himself, of course.

Still, I thought—rather naively, as it turned out—that I had finally won. I truly believed that logic and reason would prevail from now on. I could go on with my work peacefully, sliding back into the anonymity that I had cherished. I could not have been more wrong.

The Chief Minister's Advice

At daybreak on October 20, I woke up feeling an electric surge of excitement around me. Khaki-clad policemen were swarming all over the Nagarahole campus. The forest department wireless crackled nonstop, relaying messages back and forth between the department's eight-story headquarters in Bangalore and the ranger's ramshackle office in Nagarahole.

Soon, jeeps arrived from Mysore laden with supplies of fresh meat, poultry, vegetables, and, of course, imported cigarettes. The rest house caretakers were sprucing up the place as though it were Judgment Day. Das, the cook, and his numerous greasy helpers were working frenziedly in the sooty old kitchen. Forest guards and rangers in starched uniforms studded with gleaming brass buttons trotted back and forth, looking impossibly busy.

No wonder: on his way to Nagarahole, on a surprise holiday visit with his family, was none other than SB, the chief minister of Karnataka State! Around noon, he arrived in a convoy of cars, far longer than the one which had brought the forest minister, ET, seven months earlier. The convoy raised a storm of dust along the way, panicking both herds of chital and the groups of scantily clad tribal girls bathing at the roadside well.

Chief Minister SB was quite a flamboyant character. Son of a farmer from one of India's subaltern castes, he was a small-town lawyer who had risen rapidly in politics by opportunistically switching parties. He had been selected to the top job by the Congress Party chief Rajiv Gandhi, who subsequently had been assassinated.

SB was a short, wiry man of some sixty years, extremely fit from the hours he spent playing badminton. His youthful face, gold-rimmed spectacles, and fingers copiously ringed with gemstones all signaled charisma to his numerous fans.

As SB stepped out of the limousine, one flunky held his door open, a second dexterously took his briefcase, and a third curtsied while facing him and walking backward. SB cleaved through the line of deferential officials without cracking a smile, his hands folded in the traditional namaste. The chief minister radiated power, authority, and arrogance.

Beneath the portico of the forest rest house where he was camping, I joined the line of neatly dressed senior officials for the formal introductions. In my faded jungle fatigues and muddy boots, I must have stuck out like a sore thumb. The chief minister's gimlet eyes rested on me briefly, brows raised curiously.

I was introduced as the son of the famous writer Shivarama Karanth, who was greatly respected by SB's generation of socialists. SB seemed amazed by this incongruity. "Karanth, what (*the hell* was left unsaid, I think) are you doing in this remote jungle?" he asked, putting his hand out and smiling.

"Sir, I am here to study tigers," I replied, deadpan.

SB appeared nonplussed, but his curiosity was clearly piqued.

That afternoon, at SB's request, I ended up giving a slide presentation about my research. I also demonstrated how radiotelemetry worked by making the chief minister "radio-track" my field assistant Kala, who walked around the campus holding a radio collar.

At the end of it all, SB was clearly impressed. "I am a progressive leader, I embrace new technology, and I love Karanth's tiger study," he announced grandly to the forest officials standing around at a respectful distance. Everyone nodded in synchronous agreement, including, I noted, some who thought I was becoming an inconvenient nuisance.

Spotting a chance and seizing upon it, I raised my problems to him: the tiger deaths, the tabloids, the political meddling, and my fight for justice still dragging on in the court. Already, two months had lapsed since the experts had supported my work. However, I hadn't heard a peep about permission to resume my research full scale. I complained that his ministers were still hindering my research, based entirely on tabloid stories.

Ignoring the bit about his ministers, SB launched into a tirade against tabloids. It was clear he didn't like them, either. Glaring at officials around him, jaw jutting, the chief minister boasted that he never reacted to calumny in the media. "Their barbs can never pierce my skin, because it is thicker than the hide on a water-buffalo bull," he added. He held out one sinewy forearm and pinched it with his other hand. "Look here, Karanth," he chuckled. "Your problem is that you are too thin-skinned. You must grow a thick buffalo hide like mine!" Officials around dutifully tittered.

I wasn't going to give up so easily, though. "But, sir," I persisted, "your government should accept the experts' report so that I can collar more tigers." The chief minister got the message this time. He turned to the chief of wildlife, Appayya, and ordered him to "put up that tiger file" at the cabinet meeting next week. For any document crawling through the labyrinths of state power in India, being "put up before the cabinet" was the final step. This was nirvana in the kingdom of files.

Thanking the chief minister, I left. There was a spring in my step. I felt more like a ballerina than the water buffalo I had been advised to turn into. Surely, this was the light at the end of the tunnel. I had reason to hope. Both the followers and detractors of SB agreed on one thing: he was a man of his word. I was confident that neither ET nor BB could now stand in my way.

However, fate—or chance event, as the scientist in me whispered—decided otherwise. Politically things unraveled for SB very soon after his visit. In the Byzantine intrigues within the Congress Party, SB fell afoul of the prime minister, Narasimha Rao, who headed the party after Rajiv Gandhi's death. Smelling blood, SB's rivals for his throne were circling to attack him. Although SB may have genuinely intended to help my research, with this turn of events, he could no longer risk irritating his colleagues to placate a mere biologist like me. The "tiger file" was not "put up" before the chief minister for approval at the next cabinet meeting, or the ones that followed.

My last hope now rested with the High Court's final judgment. Low-priority cases like mine took years to be heard, but the grim realities of big cat population turnover would not accommodate such procrastination. The cat's naturally high mortality rates of over 20 percent per year would take a relentless toll on my collared cats. Like the ten little Indians in the nursery rhyme, soon there would be none.

Gladiators in the Jungle

My radio-tracking data showed that Das was under intense pressure from the other male tigers that surrounded his territory, including Mara to the west.

He had yielded the southern half of his earlier transient home range to Yaja-mana, the large uncollared male tiger. His range had shrunk from 77.3 square kilometers to 43.5 square kilometers.

Das was now trying to expand his range eastward, far into the roadless interiors of the park, which were covered in dry forests. I was finding it harder and harder to pick up on his signals, either from the Kuntur Tower or Faith Hill. However, having once lost him before, only to see him return after eight days, I was not unduly worried.

After a week with no signals, Gini and I began a systematic, arduous search of the entire park. We tried wandering on foot in the roadless parts of his range. On October 28, 1991, tired and sweaty under the blazing sun, I picked up a faint signal. Homing in by walk, we saw two magnificent redheaded vultures take off from a small clearing one hundred meters away. Was Das sleeping it off near a prey he had killed, or had something more sinister happened? His signals were inactive.

Lying scattered in the clearing we found the bones of some large animal. There was no meat or skin left on them. The mammalogy course I had taken back at the University of Florida told me these were not the bones of a hoofed herbivore. This broad scapular bone could have come only off a tiger. Was this Das, or a rival he had killed?

The beeps of Das's transmitter were now exploding inside my head. The device was *really* close—in fact, I was about to step on it! The ragged old radio collar lay among the scattered bones. Das, the large, heavyset male tiger for whom I had fitted that collar two years earlier, was now a mere pile of bones. This spot would be his final radio location on the wrinkled topographic map hanging in my field camp.

I estimated that Das had been dead for four or five days. Vultures had picked him clean, leaving only bones for the jackals to scatter. There were clear signs of a brutal struggle. A *Diospyros* sapling, thick as my knee, had been bent double. It stuck out from the flattened grass and churned up dirt. Imprinted on the soil were the dinner plate–sized tracks of a bull gaur.

Apparently, Das had chosen the wrong bull to indulge in his penchant for taking on these massive bovids. Due to some misstep, this time, he had failed. I was sure only a bull gaur had the power to headbutt and break such a thick sapling. There would be no room for mistakes against such a mighty adversary.

I walked away from the tiger's remains, saddened but comforted by the knowledge that a painful death was the inevitable fate of practically every living wild tiger. At least Das had not died a lingering death from starvation as Mudka had. No wild tiger dies peacefully. Some may think this a callous thing to say, but it is the truth.

After Das died, I was left with only the tigress, Sundari, and the leopard, Buddy Mackay. Stressed out by the intensity of radio-tracking, like Bopi before him, my assistant Gini also quit work to manage a roadside eatery.

Weeks passed, and my case continued to stagnate in the High Court with no final resolution. I obsessively busied myself in Nagarahole, while Prathibha and my daughter, Krithi, just waited patiently back at home for my weekend trips. Immersed in my obsession with tigers, I was failing both as a husband and a father. Months passed in this tense state.

Man and Beast: The Illusion of Harmony

At sunrise on January 17, 1992, I was alone at my customary listening post at the Kuntur tower. I listened to Buddy Mackay's signals emanating from the Kalhalla area to the north. The previous evening, when I had seen him near the Mavinahalla watchtower [**MAP 2, Point 15**] his belly had been flat and empty. He was out hunting, stealthily walking through trails in the dense *Chromolaena* brushes. Overnight, Buddy had moved eight kilometers to the northern end of his territory. I hoped he was sleeping off a meal after a successful hunt.

Next, I picked up Sundari's signal and located her. She was in the crumbling ruins of the eight-hundred-year-old Nagaraja Fort, now overrun with thick *Lantana* bushes. Although I had planned a full day for tracking Sundari, my chances of seeing her in that dense secondary forest were remote. After a hurried breakfast, I decided to track Buddy instead.

I had to first locate the leopard precisely and then stay close, monitoring its activity every fifteen minutes until sunset. I also had to plot his location on a map once every hour. Such continuous tracking was especially tough at night, when the cats moved long distances over roadless, rugged forest terrain, with my Suzuki trying to catch up. To be honest, even I hated the drudgery of those all-night tracking sessions.

On the other hand, tracking in the daytime was an enjoyable pastime. After settling down for the day, the cats usually stayed put. All I had to do was record their signals and keep filling up my data forms. In the meantime, I watched birds or other animals and listened to the wonderful jungle sounds.

I could even indulge in reading a book. Later, as the sun went down, I often had the thrill of seeing the cat when it started moving. I hoped today would be one of those perfect days. How wrong I turned out to be!

I picked up Buddy's signals when he was half a kilometer away. He was inactive. I drove closer. The leopard was in a copse of *Schleichera* trees next to the Kalhalla stream at the northern boundary of his territory [**MAP 2, Point 9**]. He went there often to establish his ownership by leaving his scent marks.

As the morning advanced, the sun got hotter. After getting inactive signals every time I listened, a vague disquiet was beginning to gnaw at me. I started listening to the signals nonstop. I did not want to miss the occasional burst of activity, whenever Buddy rolled over. But minutes passed—five, ten, fifteen, thirty, and then a full hour—without an active signal from Buddy. This was certainly unusual. Even a resting cat would roll over or stretch once in a while.

My worry turned into alarm. Something was wrong. I called Chinnappa from Nagarahole. I needed someone skilled to keep an eye out while I radio-tracked the leopard through such dense cover. As soon as he arrived, we set out on foot. I held the antenna up, focusing on the beeps in my earphones. He led, alert to the jungle sounds, and I followed close behind. We had covered about three hundred meters when the signals got louder. The leopard was close by.

At this point, I knew something was wrong. If Buddy had been sleeping, he would have heard us by now and slinked away. We pushed through some foliage: there was Buddy. It was a sight I will never forget.

In a dense grove of yellow-tinged *Cipadessa* bushes, Buddy appeared to be standing upright like a man. A chill ran up my spine. Looking closely, I saw that his hind legs were a few inches off the ground. He was still as a sculpture, apparently floating in air. Then, I noticed a thin wire hanging down from the *Cassia* sapling arched above. At its other end was a noose wound tight around Buddy's neck. An ordinary telephone wire had strangled Buddy to death.

Buddy's beautiful golden form contrasted with the gross, contorted grimace on his face. His long pink tongue stuck out grotesquely from between his tightly clamped jaws. A stub of gray excreta protruded out of his anus. The radio collar I fitted him with hung under his chin. The snare had been set with great skill. I marveled that this flimsy wire had, with such careless ease, squeezed the life out of a fifty-eight-kilogram master predator. When Buddy had tugged at the wire to free himself, the arched sapling had sprung

The leopard Buddy Mackay is killed in a snare set by a poacher.

free, hoisting him up like a victim of a gruesome lynching. Both Chinnappa and I stood staring, momentarily stunned.

The trail on which Buddy met his cruel death led down to the Kalhalla stream. Many a deer and pig followed it to drink from the stream. The poacher must have set up the snare, hoping to catch a deer or pig. Before they did, Buddy had come along for a drink.

From his faint footprints, it appeared that the poacher had returned to check the snare early that morning. I could imagine the poacher's shock at finding a leopard in his snare instead of the juicy pig he had hoped for. Worse, this leopard was wearing a radio collar no doubt fitted by the "Bones Ranger," who could arrive anytime. The poacher had dashed away from the scene of his crime well before I arrived.

The spot where Buddy was snared was deep inside the reserve, miles away from any of the villages on its boundary. The skill with which this snare had been set indicated the handiwork of an experienced hunter. The killer who had set the snare was familiar with animal trails in this locality. He would have had to check the snare every morning to claim his prey before some wild carnivore snatched it away. This poacher was almost certainly a tribesman from the Kalhalla hamlet nearby.

The veterinarian's autopsy was clear: death by asphyxiation. The veterinarian also found that Buddy's lungs were infested with cysts. This came as a small consolation to me. With his lungs' capacity reduced by those cysts, Buddy would not have struggled in agony for too long before he died.

I sent out a note to the press, together with the autopsy report, to try to get ahead of the inevitable blame game targeting me started. Deeply upset by Buddy's "lynching," I could not resist speculating that the killer could be a tribesman who lived nearby. I cited a recent survey by social activists that highlighted widespread malnutrition among tribal people living in remote interiors of the forest to suggest that the poacher may have been driven by hunger to set the snare. The only pragmatic solution to this perennial human-wildlife conflict, I concluded, was to provide decent livelihood opportunities to tribal people by resettling them outside of the reserve.

Very likely, if given the necessary support, this would be an enthusiastically voluntary resettlement. Just three months earlier, when the chief minister had visited Nagarahole, a delegation of tribal people had come to greet him. They had complained bitterly about their miserable living conditions inside the reserve. They did not have decent housing, electricity, schools, or hospitals. After forestry logging ended a decade earlier, they had been compelled to walk several miles every day to labor on the thriving coffee plantations outside the reserve. This was their only option, since raising crops and livestock inside the reserve was forbidden. In any case, such husbandry was impossible because of marauding elephants and predators.

The tribal delegation had complained, justifiably, to the chief minister: *People come from all over the world to enjoy watching wild animals in Nagarahole, but everyone is blind to our plight.* The delegation demanded an allotment of two hectares of land for each family. They also wanted roads, schools, hospitals, and other social amenities for each one of the fifty-eight tribal hamlets scattered within the reserve.

The chief minister had bluntly told them it was impossible to provide the support they sought if they continued to live inside the wildlife reserve. However, he would generously grant them all these amenities and more—if only they agreed to relocate to an area just outside the reserve boundary. Dramatically handing out a thick wad of hundred-rupee notes to the tribal leaders, he invited them to visit Bangalore the following week. "If you come to the state capital, I will organize a big meeting of senior officials and solve all your problems—if you are willing to relocate," he had assured them.

To his credit, the chief minister kept his promise. A few months later, the government earmarked a large block of degraded forest at the park's north-eastern edge for resettling tribal people. This was the genesis of the Nagapura resettlement colony [**MAP 2, Inset**].

In my press release, I had assumed that I was only reiterating what had already been agreed between the tribal people and the government. I should have known better.

The tabloids put out their own spin, with screaming banner headlines claiming I had branded innocent tribal people as poachers to mask my own culpability regarding the leopard's death. And I was using it as an excuse to get the poor tribal people summarily "thrown out" of Nagarahole to make sure there were no witnesses to my continued misdeeds. They darkly hinted that I had personally strung up the fifty-eight-kilogram leopard to cover up my own responsibility for its death. One thing became certain: I could never win any argument with the tabloids using logic and reason as my weapons.

The next week, while I was chatting with some visitors in the forest rest house, a mob of agitated tribal youth surrounded my field camp. Using thick black charcoal, they scribbled slogans that soon covered the hut's pale green walls. In Kannada they proclaimed: "Karanth the tiger killer" and "Karanth the enemy of the tribal people." One line was even added in English: "Down with Karanth." Upon seeing me they burst into new slogans of tribal power: "The rock-bees are angry, the rock-bees will sting!" They were comparing themselves to the *Apis dorsata* swarms that could indeed sting a human being to death. After shouting themselves hoarse for a couple of hours, they departed at lunchtime.

The attacks inspired by tabloids did not end with the tribal youths. A couple of days later, a group of youth claiming to be Marxists arrived from the nearby town of Virajpet. Using bamboo sticks, bundles of straw, and rags they brought, they quickly fashioned a life-size—but not a lifelike—effigy of mine. Forming a circle around their straw man, they poured kerosene and set him ablaze, chanting "Victory to the revolution!" The campaign against me had escalated from a mere local protest and become a part of the historical class struggle to unchain the world's proletariat.

Summer holidays had started bringing hordes of tourists to Nagarahole. I deliberately left the graffiti of slogans for all of them to see, as a sign of my own defiance. Meanwhile, I quietly continued tracking Sundari, the last cat with a radio collar left, while the court case dragged on. I wanted to block out the human cacophony and tune into the enchanted world of tigers. Deep inside, I tried to tell myself that all these tragic absurdities would become mere footnotes in the history of my work.

Late one evening, back from tracking Sundari, I stood on the edge of the paved road close to my camp, enjoying the tranquility of the descending dusk. My reverie was interrupted by a green tourist van that stopped near me. It had returned from the last jungle ride of the day. Four burly men got out to smoke, and started reading the graffiti on the walls of my field camp.

"That jungle ride was bloody expensive—sixteen rupees!" one complained about the subsidized one-dollar fee he had paid. "It certainly wasn't worth the money," chimed in another. "All we saw were a few hundred deer, a few herds of elephants, and some gaur. We did not see any tigers at all," whined the third man, adding he could have seen "many at the Mysore Zoo at a fraction of the cost."

"How can we hope to see any tigers in Nagarahole," complained the heftiest among them, clearly the thought leader for the group, pointing at the slogans on the walls, and continuing, "when that fellow Karanth is killing off tigers, one by one, under the guise of his research?" Then he added, "It is rumored he is secretly selling tiger skins to Americans for millions of dollars!" For these men, the evidence of my misdeeds was clinched by the charcoal graffiti.

Puffing out a series of smoke rings, the big man turned to me and asked, "Saar, don't you think all this is shamefully scandalous?" To these men, and to the public, I was only a name and not a face. I nodded solemnly.

After finishing their cigarettes, the men bade me goodbye and drove away. Rather than despair at this theater of the absurd, I found myself laughing, to my own surprise.

I had finally managed to "grow a skin thicker than a water buffalo hide," as the chief minister had helpfully suggested a few months earlier. Although I did not realize it at that moment, this metamorphosis would prove very useful when an approaching disaster finally arrived at my doorstep.

5 | A TIGER IN THE FLAMES

AS MARCH 1992 BEGAN, I felt totally under siege. Even some forest officials disliked me, because of my opposition to logging in the park. Although most realized that I had not done anything wrong, they were getting tired of the negative stories in the press. Only a few senior officers—particularly Paramesh, Alva, Lakshamana, and Appayya—were still supportive.

However, wildlife protection was once again humming with action in Nagarahole. Soon after Minister BB was moved out of the forestry department, Nachaiya had used his connections with Chief Minister SB to get Chinnappa and Devaraju posted back. Ranger GR was shunted off once again, this time entirely out of the wildlife division.

The wildlife rangers in Nagarahole now had the backing of Srinivas, the new deputy conservator in Hunsur. Although his primary mandate was forestry, unlike his predecessors, Srinivas was far more interested in wildlife. Built like a battle tank, he was a gutsy enforcer. Going against all niceties, Srinivas had once arrested a very senior civil administrator for illegal hunting. At that time, I had helped Srinivas, making sure the truth was not hushed up in the media.

Srinivas often accompanied me while I radio-tracked tigers, and appreciated the science involved. Invigorated by his support, the forest staff were going hell for leather after poachers and timber thieves. Even among the local coffee planters, I had a few sympathetic allies like Aiyanna. He was a gentle, soft-spoken soul who loved wildllife. He had been visiting Nagarahole since the 1960s. My friendship with him dated back to those days.

When Indira Gandhi's conservation laws hit home in 1970s, most local planters had stopped hunting. They had even given up their tradition of serving game meat at weddings. A few of them, however, still coveted the illegal venison. Fearing possible arrest, with its attendant social stigma, they surreptitiously hired professional poachers to supply illicit game meat.

Socially, these professional poachers were considered petty outlaws. They usually hung out in the XYZ Bar, located a couple of kilometers from the western entrance of the reserve at Nanachi. In its dungeon-like interiors, poachers, timber smugglers, and other seedy local characters found camaraderie. Sitting on rickety wooden benches, imbibing vast quantities of cheap rum, they swapped tales of clandestine adventures.

Most of the forest rangers managing the timber operations were perpetually busy men, cogs in India's gargantuan bureaucratic machine. In the forests outside the Nagarahole Reserve, these "territorial rangers" supervised logging, established tree nurseries, and even regulated timber cutting on private lands. They backed their "fieldwork" with tons of coarse paper forms filled by hand in quadruplicate and duly rubber-stamped in purple after being signed off in blue ink. The resulting bundles of ragged files, tied up with bright red strings, were then "put up" through more bureacratic layers, after which rangers recouped much more than they spent. Rather inexplicably, even as India's tall timber was virtually being mined and the forests shrank in size, the armies of government paper pushers kept expanding.

Effective antipoaching patrols, like the ones in Nagarahole, were the exception rather than the rule in the forests of Malenad. As years passed, poaching had made animals scarce in most forests. Poachers had to trudge mile after weary mile to shoot a chital or a pig. More often than not, they returned empty-handed.

Whenever the regulars at XYZ Bar discussed the scarcity of game, an air of wistfulness crept in. They were getting increasingly resentful of the intensified wildlife protection regime in Nagarahole. If only they had a free run of the forests, imagine the numbers of deer and pigs they could profitably slay—not to speak of the rich haul of teak and rosewood timber they could smuggle. Unfortunately, although the treasures of Nagarahole were right on their doorstep, accessing them had become hazardous to their health.

Only the boldest among these men dared to enter the park. They did so only on pitch-dark nights along wild animal trails, accompanied by a couple of trusted companions. One of these had to be a local tribesman familiar with the labyrinth of trails. Without him, even after spotting and shooting an animal, the poacher would find it hard to find his way home. Extra hands were also useful to quickly dismember the carcass, pack it in "gunnysacks" (bags made of jute fiber), and carry it home.

Speed was of the essence in this risky enterprise. From the moment a poacher fired a shot, he had less than an hour to get out of the forest. Wildlife guards in the nearest antipoaching camp would guess the location of the shot and try to surround the area. They called in reinforcements using handheld wireless sets. The wildlife guards tried to ambush the poacher before he got away.

In this deadly game of cat and mouse, the poacher's only advantage was the element of surprise. The wildlife patrols had more firepower, wireless communication, and vehicles to cover distances quickly. Even more critically, the patrols were guided by capable wildlife rangers like Chinnappa and Devaraju with their encyclopedic knowledge of the ways of poachers. The poacher had to sneak out before the guards took their positions for the ambush. If a careless guard smoked or talked, he could tip off the poacher.

If the ambush worked, however, the poacher was in for a nasty surprise. These encounters were always dangerous. There was utter confusion in the darkness. Men on either side could get shot. Even if a poacher chose to drop his gun and surrender, he was in for a rough time at the hands of the angry guards—and later with the even rougher policemen.

This ordeal was followed by five to six years of criminal prosecution in courts. Some policemen and the prosecutors extorted money to weaken their own cases to help the poachers. Finally, after years of social humiliation and financial ruin, most poachers were acquitted. Usually insufficient evidence, lack of independent witnesses, or some other arcane facet of the law helped them. In reality, these criminal trials were far worse than the fine or the short jail term the poacher would have endured after conviction. The entire justice system was pure Franz Kalfka; more than the punishment, the real deterrant was the trial.

There was also a long-term, ballistic aspect to the corporeal punishment suffered by the culprit. The poachers employed guns loaded with large bore bullets to kill deer, wild pigs, or gaur. If they shot a forest guard instead, he could die, or at least suffer serious injuries. On the other hand, the wildlife guards, whose mission was to incapacitate rather than kill the poacher, deliberately loaded their guns with buckshot. Because of this, they could spray the pellets in a wider area to score a hit. The pellets also reduced the chance of fatalities. Even when a poacher escaped after being sprayed, a few pellets could remain buried under his skin. They caused much discomfort, as long as the poacher lived. Forest guards contemptuosly referred to such escapees as "the men to whom the buckshots murmur." Most poachers, once ambushed, never hunted in Nagarahole again. The fact that Nagarahole teemed with wildlife was the best proof of this deterrance.

I had sometimes walked with Chinnappa and his guards when they tried to ambush poachers. These were truly hair-raising experiences. These incidents taught me, well before I earned my master's degree, that wildlife protection in India is not a mind game played by academics sitting in ivory towers. It was the cutting edge of a harsh reality, in which underpaid men in shabby khaki uniforms risked their very lives, day after day, to save rare wild animals. For the survival of many threatened species, these protectors were critical.

I had no problem if some conservation theorist labeled me as an "authoritarian" for offering this realistic assessment.

A Murder Most Foul

As the summer of 1992 advanced into the month of March, the forests turned tinder dry. The oppressive heat of the summer frayed everyone's nerves. Tensions between foresters and locals were ratcheting up. Nagarahole was a powder keg, ready to explode at the touch of a lighted match. That match turned out to be a thuggish local man, Thippa.

Thippa was a well-built school-dropout in his thirties. Karl Marx would have classed Thippa as one among the *Lumpen-proletariart*. Thippa jointly owned a small patch of coffee with his brother in Nalkeri village on the edge of Nagarahole Park. Unwilling to work at any regular job, constantly fighting with his brother over money, he usually glowered sullenly at the world around him. However, Thippa had one great marketable skill: he was a deadly marksman with a shotgun. He had turned this gift into a steady source of much-needed cash to support his many vices. However, after his arrest by the wildlife guards in Nagarahole a few years earlier, Thippa had been wary of poaching inside the reserve.

To counter the increasingly ruthless and lethally armed ivory poachers, in 1988 the government had empowered the forest guards to shoot back in self-defense. Soon after, Shikari Thimma—a legendary local poacher—had escaped after being shot by guards in Nagarahole. The forest department had reported the incident to the district collector as mandated by law. Since then, no one had seen Thimma. Some said he had died of his injuries after being admitted to a clinic where the shady doctor did not report firearm injuries to the police, as mandated by law. Others believed Thimma had died deep in the bowels of the Nagarahole jungle where, after hungry jackals and wild pigs had feasted, no one would ever find his bleached bones.

After Thimma's grisly end, Thippa realized if ever he blundered into a forest patrol in Nagarahole, he was unlikely to ever need a lawyer. He restricted his predatory activities to the forest fringes closer to home. Unfortunately, big animals like chital, sambar, and gaur, whose meat commanded premium prices, were scarce there. Thippa mostly shot hares, porcupines, palm civets, and flying squirrels, to be roasted over a wood fire and consumed. He shared the meat with his two trusted companions in crime: the hunting guide Bola, a tribesman, and Kunjappa, a migrant laborer from Kerala who helped to sell the meat locally. However, his richer clients for venison turned their aristocratic noses away from such low-class fare. Thippa's income had sharply risen during the willfully lax protection regime of Ranger GR. During this period, Thippa had begun to venture deeper into the reserve to poach the deer meat. The cash flow had dried up after Chinnappa replaced GR. Thippa and his buddies at the XYZ Bar deeply resented this unsatisfactory state of affairs.

On the fateful night of March 11, 1992, Thippa felt particularly desperate. He was so cash-strapped that he could not even afford a bottle of cheap rum. So he joined his two companions, who were drinking low-grade arrack out in his yard. After a few drinks, Thippa told the men he was fed up with the forest guards and their silly rules. Tonight they would take a chance to enter Nagarahole and shoot a chital. Kunjappa and Bola, well into their cups, had rashly agreed to accompany him.

Thippa entered his ramshackle house, picked up his trusted single-barrel shotgun, and strapped a battery-powered flashlight onto his forehead. His comrades grabbed gunnysacks to bring the meat back. Thippa could hear his elder brother snoring on the veranda after a tiring day's work at the coffee patch. He stirred and asked Thippa where he was headed. Thippa had snapped back, "Don't you know it brings bad luck to ask that? Can't you see I am going hunting? I plan to take the trail to Santapura Hadlu. There are bound to be herds of chital there at this time of the year." Inadvertently, Thippa had revealed his route to his resentful sibling.

The three men strode into the forest, their hearts full of arrack-inspired resolve. But their legs were unsteady from the same liquid. They had a hard time getting across the three-meter-deep trench bulldozed by the forestry department to mark the reserve boundary, which also kept wild elephants from raiding crops outside. Clawing their way up the trench's red-earth embankment, the three men took the trail to Santapura, walking in a single file.

As the forest shadows closed over their heads and they moved steadily along, their bravado slowly abated. The fear of being ambushed by a jungle patrol steadily rose. They would be badly outnumbered and outgunned by the forest guards.

The men entered a dense patch of *Lantana*. Thippa switched off his headlight and moved forward hesitantly. Hearing a faint rustle ten meters ahead, his imagination was in overdrive. What was that animal coming down the trail? Cocking his gun, Thippa switched on his headlight. A tiny pair of blazing emerald eyes reflected his light. A black-naped hare, frozen in terror, stood on its hind legs staring back. Enraged at the pathetic little creature, Thippa fired, dropping the offending lagomorph dead.

The trio was already two kilometers inside the park. The guards in the antipoaching camp on Bulldozer Road [**MAP 2, Point 23**] could possibly have heard the gunshot. It would be sheer madness for the poachers to push their luck by continuing to Santapura to shoot a chital. They decided to return home, posthaste. The deer could wait for another day. Bola picked up the lifeless hare and pushed it into the gunnysack. As if in telepathic communication, the three men silently turned around, and walked back the way they had come at a brisk trot.

After thirty minutes they were in the last patch of dense forest before they could cross the elephant-proof trench, and soon they would be home safe. Thippa unloaded his gun and slung it on his shoulder. No jungle patrol could ambush them now.

The poachers were walking in a single file, with Thippa in the lead, when suddenly a bright beam of a flashlight momentarily blinded them. A shot rang out. One short, ugly scream escaped from Thippa's throat as he collapsed [**MAP 2, Point 22**]. Hearing the shot, Bola had taken off, dropping the blood-soaked gunnysack. Kunjappa had sprinted after him. He found it impossible to keep up with the blistering pace of the tribesman. Kunjappa would not see Bola ever again. Kunjappa ran on blindly, unmindful of the *Lantana* twigs and

Zizyphus thorns that lashed and raked his face. He ran away from that last terrifying scream of his mentor Thippa like a man possessed.

Stealthy footsteps approached the fallen poacher. Unseen hands picked up his gun, and the footsteps receded away softly. Thippa did not hear them; he lay dead, spread-eagled under giant bamboo culms, shot through the chest. Not far from him lay the equally dead black-naped hare.

A few hours passed. The pale pink light of dawn broke through the forest canopy, infusing energy into the myriad living forms of Nagarahole. Another routine day had begun—or so it seemed. But Thippa's stone-cold body, inert on the forest floor, was about to set off an explosion like one never before witnessed in this remote corner of Malenad.

Burn, Tiger, Burn

I got the first hint of the bad news twenty-four hours later, when my doorbell rang in Mysore. I had just returned from a short trip to New York. It was my old friend, the planter Aiyanna. He had been a consistent supporter of conservation efforts. Aiyanna anxiously related the crisis building up around Nagarahole.

The previous day, after being tipped off by a terrified Kunjappa, Thippa's buddies had found his body on the edge of the forest. Finding that Thippa's brother was not up to the task, Thippa's friends at XYZ Bar had immediately taken charge of the situation and appointed themselves as spokesmen for the dead man. They claimed that before he fled from the murder scene, Kunjappa had seen "a very tall man wearing a brown balaclava cap shoot down Thippa. It seemed the man resembled Ranger Chinnappa." It was known that the legendary ranger, who was six feet, five inches tall, usually wore a brown balaclava cap on cold nights when he went out on patrols.

As to what Thippa and his two companions were doing within a protected reserve in the dead of the night, they had a simple explanation: the poor man had been searching for a lost water buffalo. Before more villagers gathered, the conspirators had quietly removed the blood-soaked bag with the dead hare, a piece of evidence that contradicted their story.

Conveniently for them, the tribesman Bola disappeared. He would lose himself in the anonymity of his seminomadic forest culture. His tribe lived in dozens of isolated hamlets scattered over three thousand square kilometers of deep jungles, spread across three state boundaries and under multiple police jurisdiction. Someone in Bola's position would be really foolish to go to the police, who were under tremendous pressure to find a suspect. An inconvenient witness, Bola had vanished not only physically but also from the entire narrative.

Thippa's comrades immediately sought support from a couple of local politicians who bore old grudges against Chinnappa. The duo agreed to lead an agitation to secure justice for the dead poacher. Their fiery rhetoric soon inflamed the crowd, which was swelling by the minute. Almost every man had a grudge—legitimate or illegitimate—against the forest department. Each man believed this was the most opportune moment to settle all old scores.

The previous day, Aiyanna had gone to the spot and tried to reason with the crowd. He had been heckled and sent away, accused of supporting a merciless ranger who had shot, in cold blood, an innocent man looking for a lost buffalo.

A posse of policemen from Kutta had come to take away Thippa's cadaver for the mandatory autopsy. The large and by now armed mob had held them at bay. During the daylong standoff, the crowd's rage had risen. The situation looked ugly; a lynch-mob mentality was taking over.

Aiyanna told me that Thippa's body was still in the custody of the mob. He feared the situation could spin out of control at any moment. After all, taking a dead body in a procession to whip up mob frenzy—against any grievance, real or imaginary—was a time-honored tactic of "peaceful agitation" in India. Nothing could incite an Indian mob to violence more effectively than a gamey human cadaver.

On his way to Mysore, Aiyanna had stopped at Nagarahole and warned Chinnappa of the impending danger, urging him to leave the place immediately. After alerting me, Aiyanna drove off to visit his son at a boarding school in the salubrious hill station of Ooty, a hundred miles away. I felt sorry for this kind, friendly man. He was worried about being targeted by the enraged mob because of his friendship with Chinnappa and me.

My heart sank as I absorbed the full story. This was far more dangerous than anything I had faced before. However, I knew the story of an unarmed man being shot while looking for a lost buffalo was just that, a story. In these elephant-infested forests, nobody in his senses would search for buffaloes at night. The law was also clear: the forest staff had legal powers to shoot a poacher if confronted. All they had to do was to immediately inform the district collector.

In the past, following such encounters, rangers had done exactly that. This protocol protected forest staff against prosecution for just doing their job. It would have been foolish not to have filed such a report if any forester had really shot Thippa. Chinnappa was an experienced ranger who was anything but foolish.

I also knew that nothing would remain a secret for long around Nagarahole. The mystery surrounding Thippa's murder would eventually be solved, when confidences were shared in the local liquor stores and bars. The police planted their stool pigeons in such places precisely to gather such secrets.

However, right now an explosion was imminent. I tried to call the range office at Nagarahole, but the phone lines were dead. I called Srinivas at Hunsur and was told he had rushed off to Nagarahole. I felt angry and helpless.

I hoped that the district collector (DC) and the superintendent of police (SP) would pacify, disarm, and disperse the mob. In India, "DC" and "SP" are the two most powerful officials in a district. I heard a battalion of special riot police from Mysore had been called in. If the SP ordered them to, they could quell any mob violence. They had the necessary gear: helmets, shields, truncheons, tear-gas canisters, and even loaded rifles. However, unless authorized by the SP, they were like caged tigers.

Preparing for the worst, I called up Krishna, Praveen, and Prasad in Bangalore, asking them to alert the press about the trouble brewing in Nagarahole. If the "Karanth tiger scandal" taught me anything, it was how the media optics significantly shaped public opinion. The calculus of politicians tracked that public opinion, and the bureacracy obeyed its political masters.

Above all, I wanted to make sure that Chinnappa was not falsely accused of murder, jailed, or humiliated once again. Although only a small number of local thugs and politicians were at the core of the brewing conspiracy, they had riled up public opinion sufficiently to gather a frenzied mob. No leader would ultimately have much control over such a mob after the rioting started.

There was no news from Nagarahole all through the day. I paced restlessly at home, unable to work. Prathibha had cooked a nice meal for her sister who was visiting. I was too distracted and grouchy to enjoy either the lunch or their company.

Finally, the phone rang at 2000 hours. It was Srinivas, back in Hunsur. "I am sorry, Ullas, I have some bad news for you," he began. My heart sank again, for Chinnappa and for Nagarahole. Srinivas quickly quelled my worst fears, saying Chinnappa and his courageous wife, Radha, had left Nagarahole that morning and were now safe in a forest rest house in the south of the park. However, that was the only good news.

I learned the SP had finally arrived that morning to the spot where Thippa's body still lay. This senior policeman had a doctoral degree in sociology, but neither the savvy necssary for negotiating with ruffians nor much experience with crowd control. The angry mob had bullied the SP into permitting them to carry the poacher's body in a ceremonial procession to the hospital in Kutta for the autopsy.

At the head of the grim parade—strapped to the roof of a jeep—was their grisly mascot: the body of the dead poacher. By then the crowd had swollen to over three hundred men, many of them drunk, angry, and armed with shotguns and clubs. When the SP yielded to their illegal request, they smelled blood. The men piled into dozens of jeeps and cars, and, instead of heading to the hospital at Kutta, turned the convoy to the left, near XYZ Bar, and drove to the park's entrance gate at Nanachi [**MAP 2**]. Breaking through the barrier, the mob reached the Nagarahole campus around noon.

The mob saw the riot police sitting inside two fully fortified police vans, fierce caged animals ready to attack. The mob suddenly became wary and hesitant.

Almost everyone in the mob had a grouse against the forest department. They disliked the seventy-kilometer detour they were forced to make because of the ban on driving through the park at night; some resented the bribes they had been coerced to pay, even to cut trees on their own lands; and others who lived right next to the reserve boundary were upset because their cattle had been barred from entering the lush pastures inside. There were frustrated petty traders of illegally collected forest products, and traditionalists angry that their erstwhile right to hunt wild game had been taken away.

All of them sullenly waited for guidance from two dozen hard-core poachers at the front of the convoy, the same men who had borne much pain and humiliation at the hands of the forest rangers and the guards. These men fumed at memories of the past beatings, public paradings in manacles, and the financially ruinous prosecutions. The buckshot pellets under their skin were murmuring to them today, louder than ever before. Instinctively, the thugs sesnsed a once-in-a-lifetime opportunity to break the morale of their tormentors.

However, the police chief still did not order the riot police to get out of their vans and stand ready to baton-charge the mob. If their truncheons did not work, the riot police had tear-gas shells, and even rifles as backup. The SP was still hoping that his social science talents would pacify the mob. He walked away to the forest rest house, taking the two politicians with him for further negotiations.

Emboldened by the absence of any authority figures, as well as the paralyzed inaction of the riot police, the thugs decided to act. Suddenly, one of them hurled a rock at the glass window of the forest range office, which shattered. Some others caught hold of a guard on sentry duty and thrashed him senseless. They started chasing and beating up the dozen of khaki-clad forest staff who were around. Even the obese cook Das was not spared.

Srinivas had desperately urged the SP to unleash the riot police. Instead, the police chief ordered tea for the political leaders, trying to soften them up. Meanwhile, more vehicles had arrived from the villages, bearing more men. Ominously, these men also brought cans of gasoline.

Thirsting for Chinnappa's blood, and I presumed mine too, the mob searched the campus. A group of men entered the range office, smashing its windows and furniture. They set fire to whatever papers and files they could lay their hands on, including forestry records of Nagarahole dating back over a century.

Another group ransacked my field camp. My green Suzuki, a witness to many tiger-tracking expeditions, was torched and reduced to an ash-gray hulk. The gasoline in its tank exploded, and the flames quickly engulfed the building's tiled roof and burned it. Some of the rioters raided the bamboo shed and stole dozens of scientifically precious animal skulls, antlers, and horns, collected and meticulously tagged as my "predator kill data."

The worst was yet to come. Their blood now fully up, the rampaging men fanned out, driving their jeeps into the surrounding forests along tourist roads. They splashed gasoline on the tinder-dry leaf litter on the forest floor, followed with lighted matches. The sparks streaked through the short, dry grass on the roadside, and then leaped up, ready to consume thousands of tons of combustible biomass. The dry taller grasses, dense shrubs of *Lantana* and *Chromalaena*, and the bamboo culms continously fed the voracious flames. Soon, fallen logs and standing dead trees were also aflame. The scorching fire spread fast and far, carried by the strong afternoon winds.

The rioters burned down Ullas Karanth's vehicle and the field station.

The emerald jungle of Nagarahole, a treasure trove of biological riches, a repository of many as-yet-undiscovered species and unexplored knowledge, had been protected for over a quarter century. Now it was going up in flames. The forest staff and the tribesmen, who should have been dousing the flames, had run away fearing for their lives.

The fire would soon spread over eight square kilometers of lush forest. Teak logs from the plantations worth millions of rupees—cut, stacked, and ready for transport—went up in smoke. The clouds of white smoke from the vast conflagration even caught the attention of Indian space agency satellites circling six hundred kilometers above the earth.

But the satellites missed another strange spectacle unfolding below. The riot police were watching the mob in frustration. It was now too late even for the "baton charge" using truncheons to quell this riot. The only thing that could stop it was to fire tear-gas shells, and, if that did not work, to use real bullets. That could lead to more deaths, and was politically risky. The riot raged on for a couple of hours while the poice watched.

The two politicians quickly realized that the mob they had instigated had thrashed government staff and destroyed government property that was worth millions of rupees. Would the government tolerate this massive destruction, such an overt challenge to its authority? It just so happened that these two leaders belonged to a couple of oppostion parties. The Congress Party that ruled the state had no sympathy for them. The leaders decided they had done their bit for the martyred seeker of the lost water buffalo. And they had given the forest department a bloody nose it would not forget. They had clearly established who now had command over Nagarahole. It was time to go home and act as if they had nothing to do with the consequences of their exhortations.

Although the core of the mob was comprised of hardened criminals, the rest were ordinary planters, traders, and farmhands who had rioted on the spur of the moment. Although these men felt their acts were justified, they did notice the quiet departure of the two politicians. Soon the crowd began to melt away. It was time to go home and pretend everything was just fine.

After the mob left, the police "took control of the situation." A doctor performed a hurried autopsy on Thippa's body in a firewood storage shed. Covering their noses to ward off the stench emanating from the body, policemen carried it back to the village for the last rites to be performed by the family. Finally, Thippa was on his way to the happy hunting grounds.

As I listened to Srinivas, increasingly feeling numb, he told me he had asked the policemen to salvage, intact, my radiotelemetry equipment and field data forms from my torched field camp. I guess that too was a piece of good news. Srinivas was greatly upset. We consoled each other and rang off.

I recalled the grim struggle that many unsung trench warriors of conservation—men like Chinnappa and his guards—had waged over two decades to recover India's decimated wildlife in Nagarahole and elsewhere. I thought of all the blood, sweat, and tears that had been shed to turn Nagarahole from the basket case it had been when I was a teenager, into a crown jewel among India's nature reserves.

I thought, too, of my own dreams of tracking and understanding the tigers of Nagarahole, of using science to help the big cats to survive the twentieth century and beyond. I thought of all the data I had painstakingly collected to paint the predator's portrait, one I could not possibly hope to complete now. I knew things had changed forever for Nagarahole. I realized Chinnappa would never come back to defend his animals. I was not even sure I wanted to go back again to Nagarahole.

Feeling a kind of deep, helpless anger, I went upstairs and lay down on my bed. Tears streamed down my cheeks. Prathibha came and stood next to me. We had been married eighteen years, and from one look at my face, she knew what I was going through. She ran her fingers through my hair and stroked my cheeks, softly whispering something that sounded like, "I love you. . . . Don't despair—everything will be OK. . . .You will ultimately win, you always do." She kept repeating, "Everything will be OK," in her calm, steady voice. I clutched at her words like a drowning man.

That was true, I reflected. I had rarely given up a fight as lost, a trait that I no doubt inherited from crusty ancestors on both sides of my parentage. The ultraorthodox *Kota Brahmins* on my father's side were notorious for their litigious nature and the tenacity with which they fought court cases over generations. My mother's ancestors were *Bunts*, a warrior caste known to prefer belligerence rather than finesse when resolving disputes. I had to now draw on both these strands of my genetic fabric to take on this battle. This was not a time to sit and mope about what happened that day in Nagarahole. I had a lot to do.

I was on the phone well past midnight.

Rising from the Flames

My immediate objective was to widely publicize the enormity of the crime the senseless men had committed. For this, I needed coverage of the rioting and arson in newspapers, radio, and television—nationally and internationally.

The landline telephone at home was the only speedy means of communication. Plotting to share with the media the information I was gathering in real time, I felt as Machiavellian as the tabloid press had been alleging all along. I also reached out to my contacts in the networks of scientists and conservationists within India and around the world.

Things fell into place quickly after Krishna, Praveen, and Prasad swung into action and alerted the media in Bangalore. Nachaiya put pressure on his political contacts in the Congress Party. By next morning Krishna, a champion motor rally driver, had raced to Nagarahole, ferrying a group of enterprising reporters.

When the journalists reached Nagarahole, firefighters were still trying to douse the smoldering flames in the forest. Srinivas was back at the helm, rallying what was left of his demoralized staff and few tribesmen to put out the blazes. It would take a couple of days to fully control the fire, which had raged across nearly eight hundred hectares of prime forest. The televison cameras caught the scorching flames and the grim struggle of the firefighters. They captured the burnt, gray forest and the herds of chital searching in vain for blades of green grass. It was their birthing season, and many newborn fawns had failed to escape the flames. Numerous smaller animals and ground-nesting birds had perished, too.

After recording the carnage in the forest, the reporters fanned out into nearby villages. When the savvy, quick-witted reporters from the big city encountered the rustic local leaders of the rioters, they were in for a culture shock. Among these men there was no sign of remorse, guilt, or even comprehension of the atrocity they had committed. Quite the contrary.

"It is our right to hunt in these forests," said one man, claiming to speak for a group with the ambition to establish the exclusive rights of local people over all the natural resources of the district. "My ancestors have hunted here for centuries. It is my birthright to kill and eat a deer, or a shoot a tiger. Who the hell are these forest officials to stop me?" was a common refrain reporters heard.

As to the indefensible torching of the forests, they claimed, "We did not burn the forest . . . at this time of the year the forest always burns spontaneously. The fires are caused by sparks that fly when the hooves of the fleeing deer strike the flint rocks on the forest floor. At other times, sparks are ignited when the hot sun causes the dry seeds of *Phyllanthus* berries to explode." Such profound absurdities were palmed off as "Indigenous ecological wisdom" to the increasingly skeptical journalists. By then the reporters had more than their fill of stories to report.

Late that evening, Chinnappa and his wife, Radha, arrived at my home. I was amazed at how stoically both of them were facing this heartbreaking tragedy. I felt proud to be their friend in this moment of crisis.

The following morning, the torching of Nagarahole by the vandals was huge news. That evening, major national TV channels and the BBC had carried the story. It led to a public uproar that could not be papered over by local political shenanigans. Conservationists held protest rallies in several towns in the state, demanding stern action against the culprits.

The prime minister of India, Narasimha Rao, asked Chief Minister SB to act. The chief minister immediately ordered a special investigation by the dreaded "corps of detectives" directly under his control. He summarily replaced the district collector and the police chief—who had failed to act in time—with tough men he trusted. The chief minister's alacrity in the matter was understandable: he had seen secret police reports, which identified the men who led the riot as supporters of the opposition parties. His own party men were not involved.

As the detective inquiry and harsh interrogations proceeded, the truth began to emerge. Police stool pigeons planted in local bars reported that Thippa was likely to have been shot because of a family feud over property. Kunjappa confessed to the shooting of the hare by Thippa, and that he had bolted without looking back. Most important, he had not seen Thippa's killer, as his friends had claimed. It turned out that guns issued to the foresters had not fired the shot that killed Thippa. Efforts began to trace Thippa's missing gun.

The men who led the mob in rioting were subjected to the dreaded interrogatory tactics of the detectives. Seventeen of them were criminally indicted. They also paid hefty legal fees to their defense lawyers and endured a tortuous trial that dragged on for five more years.

The local landed gentry were, by and large, a law-abiding lot, with a tradition of serving in the military. Indiscipline, rioting, and unsavory police inquiries were not their cups of coffee. They quickly distanced themselves from the thugs who led the riots.

I was beginning to sense a change in public perception around wildlife issues in Nagarahole. The torching of the forest had subtly worked to remove the perception that the main threat to Nagarahole was the good old "Karanth tiger scandal." The people who torched Nagarahole were the ones who had also accused me of killing tigers.

As the summer ended in the month of May, sitting at the very tip of leafless trees in the ghost-gray forest of Nagarahole, two vocal resident birds—the Indian cuckoo and the hawk cuckoo—mourned their losses stridently through the days and nights. A third species, the beautiful pied crested cuckoo, arrived on its annual migration from East Africa, heralding the arrival of the southwest moosoon.

Answering the cries of the cukoos, thundershowers arrived in cascades. The raindrops hit the fine powdery ash on the parched forest floor, kicking up coronets of water. The droplets coalesced and soaked deep into the fried forest soil. Fertilized by the ashes, blades of green grass sprouted. Herds of chital and gaur mowed down the grass as fast as it came up. Nature was beginning to heal and rise again in Nagarahole.

I pondered my future. If I wanted, I could return and work in Nagarahole. I had personally experienced how unpredictable social and political changes could impact my own work. Although I had very little control over these social forces, I felt I could still ride the tide of adversity to reach my goal. I had learned a simple rule: keep away from politics, but not necessarily from its practitioners.

I reflected on these matters deeply over the next eight months, while also completing my doctoral dissertation from the tranquility of my home. Sundari, the lone tigress with a radio collar, still roamed the forests, occasionally spotted by tourists. She called out to me in my dreams, too. However, I already had tons of telemetry data on Sundari. If I hoped to go back to Nagarahole again, I felt I had to remove all public misconceptions about my research.

Meanwhile, the once powerful Chief Minister SB was steadily being choked of political oxygen by the wily Prime Minister Rao. Going in for the kill, on November 19, 1992, Rao installed another rising backward caste leader, Veerappa Moily, as the new chief minister. When BB terminated my project three years earlier, as a minister in charge of education and academics, Moily had opposed the decision. He had argued, in vain, that scientific research was essential for progress in any field, including wildlife conservation.

I sought an appointment with the new chief minister and apprised him of how my tiger research was still in limbo because of the government's inaction on the expert committee's report. The experts had cleared me of all blame and excoriated the capricious termination of my research. The chief minister soon accepted the expert's report. I was free to go back and catch tigers in Nagarahole.

To Catch Tigers or Count Them?

Although I was back in Nagarahole, I had only a single tigress to track. The battery on her three-year-old transmitter would soon blink out. I now had the permit to catch her and replace the collar, and to catch more tigers and leopards if I wanted to.

However, a new problem was casting a shadow on the very future of wild tigers. A massive wave of poaching, driven by an upsurge in the international trade in tiger body parts, catering to millions of consumers of Chinese traditional medicines, was sweeping the world. After having wiped out several tiger populations in Southeast Asia, the wave hit India, the last stronghold of wild tigers. Attracted by the money to be made, traditional hunters and tribesmen of India were shooting, poisoning, snaring, and trapping tigers even in formerly secured protected reserves. I had taken the blame in Nagarahole when four—or possibly five—tigers had died from poaching during three months in 1990. The impact of this poaching wave on India's remaining tiger populations was totally unknown. Scientifically reliable estimates of tiger numbers had never been collected by the wildlife officials in the country.

Although my intensive radiotelemetry yielded important behavioral data on tigers, it was not a practical method to count tigers. At the cusp of this new tiger crisis, accurate counts of tiger populations, rather than intricate studies of individual tigers, had become the real need.

I was in a dilemma: should I continue my radio-tracking studies or switch my research focus to developing reliable methods for accurately counting tigers? Before taking that call, I decided to go ahead and replace Sundari's radio collar anyway. This time, I did not need an elaborate beat involving buffalo bait to catch her. All I had to do was to follow Sundari's signals from elephant back and dart her.

I decided to do a trial run. After I had tracked her through an all-night session, at 0857 hours on May 14, 1993, Sundari was resting in the eucalyptus planation at Kuntur. I returned to the camp for a quick breakfast and hurried back to where she was. This time I was accompanied by a riding elephant and its mahout. I wanted to home in on her signals, just to be sure I could get close enough to dart her later.

However, when I returned at 1030 hours, to my surprise, Sundari had moved north, crossed the tourism road, and was now two hundred meters deep in the dense secondary forest of bamboo [**MAP 2, Point 19**]. Something had shaken Sundari out of her slumber and induced her to go and investigate. Tracking her radio signals, our elephant pushed through the bamboo with reckless abandon. The mahout and I paid the price by getting raked by the thorns. The signals drew us to a fifteen-meter-tall *Lagerstroemia* tree sticking out over the bamboo canopy.

I saw an extraordinary sight: perched precariously on the thinnest branches atop the tree, looking down and growling in fear, was a big male leopard. Under the same tree, partially hidden by the bamboo cover, I could see Sundari. She was looking up intently. Escaping up a tree to dodge tigers is a common behavior among leopards. I realized this leopard was most likely the vigorous rival who had vanquished Monda the previous year and taken over his territory. I also realized that if Sundari caught up with him, she would snap his backbone like a matchstick. Sundari, with her fierce teeth and claws, was more than a match for the leopard one-third her size.

A leopard climbs to the top of trees to escape from aggressive tigers.
Courtesy Phillip Ross

As our elephant got closer to the tree, the leopard grew increasingly nervous. He did not like the pachyderm distracting him when the determined assassin lurked below. Jumping off his perch directly to the ground, the nervous leopard tried to dash for safety through the dense bushes. Sundari was off like a flash after him. We could hear the growls of a brief skirmish, before the leopard managed to dodge the tiger and claw his way back up the bole of the same tree. Sundari, continuing the chase, tried to grab him. However, her massive weight brought her down before she could catch up.

The tigress made one more ferocious attempt, this time reaching about five meters high before sliding back again. As the noonday sun turned hot, the two cats resigned themselves to a long stalemate. The leopard's growls subsided, and Sundari's radio signals kept switching between active and inactive modes.

As darkness descended, I headed back to the camp. When I returned next morning, the leopard was not at his treetop perch. Sundari's radio signals were fading away at a distance. I saw a jungle crow fly off with a piece of red, raw meat in its mouth. I feared Sundari had killed and eaten the leopard, which tigers occasionally do when they get a chance. However, at the bottom of the *Lagerstroemia* tree I saw the remains of a sambar fawn.

I reconstructed the scenario. The previous morning, after I left, Sundari had heard the screams of the sambar fawn when the leopard caught it. She had rushed to investigate the interloping predator, and stolen the kill. The leopard had escaped to the top of the tree, just before I had come back with the riding elephant. After waiting through the night for the leopard to come down, Sundari had tired of the vigil and left, just before I arrived. The leopard had seized the opportunity to escape, without worrying about his partially consumed prey. Sundari could easily have consumed the fawn, but had not. Her focus had entirely been on getting the leopard.

I realized how strong and hardwired this antagonistic behavior was between the species of big cats. It is a tribute to the adaptability and survival skills of the leopard that, despite being harried by two dominant big cat species, it has thrived in Asia as well as Africa. The leopard's range encompasses the distributional ranges of the tiger as well as the lion.

Two days later, on May 16, 1993, after just thirty minutes of radio-tracking Sundari from elephant back, I got to within ten meters of her. This location was in the teak plantation on BSR, barely three hundred meters from where I had first darted her three and a half years earlier [MAP 2, Point 2]. Sundari had walked languorously, without being bothered by my elephant following her. At one stage, Sundari sat down, panting gently. I took aim carefully. My dart hit her right thigh. Uttering the tiger equivalent of "Ouch," Sundari started walking again. Within a hundred meters she was down, fully sedated.

As soon as Sundari was found, I called my friends waiting in a nearby car to join me in the radio-collaring operation: Srinivas, Krishna, and Praveen, as well as Madhu and Ranger Devaraju. I was sad Chinnappa was not with me, but after the rioting and arson, he had voluntarily retired from government service.

Following the standard protocol, I replaced Sundari's old collar with a new one, now operating on a frequency of 150.152 megahertz. When I examined the wear and tear on her teeth, I realized what a tough life she had in the previous three years. Her teeth had turned yellow and worn out a lot more. I guessed that she could still hold on to her territory for a year or two more.

In the same three years, the tiger society in Nagarahole had been roiled by turmoil. Rather unusually, different parts of Sundari's territory had overlapped with the ranges of Mara, Yajamana, and Das. While Das was alive, she had mated with him as well as with Mara. Possibly she had mated with Yajamana, too.

I was sure Sundari had even given birth to a litter of cubs once: for two weeks during 1993 her movement became restricted to a small area in the dense lantana patch half a kilometer away from Kuntur Pond. It was a perfect place to hide newborn cubs. Tigresses move their cubs to a new place if they are disturbed, so I had decided not to home in on her signals on an elephant to check out her cubs. In the end the litter had not survived, and Sundari had left the location. It was likely that one or the other of the contending male tigers had killed her cubs. I marveled at how radio-tracking of even a single tigress had yielded so much information on tiger behavior.

The VHF radio-tracking from the ground that I was doing took me right into a tiger's world. Many current radio-tracking studies solely rely on tracking that employs satellite-based GPS or cell phone networks, which make radio-tracking far easier. However, these techniques do not allow the researcher to directly watch the collared animal. Watching tigers hunting, mating, raising cubs, and fighting in the jungle had provided me with unique insights into their behavior. I had observed not only my collared tigers, but also other tigers, predators, and prey that interacted with them. Watching animals was far more fun than watching LED blips on a computer screen.

However, I realized I would have to invest a lot of stressful effort over several years to catch more tigers and radio-track them. I wondered whether this was the best use of my talent and resources, given the terrible tiger poaching crisis unfolding before me.

All through the dust raised by the "Karanth tiger scandal," my supervisor in WCS New York, John Robinson, had firmly stood by me, even as the government and media were hounding me. Given the local hostility I had faced, I was sure no other international conservation organization would have risked doing that.

I reflected deeply on the choices before me, and made my decisions. As far as my research was concerned, I decided to switch my focus from monitoring individual tigers to monitoring entire tiger populations. My academic work had equipped me well for this challenge. On the conservation front, I decided to proactively go forth to engage with the society around me. My new confidence rested on the experiences I had gone through, rather than any knowledge I had gleaned from textbooks or discourses of conservation theoreticians.

6 | AUDITING THE TIGER BUSINESS

AN INTERNATIONAL BAN prohibiting the trade in tiger skins for trophies, fashion, or religious symbols was imposed in 1969. However, low levels of clandestine trade in tiger pelts persisted. In early 1990s, conservationists noticed a surge in this trade, as well the emergence of new commerce in bones and other body parts. Ancient medicine systems of China and the Far East attributed curative powers to the body parts of tigers. However, only the richest consumers could afford them. That changed when China's economic boom in the 1980s created a new class of affluent consumers. Thousands of tigers were raised purely for slaughter in dingy menageries peppered across China and Southeast Asia. However, savvy marketeers soon convinced consumers that body parts of wild tigers had more curative powers.

Wild tiger populations had almost been extirpated in China because of past eradication campaigns. The new tiger trade began to suck the remaining wild tigers from across Asia. Cambodia, Laos, and Vietnam lost their poorly protected tigers by 1995. Even in the extensive forests of Thailand, Myanmar, Malaysia, and Indonesia, there were only a few small populations, although they hung on grimly. Although the taiga forests of the Russian Far East were extensive, their inherently low densities of ungulates, further depressed by legal hunting, caused tigers to be scarce. In South Asia, Nepal, Bhutan, and Bangladesh had wild tigers, but India was the tiger's last stronghold on account of their effective reserve protection after the 1970s, when the trench warriors—the forest guards and rangers—had brought them back from the brink. However, by the late 1980s, senior forest officials had turned complacent. As more money

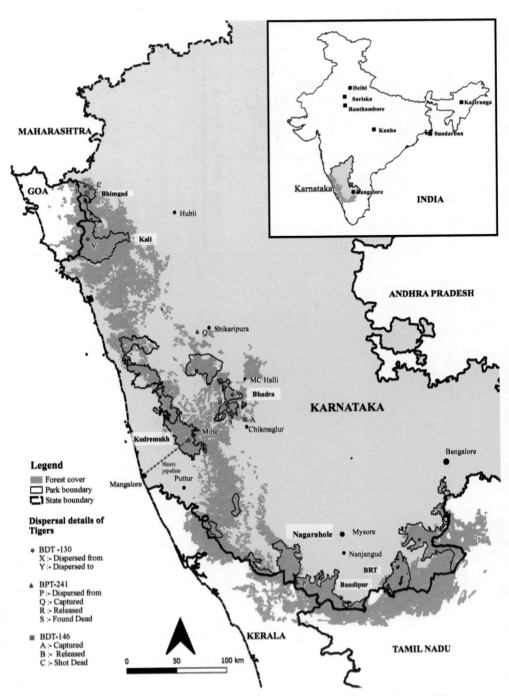

MAP 1. The Malenad tiger landscape in Karnataka State of India is a part of the vast tiger range that extends across Asia.

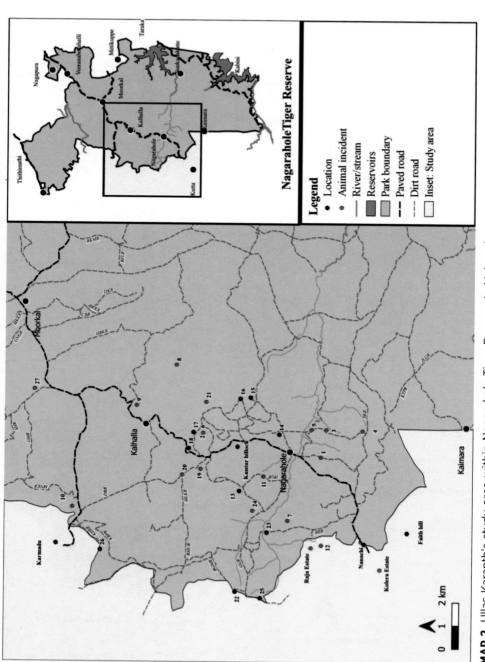

MAP 2. Ullas Karanth's study area within Nagarahole Tiger Reserve in Malenad.

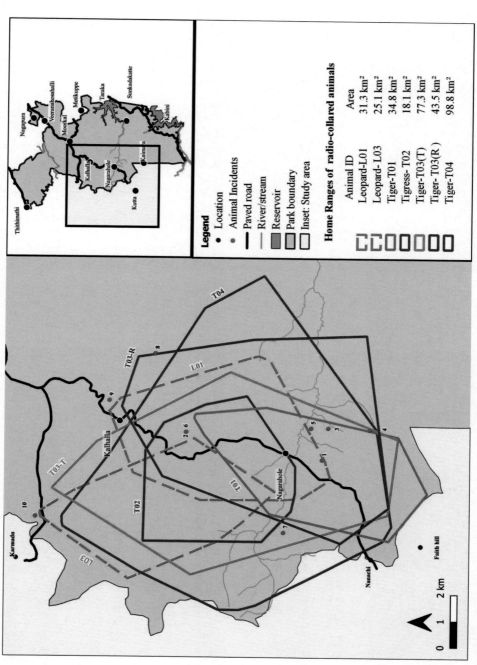

MAP 3. Home ranges of tigers and leopards radio-tracked by Ullas Karanth in Nagarahole Tiger Reserve between 1990–1996.

Legend

- Location
- Animal Incidents
- Paved road
- River/stream
- Reservoir
- Park boundary
- Inset: Study area

Home Ranges of radio-collared animals

Animal ID	Area
Leopard-L01	31.3 km²
Leopard-L03	25.1 km²
Tiger-T01	34.8 km²
Tigress-T02	18.1 km²
Tiger-T03(T)	77.3 km²
Tiger-T03(R)	43.5 km²
Tiger-T04	98.8 km²

The emerald jungles of Nagarahole in Malenad, Karnataka State, India.

Gatherings of related wild tigers are occasionally observed. *Courtesy Diinesh Kumble*

Ullas Karanth radio-collaring the tigress Sundari. *Courtesy Fiona Sunquist*

Tiger on a hunt being watched by an alert sambar deer. *Courtesy Pranav Vajapeyam.*

Ullas Karanth examining the carcass of a bull gaur killed by a tiger.

Tigers mark their passage by spraying scent marks unique to each individual.
Courtesy Giri Cavale

Tigress Sundari "parades" in front of Ullas Karanth and George Schaller.

A close encounter with the tigress NHT-116 terrified the television crew.

The economic power of tourism should be harnessed to expand tiger habitats.
Courtesy Aditya Singh

The natural productivity of tigers, if nurtured by reasoned compassion for the *species*, can lead us to a world with fifty thousand wild tigers. *Courtesy Pranav Vajapeyam*

flowed into tiger reserves, the complacency turned into a mission-drift away from strict protection.

International criminal syndicates operating from China and Vietnam reached out to their counterparts in India's urban hubs, like Delhi, Nagpur, and Calcutta (now known as Kolkata), offering premium prices for the "authentic" body parts of wild tigers. The Indian wildlife traders, most notorious among them being a man in Delhi named Sansar Chand, spread their tentacles through the spider webs of petty forest produce traders living next to thriving tiger populations, like the one in Nagarahole. The local traders, in turn, goaded dormant tiger poachers into quick action.

Nomadic hunting communities, lowly ranked in the caste hierarchy, are widely distributed across India. With the advent of strict conservation laws, they were barred from their traditional hunting of antelopes, wild pigs, and game birds in agricultural landscapes. Poorly educated and unable to adapt to rapid social changes, they hunted clandestinely. There were also forest-dwelling tribes, like my Jenu Kuruba companions, who are traditionally adept at snaring, trapping, and poisoning wild animals. Other rural folks owning firearms, men like Thippa, were also around. The booming tiger trade offering hitherto undreamed-of financial rewards was a call to arms to all these poachers.

Before the protection machinery woke up, incentivized poachers ravaged India's tiger populations in well-known tiger reserves like Kanha and Ranthambore in northern India. Some individual tigers in these reserves were habituated enough to be photographed and filmed widely. When well-recognized "star tigers" started disappearing, the global media slammed India's "tiger crisis." The cat's enduring cross-cultural appeal ensured the public and the governments across the world would take serious notice.

When India's conservationists, led by the charismatic naturalist TV-narrator Valmik Thapar, played up this new threat to tigers, the first reaction of the forest bureaucracy was to deny the problem. The director of Project Tiger calmly announced the tiger was not a "dying patient," and was "quite safe and secure."

Because of my friendship with Brijendra, I had also become a part of a tiger conservation network assembled by Valmik. Although we preferred to call ourselves the Tiger Wallahs (the Tiger Guys), disgruntled officials called us the "tiger mafia."

Soon the skeptical media was asking hard questions about tiger numbers in Indian reserves. Officials had always been ready with the exact numbers—down to the last tiger in India—going all the way back to 1970. They had been trotting out their "tiger numbers" once every four years after conducting countrywide censuses.

As a tiger biologist, I realized getting even a rough estimate of tigers across India posed many challenges. The suspiciously exact tiger numbers released by officials had shown steady increases year after year. Starting with 1,871 tigers in the early 1970s, officials claimed the population had risen to 4,005 in 1994. By then, the tiger censuses, conducted with much fanfare once in four years, had attained a cult status within the forest bureaucracy. The politicians, public, popular media, and most lay conservationists accepted the results at face value, leading to a dangerous complacency.

The tiger census method employed was invented by forest official Saroj Choudhury in the late 1960s. It rested on the breathtakingly naive assertion that forest guards wandering around in the forests of India would be able to find the pugmarks (paw prints) of every living tiger in just a couple of weeks. Choudhury and his disciples claimed that by looking at the shape of these paw prints traced on a piece of flat glass, they could individually identify and count every tiger. This "pugmark census method" had, however, never been scientifically tested.

When I tried to identify individual wild tigers in Nagarahole from the shapes of their paw prints, I had failed. The absurdity hit home after I discussed the problem with an experienced forest tracker who had participated in the censuses. He had followed the tracks of a single tiger for over a kilometer and traced multiple paw prints. Later, when his bosses back at the office were deducing tiger numbers from the tracings collected, they attributed three different individual tigers to the set of prints the tracker had found. When he piped up to point out the error, his bosses snubbed him, telling him he was not sufficiently qualified to visually distinguish individual tigers.

In 1985, I had tested the validity of the pugmark census method by conducting a trial on live tigers at the Mysore Zoo. I had shared thirty-two tiger paw prints I traced with eight official "tiger experts." The counts they came up with from the same set of prints ranged from seven to twenty-eight tigers. The truth was, my trial had traced prints from only four tigers! Even after I published my results, officials nonchalantly persisted with their census method for two more decades.

However, in 1990, with a tiger crisis looming, I had a responsibility to move beyond criticism and offer a better alternative so that the tigers could be accurately counted.

Building a Better Tiger Trap

I enjoyed the thrill of watching wild tigers in action while radio-tracking tigers. Telemetry revealed intricacies of how *individual* tigers behaved. However, at any time, I could catch and radio-track only a few cats. The problem was that meanwhile dozens of *other* tigers were born, survived, or died over the years, about whom I had no clue.

A better method of counting tigers was needed to assess whether conservation efforts were effective in the face of this new scourge threatening their last surviving populations. As a conservationist, I had a responsibility to go beyond proving that official tiger counts were flawed. A deeper understanding of how many tigers there are in a population, as well as how many are being added or lost each year, was necessary to assess the impacts of poaching and other pressures on tigers. Comprehensively understanding the dynamics of wild tiger populations became my new research goal.

I had to first develop a rigorous method to count tigers that worked not only in Nagarahole but also across the tiger range. Furthermore, I also needed to develop a simpler way to assess how many tigers could *potentially* live in an area, even if I could not count them directly.

As with science in general, in order to count tigers better, entrenched human behavior also had to be changed. Beginning in the 1960s, wildlife officials in India, Nepal, Bangladesh, and Russia had all attempted to "census" tigers by counting their tracks, using different approaches rooted in local tiger lore and tradition, rather than robust science. As a result, clouds of pseudo-data on putative tiger numbers already existed in many countries. However, these misguided attempts tried to *count all the tigers in a population*, or, in other words, conduct a census. The officials who came up with them did not appreciate the statistical challenges involved in such an enterprise. Some were not even familiar with aspects of tiger biology revealed by modern scientific research. For instance, Choudhury, the inventor of the "pugmark census," assumed that tigers lived in monogamous territorial pairs like hawks.

Moreover, the science of wildlife biology had progressed rapidly, absorbing developments in fields as diverse as mathematics, statistics, computer science, automated photography, and genetic analyses. I wanted to adapt the universally applicable science to counting tigers, rather than cook up a unique homegrown method disconnected from it.

I decided to identify individual wild tigers from their photographs: the stripe patterns on tigers are individually unique, just as human fingerprints are. The challenge was to get photographs of many tigers in a wild population.

Because tigers are elusive, scarce, and hard to photograph, in the 1920s forester Fred Champion used primitive automated camera traps triggered by tigers that walked past them. Fifty years later, anthropologist Charles McDougal used more sophisticated traps. Champion employed a trip wire tied to a dead bait, whereas McDougal relied on a pressure-activated foot pad. Both had obtained a few spectacular photos of tigers when their cumbersome traps worked, yet after a lifetime of effort, Champion had gotten only nine photos of tigers. Furthermore, those camera traps were expensive, failure-prone, and easily damaged by wild animals or stolen by people. I had tried out such camera traps just for fun, but soon gave up. It was no fun at all to see my camera trap worth a few hundred dollars smashed to pieces by a playful elephant or stolen by a poacher.

After 1990, I experimented with a newer breed of camera traps made by Bill Goodson, a tech-savvy entrepreneur in Kansas. His usual customers were American deer hunters trying to figure out where the big trophy-sized bucks roamed. Coming across Goodson's "trail master" traps was a eureka moment for me. These idiotproof, auto-everything cameras were triggered electronically, like a simple burglar alarm. Mass-manufactured for deer hunters, they were cheaper, too.

Because patterns on two flanks of a tiger (or leopard) were not symmetrical, I required two cameras at each trap, doubling my budget. Had William Blake's "fearful symmetry" of the tiger been real, I would have saved a lot of money. With a few more traps on hand, I hoped to crack the tiger counting problem.

Just before Minister BB disrupted my research in June 1990, I had tested Goodson's traps and gotten photos of some tigers, including four radio-collared cats—Das, Sundari, Buddy, and Monda. After I resumed work seven months later, I was able to identify the now collarless Mara from his stripes. He had carved out a stable home range that overlapped Sundari's and extended to the west and north beyond [MAP 3]. Right at the center of my camera-trap array, I photographed the biggest male tiger, Yajamana. I labeled the camera-trapped cats with a new series of numbers, beginning with NHT-100. The letters NH identified the park, and the three-digit number was a unique ID for that tiger.

The tiger Das photo-captured by a camera trap.

The tiger Mara photo-captured by a camera trap.

A young man named Javaji was a weight lifter and, somewhat incongruously, a clever engineer, and he loved volunteering on my line transects. He designed an ingenious steel shell that effectively protected my traps from naughty elephants and sneaky thieves. With dozens of robust camera traps set along the tiger trails that crisscrossed Nagarahole, I could photo-capture a lot of cats.

However, one nontrivial challenge remained: I could never be sure I caught every individual tiger in the population. I could trap some tigers—perhaps even most—that cruised around. However, I could also miss other cats who did not pass through my traps. This statistical problem, known as "imperfect detection," is a well-known bugbear in wild animal population

Yajamana, the big tiger who escaped being radio-collared, was photo-captured later and labelled NHT-103.

surveys. If I sampled a real population of one hundred tigers with camera traps, and caught only seventy-five of them, my imperfect "detection probability" would be 75 percent.

If I could somehow also estimate this detection probability—derisively called a "nuisance parameter" by statisticians—getting the total number of tigers was possible. This sounded like magic, but it was simple mathematics. It was a general problem the great eighteenth-century French mathematician Pierre Simon Laplace had solved to estimate the human population of France from birth and death registers kept in churches. My collaborator Jim Nichols at the US Geological Survey (USGS) was an expert in these "capture-recapture" statistical models. With my knowledge of tiger biology and Jim's modeling expertise, we finally cracked the problem of reliably counting wild tigers. Extraordinarily brainy people who are fun to be with are hard to find: Jim was both. Based at the famed Patuxent Wildlife Research Center of the USGS, Jim cracked one statistical problem I posed after another, fueled only by mugs of Guinness beer he loved.

I published my first results from "photographic capture-recapture sampling of tigers" in a reputed international journal in 1995. The reactions were startling. Most biologists across the world working on tigers, leopards, jaguars, and other uniquely marked cats rapidly embraced the method. In my own country, however, officials of the federal government's Project Tiger, and scientists of the Wildlife Institute of India (WII), closed ranks to pronounce my method unworkable, opting to cling to the pugmark census.

I took comfort in history. Scientific realities, such as the spherical shape of the earth, the planetary system revolving around the sun, or the fact of evolution of life on earth, had all met centuries of resistance from traditional authorities. I hoped my tiger-counting method would be accepted a bit more quickly, given the Indian government's proclaimed commitment to a "scientific temper." I could never have guessed it would take ten more years!

It's the Prey, Stupid

My dream of becoming a tiger biologist was inspired by George Schaller's *The Deer and the Tiger*, published in 1967. Unlike most big cat biologists of that era, Schaller had speculated how the number of tigers could be related to the abundance of their prey animals. Later in Florida, my teacher, the great zoologist John Eisenberg, had brilliantly elucidated how the diet, body size, and population density of mammal species were interlinked. To fully understand how the tiger population in Nagarahole worked, I had to untangle these relationships.

A tiger or leopard is like a shopper searching the supermarket shelves for food packets. The packets, in this case, ranged in size from twenty-kilogram muntjac deer to bull gaur or elephant calves that weighed one thousand kilograms. Leopards preferred the same prey species, but typically took smaller, younger individuals. Moreover, because leopards could climb trees, they also hunted the abundant gray langurs.

I had counted prey animals using the line transect method without fully appreciating their analytical complexities. I already had vast quantities of line transect data collected systematically by my army of citizen scientists. Now statistical ecology had to come into play. I had to again solve the same problem of imperfect detection, as with the camera-trap counts of tigers: what proportion of all the prey animals in the forest had been detected by the observers who counted them? It boiled down to the pesky problem of estimating the imperfect detection probability. As I had done with Jim Nichols for the photo-capture analyses, I reached out to David Anderson at Colorado State University, who pioneered line transect analyses.

Anderson (and other pioneers) had figured out that animals were almost certain to be detected and counted if they happened to be straight ahead on the transect line. If they were off the line on either side, the probability of detecting them rapidly decreased because of vegetation and other factors. The farther they were from the line, the lower the detection probability. Ultimately, beyond a maximum strip width, the animal would not be visible to be counted. The percentage of animals detected within this strip was the detection probability; I had to estimate it from the data on how far the detected animals had been from my transect lines. This was simple high-school geometry if the distance from me to the animal group, as well as the included angle between the transect and the animal group, could also be measured in the field. I had ensured my citizen scientists did make these two measurements, using an optical range finder and magnetic compass, respectively, each time they sighted prey animals.

From such sets of "distance data," smart statistical models could estimate the detection probability for each prey species. If we saw five thousand chital deer during the season's field survey, and the "distance model" estimated the detection probability had been 25 percent, the total population estimate, including the missed animals, would be twenty thousand chital. Sounds like magic again, but this was also based on simple mathematics.

My line transect surveys, the first ever conducted in India, yielded rich data on the numbers for important prey species in Nagarahole. I was astonished to find that Nagarahole supported prey densities of forty to sixty large ungulates per square kilometer. There were fifteen thousand kilograms of "meat on the hoof" in a square kilometer. Even ignoring the elephants that formed half of this biomass, prey species hunted by tigers, leopards, and wild dogs were still plentiful.

Once human hunters were kept out, Asian tropical deciduous forests, like the one in Nagarahole, turned into virtual supermarkets for the predators. The take-home conservation message was loud and clear: if strictly protected like Nagarahole, most other presently empty tropical deciduous forests of Malenad, and elsewhere in Asia, could support many more tigers.

This finding flew in the face of academic ecology I was taught, which assumed tropical forests were poor habitats for ungulates. These animals were said to attain such high densities only in the woodlands and savannas of Africa.

The ungulate densities I measured in fact exceeded estimates from comparable habitats in eastern and southern Africa.

After 1994, my WCS colleague Dale Miquelle also began radio-tracking tigers in Russia. Dale was discovering territories of tigresses in the cold and wintry Russian Far East that exceeded 600 square kilometers, and territories of male tigers that were over 1,200 square kilometers. However, biologically the tigers I studied were exactly like his "Amur tigers," but had territories that were twenty to thirty times smaller. I speculated the reason was the difference in the abundance of prey animals. The mathematical relationship between prey and tiger numbers held the key to the mystery.

Uniquely, I had the ability to test this idea because I had figured out how to accurately count not just tigers, but also their prey species. If I could work in multiple tiger reserves across India, which harbored tigers and prey populations at different densities, I could understand the form of the relationship between the two. This was the key that opened the door to estimating how many tigers any type of habitat could potentially carry.

In addition to advancing tiger science, such a study offered major benefits for recovering tiger populations in presently depleted tiger habitats that covered 90 percent of tiger range across Asia. I was raring to go!

Tiger Science, the Art of the Possible

In 1994, with encouragement from Valmik and others in the Delhi tiger network, I applied for a federal government permit to conduct surveys to estimate the populations of both tigers and prey species in several reserves across India. They represented a diversity of tiger habitats: the *Shorea* forests of Kanha and the mixed forests of Pench, both in central India; the semiarid forests of Ranthambore in western India; the mangrove forests of Sundarban in the east; the alluvial grasslands of Kaziranga; and tropical evergreen forests of Namdapha, both in the far northeast.

WCS and the US Fish and Wildlife Service agreed to fully fund the project. I did not need any funds from the Indian government. I also promised to share the results of my studies with the officials of Project Tiger. Despite all these benefits, my request for a research permit was rejected by the forest bureaucracy without providing any reason.

The bureaucrats were waking up to the tiger's global appeal. And, as is often the case, their next step would be to make "tiger business" their own monopoly. Obviously, that would make forest officials the judges while also evaluating their own performances—clearly a fundamental conflict of interest. While I favored the idea that forest officials should enforce the wildlife protection laws, I felt establishing a government monopoly over tiger research would not only stifle science but also lead to a self-serving management model rife with conflicts of interest.

Based on my recent experience at the interface of politics and tiger conservation, I sought an urgent meeting with the federal minister of environment Kamal Nath. He was a savvy businessman from Calcutta who had morphed himself into a powerful congress politician in central India. He was also a friend to both Valmik and Brijendra, who backed my request.

Nath summoned senior officials to the meeting to ask why my proposed research was a problem to them. The officers hemmed and hawed about the accuracy of their own "pugmark census" that obviated the need for any further studies of tigers. Nath cut them short with a whiplash command: "You are evaluating Karanth's cricket game, applying the rules of your own soccer game. Clearly you don't get it. Please 'put up' that file for my approval before the end of the day." My problem was instantly solved, not because of the logic of my science, but because of the savvy politics I was compelled to play.

Following this breakthrough, I conducted both camera-trap surveys and line transect surveys at several sites across India through the next decade. These were the first such macro-ecological tiger studies—population assessments made at large scales. They showed population densities of tigers could range from as low as 0.5 tigers per one hundred square kilometers to as high as twenty tigers per one hundred square kilometers. Looking at my results, it became clear why tiger densities varied so much among these different habitats.

My radio-tracking of tigers in Nagarahole showed a tiger killed about fifty prey animals in a year, roughly at weekly intervals. To produce such an annual "dividend," there had to be sufficient "capital" of prey animals. Given the reproductive potential of these ungulate prey species, that capital works out to five hundred prey animals, from which the tiger draws its 10 percent dividend! A single wild tiger needed a prey base of five hundred ungulates to sustain it. If a breeding female raised three cubs to adulthood, she would need 650 prey animals. This iron rule explained why there were ten to fifteen tigers per one hundred square kilometers in the protected, productive forests of Malenad, in contrast to just one to two tigers in the snowbound Russian taiga, or for that matter, in any habitat where prey density was depressed by human hunters.

In other words, if the Nagarahole forests were magically transposed on to the Russian Far East, instead of the twenty-five breeding tigresses it supported, it could hold only a single tigress. Prey density was the single most important determinant of how high tiger densities could go.

While I spread my sampling efforts across the country to obtain onetime ecological snapshots of how tiger densities and numbers varied across space, I also continued my studies in Malenad across years in a few key sites. I extended annual camera-trap surveys beyond Nagarahole to Bandipur, Bhadra, Biligiri Rangaswamy Temple (BRT), and Kali tiger reserves [MAP 1].

The long-term studies required complex analyses that dealt with the reality that tiger populations that I sampled for four to eight weeks each year were open to both gains and losses of individual tigers. They lost individuals due to deaths and outward dispersal and gained new tigers through births and immigration. The combined analyses of long-term capture history data from each individual tiger could provide estimates of not only tiger numbers in each year, but also yielded rates at which tigers were being lost or gained in each population. Such complex monitoring schemes were urgently needed for each tiger reserve in the face of the multiple threats tigers were facing.

Assisted solidly and reliably in the field by my able deputy Samba Kumar—one of my first transect volunteers, and later my first doctoral student—my macro-ecological studies yielded rich insights on tiger population ecology. They also led to the development of innovative methods of tracking the fate of entire tiger populations, not just individual tigers. With tiger science rather than tiger lore at their core, conservation insights they yielded were new and startling.

First, even in a thriving, reasonably well-protected population, such as the large one in the adjacent reserves of Nagarahole and Bandipur [MAP 1], tiger numbers regularly rose and fell every few years, ranging between one hundred to two hundred tigers. These fluctuations were the consequence of the varying numbers of breeding females that successfully raised litters of cubs to adulthood in the previous year. These ups and downs were a natural feature of any healthy tiger population. They resulted in periodic "surpluses" of tigers that were compelled to find new habitats to occupy and breed.

My studies also provided a clue as to how tiger populations had persisted despite massive killing sprees unleashed in the past by hunters. For example, over a fifty-year period between 1875 and 1925, about eighty thousand tigers were slaughtered in India by sport and bounty hunters, an astonishing average of sixteen thousand killings per year. My studies in Nagarahole between 1990 and 1999 showed why this was possible. Although the population in Nagarahole annually lost as much as 23 percent of its tigers, it also gained enough new tigers to bounce back. Overall, in a decade the population had increased at a rate of 3 percent per year, despite heavy losses.

The lesson is clear: there is nothing gained by mourning the loss of every individual tiger, or in rejoicing at the birth of every new cub. Yet this is exactly what many fans of tigers go around doing much of the time.

The concern of conservationists about the rise in poaching of breeding tigers in protected reserves of India was justified. However, the wider problem of the past and ongoing tiger extinctions across large swathes of forests had much deeper roots: the inadequate replenishment of new tigers to compensate for their naturally high rates of losses. And these high rates of replenishment depended primarily on high densities of prey animals. Historically, tiger populations were more likely extirpated because of depression of population densities of deer, antelopes, wild cattle, and wild pigs by local hunters. They had simply switched off the supply of new tigers.

Another predictive statistical model of tiger-prey populations, on which I collaborated with Bradley Stith of USGS, neatly explains this crucial insight using observed data. Of all tigers born in a healthy, thriving tiger population, such as that in Nagarahole, only 20 percent eventually get to breed and produce offspring. The model further reinforced my inference that prey depletion was a far more important causal factor for the dire status of tigers across their range. The primary reason for the depletion of prey animals in the jungles of Malenad, of course, was shooting and snaring of prey species by local people. The killing of tigers by professional poachers for the Chinese markets was only a recent secondary factor.

There was also a positive angle to my findings. Although the tiger range in India has been fragmented by human uses and abuses of all kinds, there were still a lot of potential habitats to bring back tigers. Additionally, in other parts of Asia, three times more potential habitat existed. If tigers and prey animals could be effectively recovered in even a small fraction of this extensive habitat, there was reason for hope. In India, with about 380,000 square kilometers of tiger forests, and across the Asia-wide tiger range with 1.6 million square kilometers of habitat, there is room for far more wild tigers than anyone dared to imagine.

Recovering prey and tiger populations in many habitat fragments, such as Nagarahole, Bandipur, and other parks in Malenad [**MAP 1**], is not rocket science, either. It requires the same pragmatic, determined conservation actions I had seen with my own eyes. I had even been a part of that process, however messy and difficult that engagement turned out to be.

Clearheaded science highlighted the inflexible survival needs of this physically powerful but ecologically fragile predator. These needs cannot be changed to accommodate anyone's preferred social theories or political predilections. If the tiger's vital survival needs are ignored, the species will be lost. If we can pragmatically accommodate these needs within the frame of human needs and aspirations, there is still plenty of room for wild tigers to bounce back. Despite the "crisis," the tiger was not a lost cause.

Enlightenment at the "Church of Prey"

Even as the global media and the tiger conservationists worried about the imminent extinction of tigers because of the trade in their body parts, it seemed to me this explanation, as well as the remedies they suggested, were far too simpleminded. The bigger overarching challenge was to make more room for wild tigers. This meant protecting far more quality habitats packed with prey—across India and the rest of Asia. Such thriving populations in reserves, producing surpluses, would not be at risk even if there was some poaching outside. I felt there was reason for hope, despite media predictions about the imminent extinction of tigers.

Meanwhile, some economists with unfettered faith in the power of free markets were proposing a radically contrarian solution to the tiger trade problem. These supply-siders insisted that breeding and slaughtering enough tigers in captivity could meet the demand from traders, eliminating the poaching of wild tigers.

The problem with their model was that there already were numerous legal (and illegal) tiger farms in China and other Southeast Asian countries. Mushrooming of such supplies had only spurred the demand for tiger body parts, not dampened it. Moreover, the cost involved in raising a captive tiger would always be higher than paying a village poacher to kill a wild one, at least while the supplies lasted.

Furthermore, consumer surveys showed customers preferred wild tigers with a premium market value, compared with captive ones. Despite the supplies from tiger farms, poachers were still killing off the last wild tigers, wherever they were not deterred by armed forest guards.

Finally, several other wild animal species—wild cattle, sheep, and goats—had been farmed for thousands of years. Yet the wild relatives of these species were under severe hunting pressure or even extinct. However, because I was sure India's traditional Hindu culture was unlikely to accept the recommendations of the "tiger supply-siders," I chose to ignore rather than argue with them.

Tiger poaching could not be tackled solely by curbing the trade, which occurred after the tigers were killed. More extensive and effective patrolling of tiger habitats to prevent such killings was needed. Additionally, passive deterrence by means of separating tigers from potential poachers, simply by putting more physical distance between them, was also an option. Millions of livestock, which competed with the wild prey species as well as infected them with dangerous diseases, needed to be similarly distanced for tiger reserves. Both these outcomes would require inducing people to voluntarily resettle away from prime tiger habitats. Furthermore, at least in prime tiger areas, which occupied less than 5 percent of India's land, development such as mining, dams, and energy generation had to stop. Making room for more tigers was going to be a complex challenge, but I knew it was not an impossible one.

However, the complexities of the tiger crises were far too nuanced for a media in a hurry to ride the current news cycle and move on. Even my friends in the tiger conservation community found the story of the greedy Chinese consumers eating up the world's limited supply of tigers easier to understand and get agitated about.

In March 1994, EL, a senior reporter from *Time* magazine covering the tiger crisis, wanted to visit me in Nagarahole. However, with all the media coverage of the crisis, and my persistent critiques of the official tiger counts, forest officials in Karnataka were jittery. When I sought permission for EL's two-day visit, I was asked to submit his full itinerary from the time he landed in Bangalore until he departed.

I was waiting for EL at my home in Mysore, ready to drive him to Nagarahole, when I heard the doorbell ring and welcomed EL into my home. He was a tall, handsome man, a respected reporter with a track record of covering environmental issues. He also was the China expert for *Time*, and knew a lot more about that society beyond his current assignment. I was eager to learn much from EL.

Looking somewhat worried, EL quickly paid off his hired limousine. He turned to me and said that as soon as he had landed, he had been accosted by an official "minder" who tried to pass on a sheaf of papers to him. Being familiar with the ways of official "minders" in China, who often tailed him, EL had adroitly dodged the man by jumping into his waiting limo, asking the chauffeur to drive full throttle to Mysore, leaving the nonplussed "minder" behind.

Whatever the other peculiarities of India's open society were, it seemed impossible to me that an official "minder" in the Chinese mold would be assigned to tail a mere reporter, even one from exalted *Time* magazine. Brushing off EL's apprehensions, I offered him some coffee and chatted about our plans.

Fifteen minutes later, the doorbell rang again. Indeed, it turned out to be EL's dreaded "minder": a tubby and none too bright junior forest official named JM, whom I had known for years. JM had his own story. Pointing at EL, he complained in Kannada, "Saar, my boss assigned me to meet this crazy White man and hand over some brochures on the good work we are doing to save tigers. Instead of appreciating our goodwill, this arrogant foreigner avoided me like the plague and sped away in his fancy limo. There was no way my old buggered-up jeep could catch up. Even my boss does not have such a fancy car. So, I had to drive all the way to Mysore, hoping to find him at your place or in Nagarahole."

JM only wanted to hand over those brochures to EL. Having performed his duty to the state, he disappeared. The thought of this tubby, comical man in the role of a sinister government gumshoe made it impossible for me to hold back my laughter any longer.

EL spent the next two days with me in Nagarahole, watching the superabundance of wild hoof stock wherever he turned. I was able to radio-track Sundari as she strode casually along. On his last evening, purely by chance, I showed him a large male tiger stretched out in the open, in the lush green Kaithole Hadlu. Even at one hundred meters, through my binoculars I could recognize Mara, who was watching my Suzuki calmly.

Our communion with Mara was disrupted when he suddenly perked up his ears, rose to his feet, and quickly slunk away into the tall grass. The reason became clear soon, when a van bearing chatty tourists lumbered up the slope.

Mara's ultrasensitive ears had picked up their chatter from two hundred meters away, while I had heard nothing.

It was clear to me that even a science reporter like EL was skeptical of my analysis of the tiger declines and the recovery model that prioritized protecting the prey base. It seemed EL had already concluded that tigers would go extinct soon. When I argued making my more nuanced case, EL retorted that I seemed to follow a unique faith—some kind of "Church of Prey." The *Time* cover story that soon appeared was titled "Doomed!" However, the magazine did publish my response as a short letter to the editor. Much of the global media coverage of the "tiger crisis" toed the same line.

By now, I had seen it all. When I was a schoolboy, wild tiger populations were in terminal decline across Malenad as a result of killings for bounties, as well as overhunting of their prey for the pot. Later in my youth I had witnessed pragmatic policies and actions, which led to sporadic tiger recoveries in places like Nagarahole. I had also faced the consequences of the intense social conflicts these policies had unleashed. As a conservation professional, I had developed new research methods and gained insights into the tiger declines, and possible paths for recovering the magnificent cats.

The cultural popularity of the tiger, however, was attracting attention and money from people and organizations who were either ignorant of tiger biology, or even cynically ignoring its implications for conservation. This emergent conservation narrative promoted a mythical golden era when tigers and people had lived in traditional harmony. Advocates of this model were essentially demanding the abolition of protected areas for tigers and a free rein for loosely defined "local communities." If we did that, they seem to believe, people would use tiger habitats wisely and sustainably, all the while living cheek by jowl with thriving populations of wild tigers.

The only villains in their story were the forest staff who had enforced the wildlife laws since the 1970s. Also objects of their scorn were a handful of "authoritarian" big cat biologists and conservationists—yours truly conspicuously included—who dared to contradict their narrative with some inconvenient facts.

With all this polemical noise overwhelming the signals of science and pragmatism, a nuanced narrative of how the wild tigers could be recovered was becoming difficult to convey. I had to reach out to the public through the best media at that time in India: the newly introduced private television channels.

I was pleased when I finally got my opportunity: Britain's Sky Television, a part of Rupert Murdoch's media empire, wanted to film my work. On May 12, 1994, the TV crew landed in Nagarahole. They had only three days to film. The director, Prescott—a sharp, chubby man with an Oxbridge accent—understood the issues and was happy to tell my story. However, he wanted compelling footage of wild tigers to hook his audience.

A couple of days before the crew arrived, Sundari had killed a sambar yearling near Bison Road, and had been dining off it. After she finished the small kill, I was sure she would start moving around and I could radio-track her down for Prescott and his crew, two very tall and very hefty young men— the cameraman and the sound guy. However, for two days, Sundari refused to budge from her carefully hidden kill.

The morning of May 14, 1994, was our last possible jungle drive, after which the TV crew would leave Nagarahole. A story on my tiger work bereft of live tiger footage was not likely to air. I, too, was feeling the crunch. As the "tiger expert," I was expected to somehow conjure a wild tiger out of thin air. Our expressions were sullen as I drove the Suzuki, with Prescott fitting snugly like an egg in a crate into the bucket seat next to me. The two big guys stood up on the open deck behind us, camera on the tripod ready to go.

It was a beautiful Indian dawn, with the curtain of mist just beginning to lift from the luminous tropical jungle around me. A younger tigress, labeled NHT-116, a daughter from Sundari's last litter, had settled into the adjacent territory. I had not radio-collared her, but occasionally saw her by chance. I knew she had two young and voracious cubs and would be out hunting a lot to feed them—a real soccer mom of a tigress.

The dirt road to Bommadu [**MAP 2, Point 20**], cleaving through swathes of dense bamboo, marked the intensively patrolled territorial boundary between NHT-116 and her mother Sundari. By now, the gossamer veil of mist was lifting, turning the dawn-lit jungle into a Renoir painting. Suddenly, I spotted a flicker of movement, about fifty meters ahead. Two tiger cubs the size of cocker spaniels were playing "catch me if you can" on the grassy track. I braked to a halt, cut the engine, and shushed my companions into silence. The big boys in the back started filming. The cubs frolicked around like a pair of adorable kittens as though they were performing for television.

Then I spotted their mother. Even after years of studying tigers, the cat's expertly camouflaged stripes, honed by evolution's blind intelligence, had obscured her from my view. The tigress was lying down thirty meters beyond her carefree cubs, calmly watching my car.

Silhouetted behind the tigress, I saw a peacock walk up, see her, and take off with a frightened, metallic cackle. Prescott was trembling with excitement. He had captured Renoir's magical scene, with tigers in the frame in place of the usual French bourgeoisie family.

The tigress, who was born in the best protected part of Nagarahole, knew that my car posed no danger to her cubs. Human presence near them, however, was another matter. Absolute silence was the key to filming this close encounter with tigers. After recording twenty minutes of stunning video footage of the tiger family, the big boys in the back became a bit cocky and noisy: the tiger cubs froze. The larger male cub sat up and watched us curiously. Then the precocious youngster decided to approach and investigate.

While the crew filmed the curious kittens, I concentrated on their mother. She had also stood up and started to move, first ambling, and then cantering quickly toward us. Sensing the tension building, the cubs dashed back toward their mom.

Suddenly my companions were in a panic. In the open car there was no barrier between us and this 150-kilogram tigress heading our way. "Ullas, we are not welcome anymore, let's go," Prescott whimpered urgently. I said nothing.

"Ullas, back up, please back up—can't you see she is going to attack us?" squeaked one of the big boys at the back. "Don't be crazy, Ullas!" admonished the other.

I calmly continued taking photos, whispering to them under my breath to continue filming. As the tigress got to within ten meters, she flattened her ears and charged at the car in full fury, emitting a series of bloodcurdling growls. I reached back to grab the leg of the cameraman, who seemed ready to jump off and make a run for it. Bad idea.

When the tigress got right up to the front fender, both the big boys instinctively ducked, fully expecting the tigress to land on top of them. Prescott, wedged into the seat next to me, looked like a very scared, very pink rabbit. I knew what would come next.

Just as abruptly as she had charged, the tigress braked to a halt, turned, and walked back a few strides, swishing her tail and admonishing her cubs to disappear into the bamboo thickets. She then turned around and made another, even more ferocious mock charge. Her point fully communicated, the tigress turned around and disappeared, following her cubs.

The panic on the faces of my companions quickly dissolved into absolute delight. Fortunately, unlike them, their camera had calmly kept rolling. They had successfully captured stunning footage of wild tigers, both at play and at war.

I knew all along, however, even the war had just been a form of play. I had spent the last four years tracking and observing tigers. Day after day, I had been living with wild tigers, learning the nuances of their behavior. I knew for sure this day that we were not at any risk whatsoever. The tigress was simply trying to shoo us away.

Throughout history, tigers have had many more reasons to be terrified of us than we of them. The big cats soon learned that humans are super predators to be feared, who had ultimately pushed them to the brink of extinction. Those tigers that did not fear and avoid the two-legged predator did not leave many offspring. Those that did survived, passing on their instinctive fear of humans through subsequent generations.

Turning Adversaries into Allies

Even as I tried to reach out to a broader audience with my own narrative on tiger conservation, it was important for me to demonstrate the effectiveness of the alternatives I proposed. My dilemma echoed Karl Marx's famous concern: "Thus far, philosophers have only interpreted the world in different ways. The point, however, is to change it." Replace "philosophers" with "conservation academics," and you had it.

Making Malenad a better place for tigers would require more—far more—than sound tiger science. I had to win over people with the capacity to influence what went on in the real world. Toward this end, I had already assembled a small but determined group of backers: Krishna, Praveen, Girish, and others like them. Among forestry officials, I had unstinting support from a handful of officers like Alva, Paramesh, Lakshmana, and Srinivas. In Delhi I had connected to the tiger network coordinated by Valmik.

However, these men were all conservationists by profession or by choice. While they were effective in urban India, none was from the hostile village communities that ringed Nagarahole. I needed allies among villagers living next to tigers and the tribal people who lived among them.

Although the gang of thugs who had raided Nagarahole in 1992 had since been rendered powerless after legal prosecutions, I still had to find new allies among the general populace, which had passively supported the rioters. I persuaded Chinnappa, who had retired after the riot, to launch a conservation outreach program targeted at local students and youth. WCS and Global Tiger Patrol, based in the United Kingdom, provided the necessary funding.

When local people heard Chinnappa speak with passion and eloquence about the value of Nagarahole, public sentiment gradually swung in our favor. A dramatic turn of events occurred when two leaders of the movement for local rights, Thamoo and Satish, met and apologized to Chinnappa for the rioting and arson by their local supporters. Soon after, they visited me in Nagarahole.

Thamoo was an enterprising businessman and charismatic community leader with a substantial following within his Kodava community. Satish was an erudite, scholarly coffee planter who was the environmental conscience keeper for their movement. Over a simple lunch of rice and curry in my field camp, I explained to both men the purpose of my conservation mission.

Later in the evening I took them radio-tracking Sundari. Luckily, she was in estrus and cavorting with a big male tiger, who on closer look turned out to be Mara. It was a magical moment. We all watched the two mating tigers in rapt attention. To any layperson, it looked more like mixed martial arts combat than tender lovemaking.

An hour passed, and the curtain of dusk descended. Although we could not see the tigers, alternating bouts of explosive growls punctuated by periods of deep silence would continue through the night and over the next four to six days. Two hundred or more such couplings, each lasting barely thirty seconds, were needed for the tigress to be induced to ovulate. Her fertilized eggs would emerge as cuddly cubs three and a half months later.

I could see my guests were deeply moved by this rare spectacle of amorous tigers in the wild, just as nature had created them two million years ago. Seizing the moment, I softly popped the question: "The movement you folks lead aims to protect your heritage like your land rights, dialect, and rituals, including that spectacular war dance holding those fearsome swords. Do you really think these magnificent tigers, in your own forests, are not a part of that proud heritage?" There was a moment of deep silence. However, at that exact movement I knew we had formed a bond that would endure.

Later, well into the night, we seriously discussed how their social movement could collaborate with our network on a focused agenda to protect tigers. I was finally creating a social network that could move me beyond interpreting the world of tigers to the one trying to change it. From a schoolboy who had helplessly rued that the tigers of Malenad were being pushed toward extirpation, I had grown up to be a man doing his best to bring them back.

This rural conservation networking was something new to me. My original volunteers were all bound by a shared passion for wildlife. In contrast, people like Thamoo and Satish were throwing their weight behind me, not because they were keen naturalists. Their agenda was a wider one of protecting their heritage into which I had persuaded them to include wildlife. This collaboration proved to be a major force-multiplier in making more room for tigers in the Malenad landscape also packed with ten million human beings.

Nagarahole, Bhadra, and Kudremukh became the testing grounds for my tiger conservation model. My experience as an engineer, and later as a farmer, taught me that tiger recovery here must necessarily balance the needs and aspirations of ten million humans against the survival needs of a few dozen tigers.

In fact, to some degree, I agreed with the social activists and academics who demanded that people and tigers must coexist. If the proposed coexistence was at the scale of the country, the state of Karnataka, or the Malenad region, I was fine with it. However, it was impossible for me to imagine such coexistence when the idea was proposed at the spatial scale of a protected reserve like Nagarahole. My experience, common sense, and later research had convinced me that the coexistence of people, crops, and livestock, amidst breeding populations of tigers would not work, either for the people or for the tigers. If this fantasy was imposed on the last few clusters of breeding tigers that occupied a mere 1 percent of the country, ultimately tigers would be overwhelmed by surging human needs and greed.

Gradually, with funding support from WCS, our conservation network in Malenad expanded. After 1995, Girish built up his own group, which focused on the Bhadra Reserve in Chikmagalur. He dug in and relentlessly fended off threats to Bhadra.

Niren, a talented young architect from Mangalore, joined my field research team in 1998. Soon, his passion for wildlife drove him toward active conservation advocacy to defend Kudremukh National Park, close to his home.

Ullas Karanth engaged passionate volunteers and staff to build a strong conservation network in Malenad.

Although these passionate naturalists were willing to invest their time, energy, and social connections to protect tigers in their neighborhoods, they still required funding to keep conservation activities going. Fortunately, based on my track record, WCS now gave me enough authority to provide support to these groups. Thanks to steadfast leaders like William Conway, George Schaller, John Robinson, Josh Ginsberg, and Alan Rabinowitz, WCS had not strayed off the path of science-based wildlife conservation. Most other big international NGOs—"BINGOS" for short—were embracing the "people-friendly" conservation models proposed by naive academics as well as politically correct donors like the World Bank.

From its inception in 1895, WCS had been an idea factory for wildlife conservation, supporting Western scientists like Schaller to explore the world's remotest wild areas and generate new knowledge about wonderful wild animals. After 1990, under Robinson's leadership, its conservation approach broadened from just studying rare species to their conservation in the real world. As a corollary, WCS staff also became more international and diverse. Things came full circle in 1993, when John Robinson asked me to lead a long-term conservation program in India. WCS was going native; I was the first Asian to lead a country program.

My expanded role included mentoring local researchers and conservationists to advance science-based conservation. However, I was also expected to continue my own tiger research, influence policy, and raise funds to support my program. These were new challenges. It would be impossible for me to effectively lead such a complex program while camping in the jungles of Nagarahole.

I was forty-eight years old, and my living with tigers had to end. Balancing contradictory emotions, I finally moved to the state capital of Bangalore in 1996. Around the same time, Sundari's transmitter, having exhausted its second battery, stopped broadcasting. The last time Sundari was photographed in my camera traps was on May 16, 1995. Henceforth, I could only guess her fate, but would never know for sure.

Nagarahole was now a six-hour drive away on a bumpy road choked with trucks and oxcarts. However, for me it would forever be the nearest thing to a spiritual home. Regardless of where I lived, I would always pray at this "Church of Prey."

7 | MAKING ROOM FOR TIGERS

WITH THE TIGER CRISIS hitting the headlines daily, nonprofit conservation organizations across the world, including WCS, launched their own tiger programs. Alan Rabinowitz and I were tasked with drafting the WCS tiger conservation strategy.

Alan's experience with tigers was somewhat limited, because they were either extinct or scarce in the Southeast Asian region where he worked. When Alan visited me in Nagarahole in 1994, he was surprised by the large herds of ungulates observed in broad daylight. Inching my Suzuki slowly forward, I was once able to literally drive through a herd of thirty gaur. The massive bovids continued grazing placidly, literally at arm's length from us. Alan had exclaimed, "This is more gaur than I have seen in all my years in the jungles of Southeast Asia!"

Having worked both in Latin America and Asia, Alan was very astute at capturing the essence of human cultures. I always recall his Alan's perceptive remark, after that first visit to India: "Ullas, it seems to me all the human cultures in Southeast Asia are just cocktails mixed in various proportions out of two ancient civilizations, the Chinese and the Indian." Funnily enough, in real life, both Alan and I preferred single-malt whiskey over cocktails.

Our conservation strategy document titled *Saving Tigers* was a call to action rooted in ecological knowledge of both tigers and the Asian cultures that posed threats to their survival. Most Asian cultures attributed spiritual divinity to the tiger. Yet the fact remained that the people who prayed at tiger shrines were also relentlessly eliminating tigers, prey species, and their habitats. Their behavior was driven by economic realities and could not be changed through gentle persuasions alone. An element of coercive law enforcement was essential if tigers were to be brought back from the brink of extinction.

The romantic notion that dense populations of wild prey animals and prolifically breeding tigers living off them could *harmoniously* share space with vast numbers of hunters, farmers, and herders desperately seeking prosperity and modernity was absurd beyond belief. Yet this tale has gradually become the central tenet of the international conservation movement. This transition took place in the early 1980s, as pragmatic pioneers of global wildlife conservation faded away and ceded leadership to environmentalists, social activists, attorneys, financial wizards, and theorists from academia. This transition is best captured by Harvard biologist Ed Wilson's phrase "the social conquest of nature."

The WCS tiger strategy emphasized the need for incentivized, voluntary relocation of human settlements out of critical tiger habitats as a key intervention to make more room for thriving tiger populations. This was a contentious issue around which most conservation BINGOs danced delicately, with eyes averted.

Opposition to the idea of human resettlement for wildlife conservation was widespread among social activists. Their explicit goal was to improve *human* livelihoods and welfare. They trumpeted the hypothetical human–tiger harmony model merely as bait to seduce conservationists whose primary goal is, or should have been, saving *other wild species*. Even those conservationists who knew better dodged this fundamental dichotomy, instead of challenging it.

A scholar at Yale tore into our tiger strategy in the journal *Conservation Biology*. He asserted local people should decide whether to relocate, not those who lived in New York or New Delhi. Madhu, the same young volunteer who had escaped with me from the gaur attack, had joined me in retorting that while we agreed with this proposition, it should be extended to include residents of Yale and Harvard.

I had seen too many tragedies resulting from the enforced coexistence of deprived people with dangerous wildlife. Encounters with wild elephants killed about five hundred human beings *every year* in India, about eighty of them in Malenad alone. Over the years, I had seen many poor human victims, their innards squeezed out like toothpaste out of a tube. I simply could not conjure up a romantic vision about the conditions that led to such tragedies.

A specific instance was a Jenu Kuruba tribesman named Kuniya, who illegally collected wild honey for selling to petty traders around Nagarahole. Men like him located the beehives by following the flight paths of bees. After silently sneaking up to the hive, they repelled the angry bees with wood smoke, killed off the queen bee and larvae, and made off with buckets of honey and wax. Sloth bears, heavily furred denizens of these jungles, which weighed 100–150 kilograms, also hunted for honey in preference to their normal diet of termites, berries, and small animals they could catch. Bears raided the same beehives, unarmed with wood smoke, yet surviving the stinging swarms, all the while howling in much pain.

Sloth bears, like most other wild beasts, are usually afraid of humans. Given sufficient notice, they sneak away, seemingly muttering curses, but pose no real danger. Often the bear will stand up on hind legs and curse or do a "mock charge." I had shooed off sloth bears many times, simply by standing still, yelling curses back, and clapping my hands. However, because of its poor eyesight, if a bear gets too close and feels threatened, it will attack an intruder.

On that fateful day in 1994, following a jungle trail tracking bees back to their hives, Kuniya failed to detect a sloth bear until it was too late. That morning Kuniya was just too close to the startled beast. The bear attacked and mauled him briefly but brutally, before running away. As Kuniya was bleeding and screaming in agony, other tribesmen carried him back to Nagarahole.

I was horrified at the sight of Kuniya: one of his eyes was completely gouged out. His scalp had been ripped off, and his exposed brain pulsated eerily. Blood streamed from the bites and claw marks on his near-naked body. The tribesmen, including Kuniya's hysterical wife and little children, were begging me for help. The only hope was to rush him to Mysore in my Suzuki, the only readily available vehicle. There was not a moment to lose.

At the hospital in Mysore, Kuniya miraculously survived. He lost one eye, and his scalp and face were horribly scarred. He would go around covering his head and face with a dirty checkered towel, peering out at the world with his single functioning eye that watered constantly. Through all this misery, whenever he saw me, Kuniya smiled broadly. His days as a "traditional honey hunter," so beloved by social activists and anthropologists, were over.

I recalled dozens of interactions with settlers in remote hamlets ever since my youthful forays into the jungles of Malenad. Many of these folks had no easy access to roads, hospitals, schools, telephones, and markets to sell their crops. Their lives were an incessant struggle against forces of nature: crop raiding by elephants and herds of ungulates, as well as the persistent predation of livestock by tigers and leopards, not to mention sloth bear attacks. They desperately needed the same economic development and social progress unfolding in villages and small towns not too far away. They wanted freedom from dangerous beasts, not coexistence, harmonious or otherwise.

As Vishwanatha, a teenager in the remote Singsara hamlet in Kudremukh narrated: "My elder brother, the breadwinner of the family, had fallen seriously ill. We had carried him on a bamboo stretcher, force-marching across twenty kilometers of rugged forest trails to reach a rudimentary rural clinic. Even that effort was futile. We had to carry him back on the same bamboo stretcher for the traditional cremation at our homestead."

The impassive, almost matter-of-fact manner in which hundreds of forest-dwellers like Kuniya and Vishwanatha narrated their tragedies, simply stunned me. Their life in the remote wilderness was not a happy picnic with tigers in attendance, as the campaigners for these forest-dwellers believed.

Largely because of the pragmatism of India's first generation of conservationists and foresters in the 1970s, backed by the ironfisted Indira Gandhi, India's tiger conservation policy supported voluntary relocation of remote human settlements . . . at least in theory. However, there were major problems with how the theory had been put into practice.

The track record of hundreds of village resettlements in India, executed to accommodate giant irrigation reservoirs, strip mines, or even wildlife reserves, had been less than stellar. Bureaucratic corruption, inefficiencies, and lack of social empathy for the "beneficiaries" had plagued resettlement projects. However, it was also equally evident that tigers and prey species had benefited from the resulting habitat recovery. Ironically, rebounding animal numbers were now piling up even more misery on people still compelled to coexist with them.

If tigers were to return to Malenad in significant numbers, such resettlement projects had to be win-win solutions for both people and tigers. I was confident, unlike in the past, chances of successful resettlements were now far greater. Thanks to the wise leadership of Prime Minster Narasimha Rao in the early 1990s, India's economy was now chugging along, full steam ahead. After accelerating from the old "Hindu growth rate" of 3 percent per year, it was hitting double digits. New opportunities for employment and livelihood were mushrooming in small towns and cities. There was a steady migration of rural folks in Malenad to small towns and cities. Those who chose to migrate in search of livelihoods or education now also had access to television, movies,

Internet, and omnipresent cell phones for the first time in their lives, changing their fundamental perception of what a good life was. In contrast, agriculture was becoming harder in Malenad. It was increasingly dependent on migrant laborers from hundreds of miles away.

For resettling the willing families of forest-dwellers, farmlands and even some degraded forests were available not too far from the interiors of tiger reserves. Because these reserves were small, resettlements were feasible in locations familiar to the beneficiaries. Unlike in the past, the surging economy was filling the government's coffers. It was now possible to compensate people fairly and generously if they agreed to relocate.

I felt strongly that nongovernmental organizations should play a pivotal role as intermediaries between beneficiaries of resettlement and the government. I believed nongovernmental organizations that claimed to promote human rights, economic development, and social welfare were best equipped to be such intermediaries.

Unfortunately, most social activists in India remained bogged down in the notion that forest communities marooned in nature reserves should continue to live in "traditional harmony" with tigers. At the same time, they also wanted remote communities to enjoy nontraditional products of economic development such as new markets, job opportunities, schools, hospitals, roads, and communication, all in the heart of the jungle.

There was another issue with some groups espousing the cause of forest-dwellers. Their functionaries had become addicted to streams of steady donor support, which over time had turned into quite a flood of money. These groups now had inflated budgets to support developmental activities, which often merely duplicated the work of vastly better funded government agencies.

Ironically, the leadership of these social activists came from the same educated middle class as the tiger conservationists. They had successfully parleyed their catchy narratives around "Indigenous natives" versus the "colonial intruders" to tug at the heartstrings (and purse strings) of donor agencies only familiar with the social context of colonized Africa and the Americas.

This illusion masks the vastly more complex reality of human colonization of India. Starting with African immigrants seventy thousand years ago, many subsequent waves of ethnic, racial, and cultural groups arrived in India over millennia, intermingling and churning to produce the present societies. Indian society had frozen into a professionally and economically stratified caste system around 1000 CE. There really were no clearly distinguishable Indigenous natives battling "colonizing aggressors." The last White colonizers from Britain had been packed off by the Congress Party, which, ironically, had been founded by Englishman Alan Hume, to fight for India's independence. (Not many know that Hume was also an avid birder with many species named after him.)

Yet promoting the cause of the Indigenous people helped activists to raise funds from guilt-ridden Western donors. In this context, it seemed to me the self-appointed shepherds of the oppressed folk had an interest in corralling their herds in their present poverty traps inside tiger reserves by fortifying ideological barriers against their aspirations of seeking modernity.

A glossy brochure of one such emancipatory outfit said it all. It boldly proclaimed its goal was to "put people back into the woods." It seemed nothing less than reversing the Darwinian evolution of Hominins from apes over the previous 2.5 million years was their ultimate emancipatory goal. Despite their radical-chic rhetoric, some promoters of forest-dwelling as a way of life were also raising huge donations from faith-based groups whose mission was to save heathen souls in Malenad through proselytization.

Despite these reservations, in 1996 I reached out to a leader among these social activists operating in Nagarahole, relying on a mutual friend as an intermediary. I hoped to convince the man to get involved with our resettlement efforts in Nagarahole. Although his initial response was positive, later he backed out because other activists told him not to rock the ideological boat they were all sailing on.

I was sure if we could demonstrate a resettlement solution that truly was a win-win for both people and tigers, genuine hesitancy among local people would crumble. Then it mattered little even if opponents of voluntary resettlement continued to remain impervious to biology, economics, and history.

I decided to test the waters in three wildlife reserves of Malenad, which were ecologically distinct and offered very different social challenges for recovering tigers. There also was an emotional tug: during my teens, desperately seeking to watch tigers, I had visited Kudremukh in 1965, Nagarahole in 1967, and Bhadra in 1972. I had instantly fallen in love with all three spectacular jungles, visiting them year after year. I was convinced that successful voluntary resettlement projects were desperately needed at all three of these marvelous lairs of the tiger.

I realized, however, that my network of partners consisting of naturalist volunteers lacked the social traction necessary to execute the voluntary relocation projects I was conceiving. While their passion for wildlife ran deep, their attitudes toward potential beneficiaries of resettlement sometimes ranged from disinterest to lack of sympathy or even disdain. They were all passionate naturalists, but I could not overnight turn them into clones of Mother Theresa.

I had to find individuals with the empathy and aptitude suited for this specific conservation mission. And I had to find them through the same careful filtering I used to pick my naturalist partners. My experience in the 1970s selling tractors in rural Karnataka, and subsequent years spent in the company of farmers and tribesmen, did teach me some lessons not taught in the ivory towers of academic conservation.

My very first volunteer naturalist, Krishna, was by now a savvy technocrat. He had some smart advice for me. Krishna argued that going forward I could not depend solely on volunteers for implementing the complex tiger-recovery projects I dreamed about. I had to find, recruit, train, and mentor a core cadre of professional staff with the necessary range of skills to deliver the results I wanted. Ironically, I was also noticing that most of my early volunteers—Krishna included—had secure jobs and families and had to assume new responsibilities. Although many still turned up for the annual line transect surveys, except for a handful, they did not have time for sustained conservation action over years. I had to build an additional tier of committed, full-time conservation staff.

Increasingly, my challenge of finding conservation warriors was beginning to look like the model perfected in *Star Wars* by Yoda to recruit his Jedi. The conservationists I hired had to be good at dealing with sluggish bureaucracies, combative social activists, and fickle-minded forest-dwellers. Passion for natural history could not be the defining filter when selecting my relocation team.

Nagarahole: From Killing Tigers to Committing Genocide

Tiger populations had attained high densities in Nagarahole after serious protection began in the early 1970s. However, Nagarahole was peppered with dozens of tiny tribal hamlets, called *Haadi*, enclaved within its boundaries. In a few settlements on the park's northeastern and southwestern fringes, non-tribal occupants had land titles of dubious pedigree. These would take years of litigation to resolve.

Meanwhile, the real elephants in the drawing room were the fifty-eight hamlets of varying sizes inhabited by Jenu Kuruba and *Betta Kuruba* tribes.

They had existed in these jungles for centuries. They had originally lived off the land as hunter-gatherers, at far lower population densities. Later they took up slash-and-burn cultivation as their numbers rose. After systematic forestry and logging began in the late nineteenth century, they worked as logging labor.

Following Indian independence, when malaria, smallpox, and other lethal diseases were controlled through public-health measures, the population of tribal people living inside the forests rose steeply. At the same time, intensified logging employed them as well as attracted nontribal immigrants into the reserves. Cultivation of paddies in the productive Hadlu grass swamps, forest fires to aid collection of nontimber forest produce, illegal liquor stills, and clandestine logging all thrived. The government had tried to resettle the tribal people in "colonies" outside the reserves by allotting them farm plots, building houses, and establishing schools and clinics.

Quite a few of these tribal relocation efforts faltered because of the easygoing work ethics of tribal folks, as well as lack of meaningful post-relocation support. These farm failures and indebtedness had led to the grabbing of tribal lands by powerful agricultural and trading castes, who socially dominated the scene around the colonies. Many failed tribal farmers headed back to forestlands and encroached even more. Put bluntly, it was all a big mess.

On one of my early visits to Nagarahole in the 1970s, riding my motorbike, I stopped to chat with a prosperous-looking farmer in Karmadu [**MAP 2**]. Ramaiah had come to these forests in 1950s as a petty logging contractor. He had cleverly invested his profits to become a loan shark to dozens of newly resettled tribesmen trying to grow crops on their government-allotted land. As Ramaiah had shrewdly anticipated, failing at farming, and unable to repay their debts, the tribesmen had sold their lands to him. Consolidating this land and farming it efficiently, Ramaiah had become a prosperous coffee planter and a politician. The well-kept coffee bushes and the neat bungalow that I could see behind him were testimony to his enterprise, and to the helplessness of the tribesmen. Another testimony was the dusty logging road on which I had come riding. Using his political traction, Ramaiah later got it converted to a paved public road cutting diagonally through the reserve, thus ensuring the steady supply of migrant laborers to him and other rich planters in his village.

A project for resettling tribal people from Nagarahole required not just land and financial resources, but also sensitive, long-term hand-holding of the settlers. Such effort needed much skill and empathy, the very qualities in short supply that led to the failure of earlier relocation projects. However, I felt encouraged by Thamoo and Satish, who had overcome their biases to offer staunch support for resettlement, not because of passion for tigers, but because they felt it was the right thing to do.

As I was wrestling with these dilemmas, Thamoo suggested that I consider a young journalist who owned a tabloid, *Malenadu Varthe* (News from Malenad), to lead the project. My experience with tabloids being what it was, I was a bit hesitant. But Muthanna turned out to be an intelligent, enthusiastic man. Built compactly, the slightly balding young reporter had bright burning eyes. As I drew him into a deeper discussion, his intellect, deeply held values, and empathy for the underdogs impressed me.

Muthanna also seemed to possess the necessary shrewdness and savvy to deal with social complexities of tribal resettlement from Nagarahole. I felt he could lead the tribal folks out of their poverty trap to a better life outside. In the year 1999, I managed to convince Muthanna to shut down his tabloid and join my staff.

The planned government relocation project, initiated in 1991 by Chief Minister SB, was a massively complicated one, involving many agencies besides the forest department. It also involved other local stakeholders with their own

Muthanna's genuine empathy for the tribal people impressed Ullas Karanth.

conflicting agendas. The planters outside wanted tribesmen to live inside the forest, to be ferried every day for work and returned in the evening, rather than be provided with housing on the estates and benefit from compliance with complex labor laws. The petty traders wanted them to forage inside the reserve, to collect forest produce for lucrative markets. Even some foresters wanted cheap and pliant labor for logging and other "works" from which they benefited.

Muthanna and his hand-picked team of assistants, which included tribal youth, would have their hands full for years to come.

I was by now on the steering committee of the federal government's Project Tiger. I could network with senior officials to make sure they released the necessary funds for relocation. By June 1999, all these assets were brought into play to get necessary land allocations for the new colonies to be established outside, to build the first houses. The first fifty families of tribal folks from Nagarahole who volunteered to relocate chose to name their new colony Nagapura [MAP 2, Inset].

Our challenge was to convince more potential beneficiaries to move out. Given the history of earlier failures of such government projects, there was indeed a trust deficit. The rocky relationship the tribesmen had with the forest department did not help, either. Muthanna's skills were really put to the test. His team of "motivators" visited tribal hamlets to identify families willing to relocate. They were initially abused, threatened, and even beaten up by inhabitants led by the well-entrenched, antirelocation activists. While these activists advocated people's harmony with tigers, they chose to sow discord against those willing to move out. I soon became a marked man in the eyes of social activists, as well as their international patrons promoting emancipatory causes.

My participation in the World Parks Congress in Durban, South Africa, during September 8–17, 2003, opened my eyes to how the global agenda for nature conservation had been hijacked by promoters of other—no doubt equally worthy—emancipatory causes. The soaring rhetoric I heard from the leading lights of global conservation papered over hard issues of how to recover parks under serious threat from human pressures. It was all about helping people to penetrate even deeper into these dwindling natural areas, to exploit them more intensively—"sustainably" and "harmoniously," of course.

Sadly, many first-generation African conservation biologists appeared to be willing to genuflect before this empty rhetoric of consuming yet saving wild nature at the same place and at the same time. Some even argued that national parks should become chief drivers of Africa's future economy, a role historically played by agriculture, industry, and trade in the rest of the world.

An incident I witnessed at the front desk of my modestly priced hotel in Durban said it all. There stood a tall African man, in full Masai pastoralist regalia with a spear, beads, and all, but also holding two cell phones. He was yelling into them alternately, complaining loudly about not being booked into a better hotel befitting a renowned conservationist like him.

Then there were also pleaders of the "mobile peoples" cause, each of course carrying two mobile phones. A high-ranking Indian forest officer, always nattily dressed in a jacket and tie back home, had turned up dressed like an ethnic Indian villager wearing a dhoti and sporting a brilliant pink turban.

There was an exhibit outside the conference hall, advocating the desirability of the harmonious coexistence model for India's wildlife reserves. As evidence, there were beautiful video clips of the presently abundant tigers and other wildlife in Nagarahole, juxtaposed with images of villagers cultivating crops, weaving baskets, and bottling wild honey, implying these activities had led to the resurgence of wildlife. There was even a line describing our own voluntary relocation project as "genocide" being committed on the tribal people. I had just graduated from being a mere killer of tigers to a mass murderer of humans!

There was no way I could possibly counter this global, gargantuan propaganda machine. My only option was to effectively engage with the government's resettlement project to ensure it delivered what was promised to the tribal beneficiaries: intensive action on the ground, but without worrying too much about critics halfway around the world. Wildlife conservationists like me could only be catalysts added to the larger brewing cauldron of unfolding social change.

The fifty tribal families settled into new homesteads at Nagapura harvested their first agricultural crops in the winter of 1999. Their relatives inside the park, still hesitant to move out, came and stayed few days to consume the bounty. Around that time, through Valmik's tiger network, I had met Rajendra Singh, a savant of India's rural development, hailed as "the water man of India." He was widely respected among social activist groups. I invited Rajendra to visit the relocated families at Nagapura. They shared their earlier travails in the forest, and how much better off they were here farming and raising livestock, away from marauding elephants and predatory tigers. Rajendra's subsequent endorsement of our relocation work did mute at least some of the local critics.

I realized an effective counter to the flood of such unreasonable criticism could not be a counter-barrage of rhetoric. That would only consume all my energy, leaving little time for tiger conservation. Making sure the relocated families were truly better off was the only answer. Acting as a pressure group, we pleaded, cajoled, and sometimes fought with officials managing the relocation project in Nagarahole.

Over time, Muthanna and his energetic team of tribal youth became quite adept at these tactics. I was particularly pleased that the most articulate among these youth was a man named Rajappa. He turned out to be phenomenally successful as a farmer, and later as a trader. A few years later, Rajappa contested the elections to the state legislature. Although he lost, Rajappa had garnered over ten thousand votes from predominantly nontribal voters. I felt this was true social empowerment.

Whenever I meet Rajappa, I still tease him about the fact that decades earlier he was among the rebellious tribal youth who had mobbed my lab, scribbled graffiti on its walls, and chanted my death warrant from bee stings.

Muthanna's continuous engagement with government agencies, local politicians, and religious and community leaders gradually began to bear fruit. Throughout these years, none of India's academic conservationists who opposed voluntary resettlement bothered to see the outcome.

The momentum for Nagarahole relocation gained strength when a dynamic park director named Yatish—who had earlier successfully executed a voluntary relocation project in Bhadra—was posted as park director of Nagarahole during 2008–2009. His passionate involvement and prioritization of house construction eventually led to the successful relocation of 280 families from Nagarahole. By 2014, 816 out of 1,900 families within Nagarahole had been resettled.

However, the erratic flow of government funds, increasing corruption, and disinterest among the officials (which emerged as major problems in India as the twenty-first century dawned) began impacting the Nagarahole relocation project.

The project hit a brick wall when Yatish was moved out prematurely, because of jockeying for power among his colleagues. His successors were more interested in splurging the ever-increasing park budgets on unnecessary "wildlife management" activities. The relocation project, which was not a comparable cash cow, languished. Some officials proved greedy, others incompetent, and most were both.

As I write these lines, the Nagarahole resettlement project remains essentially stalled halfway through. This massive mission-drift away from effective conservation has also spread to the nongovernmental organizations. It has even swelled the ranks of publicity-hungry, media-savvy "tiger conservationists" of the weirdest types.

On the other hand, as India's economic progress tries to catch up with the aspirations of its people to escape poverty and deprivation, new opportunities to make more room for tigers through voluntary relocations are inching forward, not only in Malenad but also in many other tiger habitats across India. Major successes have been achieved in the central Indian states of Madhya Pradesh and Maharashtra because of the savvy political and bureaucratic initiatives of key officials and nongovernmental players.

Bhadra Relocation: Unleashing the Animal Spirits

I had first visited the Jagara Valley, which forms the southern half of the kidney-shaped Bhadra Reserve, in 1972 [**MAP 1**]. This landscape was even more spectacular than Nagarahole. The valley is a 250-square-kilometer "crater" encircled by the towering Bababudan Mountain arc, named after an Indian mystic said to have brought the first seeds of coffee to India from Yemen in 1670 CE. The arc is an out-spur off the ridge of the Western Ghats. The northern half of Bhadra, known as the Lakkavalli forests, lies on the outer slopes of the Bababudan mountains. The reserve is the major water catchment of the Bhadra River that originates in Kudremukh, one hundred kilometers to the west.

The Bhadra River had been dammed at Lakkavalli in 1965 to irrigate 1,055 square kilometers of semi-arid flatlands on the eastern plains of Karnataka. Overnight, the land transformed into bountiful fields of rice and sugarcane. Historically, such large dams had spelled disaster for wildlife because they submerged extensive forests. And though the 112-square-kilometer Bhadra reservoir did submerge 7.2 square kilometers of forests, it also cut off a major paved road that connected villages in Jagara Valley to the towns located outside the reserve. Before that, the paved road provided easy access to swarms of outside poachers and timber smugglers who pillaged these forests. It also enabled the forest department to intensively log valuable timber. Just as devastating was the massive extraction of four species of bamboo that grew luxuriantly in the

Bhadra forests. Additionally, parts of the forests were cut down and converted to charcoal to feed a steel mill set up even earlier, in 1923.

The construction of the dam had changed these equations. By cutting off easy access, it turned the Jagara Valley into a forest fortress protected by the high mountains on one side and the vast reservoir on the other. Seventeen hamlets were still marooned inside. The larger ones harbored as many as eighty families, and the smallest just a couple. Their inhabitants were not tribal folks as in Nagarahole. Villagers within Bhadra came from hardy, industrious peasant stock. Many of them had legal titles to some of the lands they cultivated.

Although the reservoir severed their easy access to nearby towns, the newfound isolation also gave the villagers full freedom to ravage the forests around them with even greater rapacity. The villagers illegally cut valuable teak and rosewood timber, which they floated down the Bhadra River to the sawmills on the other side. Rampant hunting of animals large and small, using shotguns and snares, went on largely unchecked.

The small number of staff deployed to protect the forests also depended on the very same villagers for food and shelter. There were no jeeps to provide them with the mobility needed to effectively enforce antihunting laws. In this context, the forest staff either colluded with the villagers, who pillaged the land, or looked the other way.

When I hiked in Bhadra during summers, I saw vast forests of bamboo scorched by fires deliberately set by the villagers. Systematically deploying clandestine arson, the villagers were steadily expanding their settlements, raising more crops and larger herds of cattle that chewed up more forest forage. These herds of unvaccinated scrub cattle spread the deadly foot-and-mouth disease to dense herds of gaur. Periodically, the magnificent bovids perished by the hundreds. I came across dozens of rotting gaur carcasses, first in 1985 and again in 1995.

The number of homesteads in the Jagara Valley, just nine in the year 1909, had reached 450 families, harboring over 2,500 people by the 1990s. As an amateur naturalist, I had surveyed the conservation status of the valley in 1978. I had reported its many problems, as well as its immense wildlife recovery potential. Carefully mapping the hamlets located within Jagara Valley, I had recommended they be resettled outside. Later, in the early 1980s, I surveyed the better connected Lakkavalli forests and urged stopping the massive bamboo extractions by the forest department, and the looting of timber and firewood by local villagers using oxcarts, bicycles, and "head loads" to sell in towns. Wood was everything in the economy of Malenad, the source of all domestic energy and structural timber.

My recommendations, however, remained on paper. There was neither the will nor the resources among local forest officials to implement them.

Although I lived in Mysore at the time, Bhadra was always on my radar. During 1982, two incidents rekindled my interest in Bhadra. I had my first ever sighting of a wild tiger in Malenad, while waiting in a machan. It was an amazing face-to-face encounter between a tigress and a young bull gaur across a pond. They both ignored each other and moved on.

Soon after, while on a visit to the Chief Wildlife Warden Appayya's office in Bangalore, I met a farmer named Sheshanna from Hebbe, the most remote and isolated hamlet in Bhadra. He was desperately pleading with the officer to relocate his village to some fertile area outside the park. I too joined Sheshanna's pleadings, trotting out my own report of five years earlier.

However, one question stymied our discussion: where was the land required to resettle over four hundred families? None of us had the answer. Without available land the relocation project was only a pipe dream.

In those days, the forest department was single-mindedly preoccupied with logging old-growth timber for cash and raising fast-growing tree species to feed the paper mill. Any open forestland available was earmarked to be "afforested"—often while borrowing huge loans from international development agencies. Much money was being spent, with the inevitable "leakages" typical of the bureaucratic systems in India.

The protected wildlife reserves, on the other hand, did not facilitate logging and raised little money. Matters important for wildlife recovery, such as the socially complicated village relocations, did not interest the bureaucracy, as the farmer Sheshanna and I soon realized.

Two exceptional officials, however, did appreciate my concerns for the fate of Bhadra. Both were very senior forest officers: my older cousin Shyam, who had been my mentor since my teens, and Paramesh, his second in command—a live wire of a forester who had just returned after serving a stint in Nigeria. I beseeched them repeatedly to find some suitable land for resettling villagers from Bhadra. Their reaction was surprising, and visionary. They soon identified a large fertile area of degraded forest, which had been earmarked to raise sugarcane plantations for a government sugar mill . . . if and when it was set up. Moving swiftly and adroitly, Shyam and Paramesh got that land reassigned exclusively for the resettlement of villagers in Bhadra, whenever that happened! For years, both deftly resisted pressure from local politicians to redistribute that land to their own voters. At least one key problem was solved.

I next met the minister for agriculture, NG, who happened to be a rich coffee planter adjacent to Bhadra, and requested that he push the relocation proposal through the state government. NG was sympathetic to the plight of the villagers landlocked within Bhadra because most of them came from his own caste, and hence were a dependable vote bank. Democracy is a serious matter in India, where every vote must be clawed out of shrewd voters by employing ideology, religion, caste, charity, and even outright bribery.

Minister NG said he would steer the relocation project, provided the beneficiaries inside Bhadra were relocated to a site within his electoral constituency. Unfortunately, the land earmarked for the project was in an adjacent constituency. With the prospect of reliable votes being lost, the minister's enthusiasm waned.

Eight more years passed.

During my line transect surveys in Nagarahole in 1990, a tall, bearded, and stern volunteer named Girish attracted my attention. His love for animals was genuine, and his commitment to wildlife conservation was fierce and total. As important, Girish lived close to Bhadra and was an established coffee planter in his community. I felt he could potentially be the catalyst who could get the Bhadra relocation project going.

However, because of Girish's commitment to the "hands-on" protection of wildlife, he could sometimes be a vigilante who thrashed the poachers he caught. In some ways Girish faced the same problem of local unpopularity among villagers within Bhadra that I was facing around Nagarahole. He needed an assistant, with the soft skills necessary to connect with local villagers.

By the mid-1990s, I had become a member of the steering committee of the federal government's Project Tiger. An extraordinarily capable senior forester named Prashant Sen had taken over as the director of Project Tiger. Sen and I had hit it off right from the time we met. He had even visited Nagarahole to walk the transect lines and checked the camera traps to understand the new survey methods I was advocating.

In the national elections of 1997, voters threw out the Congress Party and elected an opposition coalition headed by Hindu nationalists. The new environment minister, Suresh Prabhu, who also chaired Project Tiger, was keen on wildlife and was also a friend of Krishna. Working closely with Sen, I was able to get a substantial chunk of money allocated to the Bhadra relocation project. The money would be released, however, only after the state government guaranteed the land and provided legal approvals. Luckily, this time around, a public-spirited minister, GG, held political sway in the district. Being aware of the plight of the marooned villagers in Bhadra, he ensured the necessary state support.

Meanwhile, I had budgeted WCS funds to cover the social engagement with villagers to facilitate the project. I hired an assistant, named Pandu, who was a trained social worker, to assist Girish. Pandu had the social skills necessary to deal with both the most recalcitrant villagers and the most lethargic officials. He swiftly established a rapport with the beneficiaries, who had been somewhat antagonistic to hard-core naturalists led by Girish. Finally, things were falling into place, but we still needed senior local officials to swiftly deliver results.

This was an incredibly complicated project. Implementing it on ground involved allotting the available land equitably among contending beneficiaries, building houses, and providing all the other amenities necessary for them to start new lives. That responsibility was jointly shared by the park director of Bhadra and the deputy commissioner who headed the entire district administration.

In a true stroke of serendipity, Yatish, a young Reserve director who had the necessary empathy, patience, and commitment to deal with the village communities, had been posted to Bhadra. At the same time, the district commissioner Gopal happened to be an extremely upright, efficient, and energetic man. Unlike most administrators, Gopal loved wandering in the forests to watch wildlife. Working around the clock, in close coordination with Girish and Pandu, these two officials ensured all the infrastructure at the relocation site was built up skillfully and swiftly.

A former American ambassador, John Galbraith, had famously remarked that "India is a functioning anarchy." In the case of the Bhadra resettlement project, we had collectively demonstrated how that anarchy could indeed be made to function.

Within a couple of years, what once was a distant dream had magically materialized. The relocation colony, with its lush sugarcane and banana farms, excellent social amenities, and satisfied inhabitants, was promoted as a model project across the country, after I persuaded another energetic environment minister, Jairam Ramesh, to visit it as soon as he took over in 2009.

However, my other suggestion that the settlement colony be named *Huli Pura* (tiger town) to commemorate its other beneficiary went unheeded: a showboating local politician who had little to do with the project successfully got the colony named after himself!

Be that as it may, the real metric of our collective success in Bhadra was that the originally skeptical—and even hostile—villagers were now far better off in every way. And they said so clearly and loudly to whoever asked them. Sheshanna, who had worn a threadbare cotton shirt when I first met him twenty-two years earlier, now dressed up in a natty polyester "safari suit." He looked at the world through Ray-Ban glares, driving around in a red Suzuki compact. Lives of most other settlers had witnessed similar, dramatic improvements. My ecologist daughter, Krithi, a graduate student of conservation at Yale when resettlement began, showed through her long-term social surveys how the economy and welfare of the settlers were improving steadily, year after year.

For the tiger biologist in me, all this was secondary. The true metrics of any conservation success were different: with logging and fires banished, Bhadra forests have flourished and thousands of scrub cattle and most of the poachers are gone. Within a decade, the population of wild herbivores had doubled. Catching up with the rising prey densities a decade later, the tiger population also had risen to produce surplus tigers for dispersal.

A male tiger cub, BDT-130, that I camera-trapped in Bhadra in 2006, dispersed. He turned up in the camera traps in the Kali Reserve two hundred kilometers to the north in 2008.

The overall lesson was clear. To make more room for tigers in crowded Asia, conservationists, social activists, and governments should genuinely cooperate to help village communities relocate out of a few critical tiger habitats. The transformation I saw in the lives of old farmer Sheshanna and the young tiger BDT-130 were both symbolic of that optimistic prospect.

I knew I was on the right track.

Moving the Mountains of Kudremukh

In my boyhood, looking out from my home in Puttur, I had marveled at the sight of a blue mountain ridge far away, noticing its remarkable resemblance to a horse's face in profile. In fact, the peak's Kannada name—*Kudremukha*—meant exactly that. I had hiked up to the peak with some friends for the first time in 1965.

The ecology of Kudremukh, typical of higher ranges of the Western Ghats, was very different from that of the deciduous forests of Bhadra or Nagarahole. The western slopes of Kudremukh rose almost vertically from the coastal plain to a ridge 1,842 meters in altitude. These mountains blocked the moisture-laden monsoon clouds that in just four short months poured down eight thousand millimeters of rain. Tall and luxuriant evergreen forests clothed these western slopes, with the dense canopies of giant Dipterocarps filtering out much of the sunlight. This rain forest could not support high densities of large ungulates like the deciduous forests. Although tigers were present, their natural densities were low.

As I struggled up the steep, dank, rain forest slopes, my socks and pants were soaked in blood oozing from the bites of leeches, which had silently crawled all the way up to my neck. These bites were painless and went unnoticed, until the thumb-sized leeches were gorged with my blood, looking like elongated grapes, and dropped off. The bleeding continued for a while because of the anticoagulant the leech had injected into me to facilitate its blood thirst.

As I climbed up gradually, the continuous canopy of the giant rain forest broke up into smaller patches of stunted cloud forest confined to gullies and folds on the mountains. The forests on the convex slopes were replaced by vast stretches of lush green grasslands. At this altitude, with abundant grass forage, perennial fresh streams, and dense hiding cover in the valley folds, large ungulates such as gaur and sambar proliferated.

It had been a long, tough, eighteen-kilometer climb to the peak. Five kilometers below, in a bowl-shaped depression, was the hamlet of Tolali. It was occupied by a middle-aged Roman Catholic rice farmer, Simon Lobo, and his large family. Lobo's half-a-dozen progeny ranged in age from an infant in arms to a young man of marriageable age. Lobo was brought to Kudremukh as teenager, sometime in the 1930s, to be a caretaker of a small rest house built near the peak. The rest house had been a refuge for German missionaries looking to escape from the hot summers of Mangalore. After the missionaries departed for good, Lobo had stayed on in the wilderness, cultivating rice and areca palm and raising his family. The rest house and the small prayer hall next to it had collapsed into heaps of rubble years before.

After eating a sparse meal of rice gruel—and sips of a fine liquor distilled by Lobo from fermented cashew fruit juice—we had slept around a crackling campfire staring at the brilliant, starlit dome above. The night was silent except for the eerie wail of the forest eagle owl or the occasional alarm calls of the sambar and muntjac that rent the air. I was truly in the wild!

At daybreak, I scouted around for animal spoor. I saw abundant tracks of gaur, sambar, and wild pigs. Superimposed on them were the fresh, saucer-sized pugmarks of a wild tiger, the first I had ever seen in my life! Back then, with game hunting rampant across Malenad, one of the last remaining tigers had found refuge in this remote vastness of Kudremukh. I feared this tiger, too, would soon be gone, like the German missionaries before him.

I made several hikes through the wider Kudremukh landscape in later years. The entire leech-infested, rugged rain forest tract of over one thousand square kilometers was sparsely populated by people living in scattered hamlets. Like Lobo's farm, these enclaves were also confined to valley bottoms, where their owners eked out incredibly tough lives. Although their numbers were small, it was obvious their impact on the wildlife and habitats was severe.

Even after the advent of the strong wildlife laws of the 1970s, the remoteness of the Kudremukh landscape made it hard for the forest department to patrol it effectively. The homesteaders in remote hamlets shot and snared wildlife with impunity. They augmented their uncertain farm incomes by commercially extracting a variety of nontimber forest products, which were finding new global markets for chemicals, pharmaceuticals, and beauty products. Such profitable bounties from the rain forest included leaves, fruits, nuts, and seeds from numerous tropical plants. The settlers debarked trees and drilled deep into their boles to tap resin. They extracted massive quantities of rattans, lichen, reeds, and sedges for sale at outside markets. They also owned huge herds of free-ranging, hardy local cattle, known as Malenad *Gidda* (shorty), barely the size of German shepherds. The Gidda cows yielded little milk, and the bulls were useless for haulage. These cattle were essentially mobile green manure factories. The Gidda chewed up lush forest, converting it into tons of dung, which the farmers used to fertilize their fields.

To promote the early growth of fresh grass for their cattle, during late summer the farmers set fire to the grasslands around their hamlets. Carried by swift wind currents, these fires burned down huge expanses on the grassy mountain slopes, gradually destroying the small patches of cloud forest confined to the gullies and folds.

By tradition these villagers, like the boy Vishwanatha, who had buried his brother after such tribulations, believed they were fated to live this hard life.

However, as schools and education spread on the plains to their west and east, and urban economies developed in the small towns not too far away, the youth from these hamlets who had been sent out to study preferred not to return.

By early 1990s, after the total electoral collapse of India's communist parties, a tiny minority of radical Maoists in towns and cities were still preaching the creed of Chairman Mao's peasant revolution to such students from the remote vastness of Malenad. Neither the preachers nor their newfound disciples noticed that the creed had been given a ceremonial burial in its own homeland of China. A few idealists among the targeted youth, however, were sufficiently inspired to return to the villages to launch the long-awaited war of liberation. The upshot of all this was that small bands of armed guerillas found a toehold in the Kudremukh landscape, where roads were sparse, telecommunication nonexistent, and police presence minimal.

There being no feudal warlords around for them to appropriate the huge surpluses to enrich the masses, as there had been in Mao's case, the guerilla bands made a living by extorting food and cash from better-off farmers located in remote enclaves. A few of these farmers were even tortured and killed by guerillas to send a stern message to bourgeoise class enemies. When the government retaliated by increasing police patrols, the revolutionaries even killed poor villagers who had snooped for the police. Most of the local population in and around the Kudremukh Reserve were terrified of the guerillas and weary of the police harassment. They just wanted a way out.

The revolutionaries also demanded that the Kudremukh Reserve be abolished and the forests thrown open for farming and direct exploitation by the masses. The guerillas had chased off the forest guards and burned down their patrol camps. The resulting anarchy suited everyone, including those who had suffered the depredations of the guerillas. Poaching and forest encroachment were rising again.

Many ordinary folks I met on my forays increasingly expressed a desire to relocate, a compulsion compounded now by the fear of being trapped in the crossfire between guerillas and the police. I had to find a local leader— and a tough support team—to canvass for a voluntary relocation project in Kudremukh.

Niren, a young architect from Mangalore, had joined my research team as a technician. In 2000, he wanted to be a full-time staffer, with a serious plan to switch his career entirely to wildlife conservation. I was very pleased when Niren offered to lead a small team of local youth to scope out the prospects for a voluntary resettlement project in Kudremukh.

Niren was smart, savvy, and focused on his mission. Unlike in Nagarahole and Bhadra, I had an additional problem in Kudremukh. There was no formal government relocation scheme in existence, nor was there any money set aside. The area was not a federally funded tiger reserve to be eligible for finds. Moreover, unlike in Nagarahole and Bhadra, the park officials were not interested in resettlement. They were also worried about further annoying the Maoist guerillas. This project was likely to be hard to get off the ground.

I was able to find a few WCS donors, however, who believed in the model of inducing land-use change to assist wildlife conservation. This model is heavily promoted by the Nature Conservancy in the United States and is well-entrenched in parts of Africa. If I could get it going, Kudremukh would be the first example of such privately funded resettlements.

In 1995, I had met a group of enclaved settlers at Bhagavathy Valley, a beautiful piece of grassland and cloud forest, right at the center of the reserve. There were only five families at Bhagavathy, but they had dozens of scrub cattle. They had built houses and farm buildings on illegally encroached government forestland, for which the officials would not pay them compensation, even if they left.

Niren and his team had scouted to locate some farmland for sale outside the park. The beneficiaries in Bhagavathy were happy to move out to that area. After they were fully compensated using WCS funds, the families quickly moved out to their new homes. This project was not a usual kind of government-funded mass relocation. It was a precise, surgically executed operation for specific individual families in dire need. We had succeeded despite unenthusiastic officials and the threat of violence from the Maoist guerillas.

Soon, some more families moved out. But we were faced with a piquant situation. The beneficiaries had promised to take away their dozens of unproductive cattle when they left. However, at the last minute, they had dodged the headache of driving these worthless cattle all the way to their new homes. Instead, they had simply driven the animals into the surrounding jungles. Soon after they left, dozens of these cattle were back at their old pastures, undercutting our goal of making space for gaur and sambar.

I now had to think outside the box. Vinay, an enthusiastic transect volunteer, had left a federal government job to join my team. He knew a Brahmin Swamiji who was a fanatical worshipper of the holy cow. The holy man even believed cows were likely to go extinct in India—an unlikely prospect, since India possesses 18 percent of world's cattle on just 2 percent of the earth's surface.

Of particular interest to the Swamiji were the dwarf breed of Gidda cattle, which he had sworn to preserve. Around his *Matha* (monastery), 110 kilometers from Kudremukh, the holy man was building shelters for cattle to be donated by the devout, who otherwise would have sold them to butchers. Instead of being used to catch tigers like my buffalo calves in Nagarahole, these cattle would live long, unproductive lives, until their teeth wore down to the gums.

I sent Vinay as my emissary to the Swamiji, offering to populate his newly built shelters with dozens of dwarf cattle. We tactfully did not disabuse the Swamji's worry about the likely extinction of cows in India. Not only did the holy man graciously accept our offer, but also he sent his own "cowboys"—who wore dhotis instead of Levi Strauss jeans—to take away the cattle. The lesson for me was, in the business of saving tigers, anyone who offers help is your ally.

Thereafter, as more families came forward to relocate with private funding support from donors that I rustled up, the program established its own momentum. The beneficiaries were eagerly voting with their feet, defying the rhetoric of their Maoist emancipators. Economics was trumping ideology. Soon sixty families moved out, funded entirely by WCS.

In 2009, I had convinced the federal government to designate Kudremukh Reserve as a Project Tiger area, so that it could receive federal funds for village relocations. But that idea fell through because local politicians, left-wing guerillas, and even temple priests of many shrines in the region had opposed it. Some wanted the area to be mined for iron ore, others wanted new highways in place, politicians wanted votes, and guerillas wanted remote places to hide.

However, I knew that the state government routinely budgeted massive funds meant for "social welfare" of deprived groups. Much of this money was frittered away or siphoned off by a vast bureaucracy created to administer it. If village relocation could be funded out of this huge budget, a lot of progress was possible, though it was not a clearly mandated use for these funds. Once again, it was time to think outside the box.

Our team encouraged a few well-heeled farmers owning significant assets within Kudremukh Park to ask the state government to relocate them. No private donor could provide the large-scale funding required. Predictably, the government responded that its wildlife conservation budget did not have the necessary funds. So the farmers filed a case in the High Court at Bangalore, hiring smart lawyers to plead their cause on constitutional grounds. The High Court directed the "government"—not the forest department—to fund the relocations from any funds at its command. The farmers received their largesse from the overflowing "social welfare" budget and moved out, laughing all the way to the bank.

A new precedent had been set, and many other savvy farmers and ever-eager lawyers joined the fray. Over the years, 288 families out of 717 have moved out of Kudremukh using this novel funding mechanism. The blessings of a constitutional court had created it. The truth is, the Indian constitution guarantees every citizen a right to move and settle in any part of the country. So long as the movement of the beneficiaries is voluntary, relocation from a nature reserve could too be viewed as an enforceable fundamental right.

Even in the Kali Tiger Reserve in northern Malenad [**MAP 1**], the same winds of change have been blowing. Thanks to tireless efforts of Muthanna and his team, led by a young and capable reserve director—who had worked as a researcher in my team before he joined the forest service—about 220 families out of some 2,200 have moved out as I write these lines.

Meanwhile, there were even bigger wheels turning in the society around Kudremukh. The impact of social and demographic changes unleashed by the economic reforms of the 1990s were being felt. The economy was growing, and new job opportunities, urbanization, and cultural changes were allowing people to escape from hard life in remote areas. This was also happening across the country, from the Himalayan foothills to the Ghat forests of Malenad. These winds of change broadly favored my tiger conservation model over the one endorsed by romantic idealogues desiring to "put people back into the woods."

Economic development could sometimes be an ally of the tiger conser-vationists, not just a permanent enemy, as many feared. However, making room for wild tigers also required that negative impacts arising from the same economic development be effectively countered.

Once again, Kudremukh became my testing ground for this battle against a very different enemy.

Carving Up Mother Earth

During one of my field trips to the jungles in Kudremukh in 1974, not far from Bhagavathy Valley north of the towering peak, I had observed an encampment of geological surveyors trying to detect exploitable mineral deposits. They had found abundant iron ore, as expected. However, the ore was low grade, containing just 38 percent iron. The only way to extract the iron deposits in Kudremukh was to rip up and carve off entire hillsides using massive bulldozers, and then mechanically separate the fraction of iron from the bulk of rocks and mud, which were derisively labeled the "overburden." From there, the filtered iron ore would be crushed into a powder by monster-sized mills, mixed with pure water from forest streams, and turned into a blood-red soup called the "slurry." Gigantic electric pumps would then suck the red sludge into a pipeline, 120 centimeters in diameter and 50 kilometers long, which cleaved through the primary rain forests, across the ridge of the ghats, to ultimately reach the bustling Mangalore port [**MAP 1**].

A huge refining plant at the port then compacted the blood-red slurry into solid balls of iron concentrate. Giant tankers would swallow these iron pellets into their capacious holds and sail away to steel mills in faraway countries. Export of raw iron ore from India, a nation with a history of manufacturing steel going back to the tenth century, was an economic irony. However, in the 1970s, desperately starved for hard currency, the Indian government had no other option.

Back at the mines in Kudremukh, "overburden" of discarded mud and rocks, consisting of two-thirds of the hillsides that had been carved up, would be used to fill a gigantic dam built at Lakya, just upstream of the origins of river Bhadra in Kudremukh. According to the mining plan, after thirty years, in the year 1999 to be precise, Lakya Dam would fill up with mud, and mining operations at Kudremukh would cease.

A forty-square-kilometer area of grasslands at the center of Kudremukh had been leased to the mining company, owned by the federal government's Ministry of Steel. At the very center of this mining lease was an eighteen-square-kilometer wild jungle cleared for the initial mining. This area also harbored the dam storing the overburden, the sites for the plant and machinery, and a modern township to house fifteen hundred workers. That was the plan, which had lain dormant because there were no buyers for the ore. Kudremukh forests were safe for the time being, I had then thought.

Therefore, I was dismayed in 1975 when, under the national emergency declared by Indira Gandhi, the ill-conceived Kudremukh mining project suddenly took off with a tight schedule of just one year to completion.

Through the pristine jungle to the west of the mine, comprising the largest of such blocks of tropical evergreen forests in the Western Ghats, three separate swathes were clear cut, extending all the way to the boundary. One clear-cut swathe was for the pipeline carrying the slurry to the coast; another was for erecting the tall steel pylons to support the cables carrying 22,000-KVA electric power to the mine; and the third and most damaging cut was a broad new highway that snaked from west to east right through the forest. On this highway, everything from giant earthmoving machinery, trucks packed with supplies for the township, and buses crammed with pilgrims to the many temples, would ply twenty-four hours a day.

The hitherto isolated rain forest of Kudremukh was now open to pillage, not just by the mining but also for intensified logging, indiscriminate hunting, and inflow of migrants and encroachers. Wild nature and tigers would be casualties.

When the mountain sides were ripped up, carved and gouged by huge machines like in a battle scene from a dystopian science fiction movie, all that was left was a moonscape of mud and rocks. Soon it became obvious there would be human casualties, too. When the monsoon rains lashed the scarred hillsides, the runoff choked the hitherto crystal-clear jungle streams with silt. Bhadra, originating in Kudremukh and the lifeline of millions of farmers downstream, turned into a river of blood.

The giant dam at Lakkavalli that stored waters from Bhadra to irrigate 1,055 square kilometers of fertile paddy and sugarcane in the parched plains to the east, was silently and steadily filling up with the silt. Its designed ninety-year life span was being inexorably cut short, year after year. The mandated measurements of silt flows, to warn of such damage, were deliberately made only in the dry season when the river ran clear.

The clarion call of Visvesvaraya, a pioneer engineer of Karnataka who had established the steel and paper mills downstream of Bhadra, had been to "industrialize or perish." I felt the mining in Kudremukh had corrupted that slogan to "industrialize to perish." Several powerful sections of the society converged in this corruption: the federal bureaucracy that owned and ran the mine, the state that shared the mining revenues, the workers at Mangalore port who benefited

Ravages of strip mining in the rain forests of Kudremukh. *Courtesy Niren Jain*

from the shipping, and thousands of local workers to whom the hitherto useless jungle of Kudremukh had turned into an El Dorado of opportunities.

As a young engineer of twenty-seven, all I could do was to wring my hands in despair. The pain I felt was almost visceral.

In 1977, I was transitioning to a career in farming, vaguely hoping somehow to make a difference to the tigers of Malenad. The unfolding disaster in Kudremukh—where I had first seen the tracks of a wild tiger—warned me this would be a long game.

Ever the pragmatic optimist, I realized there was still 550 square kilometers of superb rain forest surrounding the mining lease area. The key to my long game lay in making sure the lease area could not expand beyond the fifty square kilometers. I thought, naively as it turned out, the mining company would pack up and go after the lease ran out in 1999.

Meanwhile, the implementation of the new wildlife laws was leading to the sporadic recovery of tigers in a few protected reserves of India, including some in Malenad. While waiting for the mining to end in Kudremukh, I had to do something.

In 1977, I had heard a talk by Steven Green, a primatologist from the University of Miami, who had just completed a study of the lion-tailed macaque, a magnificent black monkey with a lionlike mane and tasseled tail. The macaque is found only in the Western Ghats. Green's study had been conducted farther south in Kerala.

After a cursory survey in Karnataka, Green claimed that only four hundred of these monkeys survived farther south, but they were virtually extinct in Malenad.

I was surprised by his summary assessment. During my own wanderings over the years, I had seen these macaques where Green claimed they were extinct. I also knew local people in Karnataka did not hunt the lion-tailed macaque for the alleged medicinal properties of its flesh, as they did farther south. I felt this had helped the macaque to persist better in Malenad.

With a small grant from the state government, I conducted a field survey during 1982–1983 across Malenad. I estimated as many as two thousand macaques survived in Malenad, with Kudremukh alone potentially harboring a large population of three hundred monkeys.

Based on these data and using my position in the state wildlife advisory board in 1987, I managed to get 608 square kilometers of the Kudremukh forests classified as a national park. The park surrounded the mining lease area of forty-eight square kilometers. When the mining stopped in 1999, even the leased area would automatically enjoy protection under the tough wildlife laws.

The officials of the mining company were initially sanguine about the creation of the national park. They were sure no power could stop them from expanding the mine, if new buyers could be found for the iron ore. The booming economy of China had begun to drive up the demand for iron ore.

Using varied legal ruses of its clever lawyers, the company continued mining even after the lease ended in 1999. However, the ill effects of mining were by now apparent even to the left-wing militants, right-wing temple priests, and ordinary farmers along the Bhadra River. My conservation network was also now more robust, with Niren spearheading the action in Kudremukh. There were social activists who also opposed the mine. However, all these other antagonists to the mine demanded that the national park should also be abolished.

Working closely with me in Bangalore was Praveen, who had selflessly invested more and more time on conservation over the years, instead of growing his own advertising agency. He had become quite an expert in forest laws. All of us in the network were clear that the expansion of the mine could be halted only if the national park stood to bar its expansion. If the park was decertified as the social activists demanded, the powerful corporate and bureaucratic lobbies supporting the expansion of the mine would prevail.

In 2002, Niren and I were invited to a public meeting organized by the Rotary Club in Sringeri, a small town, but a major Hindu pilgrimage center located at the northeastern edge of the Kudremukh Park. We had to make our case for the ecological value of the national park, and the voluntary resettlement of people necessary to consolidate its habitats. The supporters of the left-wing militants had arrived in large numbers from the surrounding villages. Because of fears of violence, armed police protection was provided to us. In the end, Niren and I had stood our ground, with many in the audience appreciating the nuanced case we made for getting rid of the mine, as well as saving wildlife and farmers downstream, by securing the park.

After the meeting, a group sympathetic to the militants had accosted me, led by a frail but fiery woman, LM. She argued that respected scientists like me should support the cause of the oppressed peasants that she championed, rather than worry only about the lion-tailed monkeys and tigers. I had tried to convince her of my own values.

Later, LM had risen in the ranks of the guerillas and allegedly been involved in killing a local police informant. A few years later, in the waning days of the guerilla militancy in Kudremukh, I heard she was shot dead by the police. How I wished she had thrown her obvious sincerity and passion for the poor behind the rational conservation solution I was pleading for!

As far as the litigation against the mine was concerned, the cases filed by various social activist groups in the courts were dismissed. They had failed to use the strongest available legal defense: the need to preserve the national park, because it harbored precious biodiversity and priceless watersheds. The litigants also wanted the national park abolished, which is exactly what the mining company was happy with. The mining company had arrayed its best legal talents and shot down the cases with ease. The failure of these ill-planned cases made it impossible for us to litigate again in the state High Court against the mine. The company's prospects for continuing the mining had, in fact, improved because of the illogical approach underlying the cases against it.

We continued to lobby strongly against the mining before the media and public. However, legally challenging the mine's continuance at the apex forum, the Supreme Court of India, was far too expensive a proposition for us. Although some of my companions felt we needed to launch that final assault, I knew we were unlikely to succeed without a powerful attorney and solid scientific data against mining. If we failed, the last door would be shut. I counseled patience and waited.

Meanwhile, the national conservation scenario was rapidly changing. The strong political support for wildlife conservation within the Congress Party had steadily declined. The opposition parties had even less interest in conservation: the right-wing nationalists were interested only in the holy cows, and the leftists wanted all forests cleared and distributed to peasants. Ad hoc violations of even the existing conservation laws by the states and the central government had been ratcheting up over the years. Such violations were also being challenged by conservation groups in various courts across the country.

Fortunately, even as political support for conservation nosedived, the judiciary had stepped into the breach. The Supreme Court decided to form a powerful Central Empowered Committee (CEC) to advise it in the mounting pile of "environmental" cases it was hearing. The court deliberately chose Harish Salve, one of India's leading lawyers with a genuine interest in conservation, as the amicus curiae to assist it.

The effectiveness of such empowered committees largely depends on the quality and commitment of the members. In this case, the court appointed passionate conservationists with solid track records: tiger enthusiast Valmik Thapar, legal eagle Mahendra Vyas, and astute forester Mahesh Jiwrajka. The chair of the CEC was an able retired civil servant, P. V. Jayakrishnan.

The CEC suddenly opened an alternate route for us to challenge the mining in the Supreme Court without spending millions on pricey lawyers. Unlike most courts where judges vary in their comprehension of complexities of conservation, the members of the CEC were knowledgeable, as well as genuinely committed to conservation. Usually, the Supreme Court accepted their recommendations.

I decided it was time to go to the CEC seeking closure of the mine. I was ready to spring the trap I had set two decades earlier by ensuring notification of the outer boundary of Kudremukh Park, which included the forty-eight-square-kilometer area leased to the mine. We decided to file the case in the name of Chinnappa, the warrior who had defended Nagarahole and continued to be an inspiration to all of us.

Much evidence had to be marshaled and presented to the CEC. Beyond purely legal issues there were scientific ones: the loss of biodiversity, threats to endangered species, the harm from the mining operations to the Bhadra River, and its dependent agricultural economy. Shekar Dattatri, one of India's best nature filmmakers, was commissioned to make a short film that summed up all the evidence in a hard-hitting video titled *Mindless Mining*. Shekar and I had met on January 7, 1990, in Nagarahole, the day I captured Mudka, the big male tiger. We had worked closely together on conservation issues for fifteen years.

Our local outreach campaign finally woke up people and the powerful farmers groups in the vast area irrigated by the Bhadra reservoir. The public opposition to the dam massively erupted even as our case progressed in the court. Sensitive to the popular mood, the state government of Karnataka, the owner of the land, backed away from its earlier stance in favor of continued mining. Finally, in 2003, the Supreme Court ordered a graduated scaling down of the mining operations, setting a terminal date in 2006.

We had shut down Asia's largest strip mine owned by the federal government. Our victory affirmed the fact that we not only fought local pressures like hunting, farming, and herding that impacted tigers, but also could effectively confront powerful corporate and industrial interests.

I was sanguine that at least one major threat to Kudremukh had been averted. Niren and his team could now dig in for the long haul and fight to recover tigers and other wildlife in Kudremukh. I could not have been more wrong.

The Empire Strikes Back

Unknown to me, the mining company had planned its counterstrategy. With iron ore prices soaring in global markets, the company was flush with cash and its top officials had a lot to lose if the mine closed within three years, as ordered by the court. Their plan was to somehow keep mining in Kudremukh by delaying the implementation of the court's order of closure in 2006. The longer game plan was to reverse the court's judgment sometime in the future, when the political winds changed and a different set of judges ruled the Supreme Court. The company did not want us watching over its shoulders like hawks as it tried to first delay, and then stop, its impending closure.

Even as the company and its powerful allies continued their legal maneuvers, they also courted new partners to strike and put us out of action. The "coalition of the willing" backing the company included unions of the mining labor as well as unions of the port workers at Mangalore who shipped the ore. Top-notch lawyers in Delhi filed a series of "curative" petitions in the Supreme Court seeking delays of the final closure.

The company also courted forest officials who were willing to frame us for violating the very same conservation laws that we had cited to shut down the mine. This strike against us was to be followed by a strong media campaign to publicly tarnish us through accusations of financial skullduggery. It was a brilliant strategy that caught me entirely by surprise.

Up to that point in time, different forest officials who managed Kudremukh National Park had been generally supportive of us. They also wanted the mining to stop. However, when the new park director AA took over in 2004, the miners finally found their attack dog. AA was not only extremely arrogant, but also was alleged to be corrupt to the core. She had an axe to grind against us as well, because her husband, also a forest official, had been exposed in a logging scam by Thamoo's group and rusticated by the government.

Leading a posse of uniformed, armed forest staff, AA suddenly conducted a surprise raid on Niren's office in Mangalore on April 22, 2004. She claimed the mandatory judicial search warrant was not required because she had the power to summarily raid anyone suspected of possessing illegal forest products. Of course, Niren's office only had his architectural drawings and a laptop. The raiders seized the laptop, claiming it contained incriminating information.

Niren had chosen to join my team, much against the wishes of his father. He was a principled young man but a rather gentle soul. He was shocked by this brazen and violent abuse of official power, which was usually reserved for hard-core criminals. Niren's father, a friend of mine from our college days together, called me. He told me in great anguish that my reckless conservation actions had seriously damaged his son's career. I had no words to console my friend because there was more than a grain of truth in what he was saying.

Although we tried to seek relief through the CEC by linking the punitive actions of AA against Niren to our fight against the mine, senior forestry officials, their palms well-greased by the mining company, now stood fully in support of the park director. The CEC ordered the park director to stay the proceedings against Niren, while it adjudicated the matter. However, the CEC had no power to directly punish anyone for the contempt of violating its orders.

Taking umbrage at our challenge—and egged on by the mining company— AA went ahead and foisted thirteen more "criminal cases" against eighteen of us, in open defiance of the CEC order. In all these cases we were accused of "criminal trespass" in the Kudremukh National Park! There were thirteen cases against Niren, nine cases against me, and multiple cases against other key members of our team, like Praveen, Thamoo, Girish, Krishna, Prasad, Chinnappa, and even Shekar Dattatri, who had made the hard-hitting film against the mining.

AA also booked cases of "trespass" against the scientists who had documented siltation caused by the mining. Going even further, the trustees of organizations affiliated with our entire network, all respected citizens who had never set foot in Kudremukh, were also accused of "trespassing." With great cunning, AA had spread the locations of these alleged trespass incidents across the entire park, thereby apportioning the prosecution among four different court jurisdictions.

All eighteen of us had to obtain bail bonds in each case. Every time any case came up for hearing, in any of the four local courts, we had to be personally present. Each of these cases would go on for several years, after which we could be fined, at worst. There was also the prospect of more years of litigation in the higher-level courts if things came to that. It was a brilliantly devious strategy to paralyze us and drive us to financial ruin. Meanwhile, because she worked for the government, AA was immune to countersuits by us. She could merrily go on with her life while the cases dragged on. With us out of action, the mining behemoth would be free to pursue its agenda for staying on beyond the two-year deadline, which loomed ahead.

Meanwhile, a major newspaper in Bangalore that had been receiving massive revenue from the mining company lauding its own "green initiatives" via full-page advertisements, had hired a special correspondent to do an "investigative report" on us for thwarting the industrial progress of the nation with fraudulent intent. This journalistic hit job made us appear to be shady characters in the public eye, just when the "eighteen criminal cases" came up for trial.

I felt I had seen it all, and was prepared to fight back. While not a criminal, by now I was at least hardened! However, the price young Niren paid appalled me. Although he had willingly chosen conservation as a career, I felt responsible for what he was going through as the consequence.

There was only one option left. I rushed to my friend Udaya Holla's office with Niren and Praveen in tow. Holla had grown considerably in legal stature and authority in the years after he had won my "tiger case." He had the legal acumen and personal charisma to convince the state High Court that our constitutional rights had been violated by this vindictive abuse of official power. If he succeeded, the High Court could immediately stay the operation of all thirteen criminal investigations. Although these cases could still drag on for years, we would be free to effectively monitor the closure of the mine.

I was greatly relieved when Holla responded, "Why did you not come to me after the very first case against Niren? I would have stopped these rascals in their tracks." Our error of judgment in rushing to the CEC had only increased our subsequent legal burdens.

Praveen and Niren worked like beavers with me to assemble all the documentation to support the thirteen appeals filed by Holla in the High Court. A feeling of righteous indignation kept us going as we burned the midnight oil. Within a few days, all the thirteen cases against us were stayed by the High Court. To the park director AA, and the senior officials who colluded with her, this was a legal slap in the face.

Finally, after nine long years, on April 4, 2013, all these fabricated "criminal trespass" cases were finally dismissed by the High Court. The presiding judge even reprimanded AA, and she had to cry and plead with the judge that no penal action be imposed on her.

However, minor legal and administrative skirmishes continued in Kudremukh with the mining company, tour operators, temple priests, and other vested interests who wanted to grab the precious land. Praveen, who had honed his legal skills over the years, effectively led the fight against all of these threats. Thwarted at every turn, the mining company finally gave up and packed its bags to leave in 2016. We now had to get busy looking for land to resettle the unemployed laborers of the mining company, which had abandoned them.

It appeared I was in the relocation business forever. For the cause of the tiger, we had moved everybody and everything, including simple tribal families, herds of holy cows, and even massive beasts that ripped up Mother Earth's belly.

Unfortunately, Niren decided to gradually withdraw from active conservation to concentrate on his career as an architect. I could fully understand his decision, given the personal trauma he had suffered in the prime of his youth while trying to save the tigers of Kudremukh.

In the years to come, as the economies of Asia's tiger nations developed, poverty levels dropped, and increasing numbers of people demanded better lives, there would be more and more mines, dams, factories, solar farms, and windmills trying to encroach the remaining tiger habitats. There was no winding back *that* clock of progress. I was sure tigers had to coexist, harmoniously or otherwise, with this tidal wave of development.

As George Schaller often cautioned, in our business of conservation there is no such thing as a closure.

8 | WHEN EVERYBODY LOVES THE TIGER

INTENSIVE CAMERA-TRAPPING IN NAGARAHOLE showed 23 percent of the tigers were being lost each year, on average, due to deaths and dispersals. However, the births of cubs and immigration of new tigers more than made up for these losses. Furthermore, more resident tigresses successfully producing cubs during some years, but not others, causes periodic "bumps" of surplus of tigers. These animals included eighteen- to twenty-four-month-old subadult tigers evicted from their home ranges, as well as residents past their prime that lost their territories to stronger rivals.

Most of the losers in this competitive scenario perish unseen in the forest immediately after the fights, or later from injury-induced starvation. A few more died from injuries suffered when trying to take down large, dangerous prey animals such as adult gaur. Of the 161 tiger deaths I recorded in Malenad between 2006 and 2016, 46 had died from such "natural violence," 45 from poaching, and 32 were captured or killed by officials. In the remaining 38 cases, the cause of death could not be established due to decomposition of the carcasses or cover-ups.

Sometimes, these incapacitated old tigers—or inexperienced subadults— sought refuge in the farms and coffee plantations outside the park. They preyed on livestock and, more rarely, human beings. Ironically, the tiger is a highly endangered species, which is already extinct in over 93 percent of its former range across Asia. Yet locally a few individual tigers do become "surplus." When problem tigers kill or threaten human lives, officials, tiger conservationists, and local people face cruel dilemmas, as the cases below show.

I tracked the fate of many such individuals over time from their photo-captures: Tigress NHT-111 offers a good example. On February 11, 1991, Tigress NHT-105, who occupied a territory to the south of Sundari's range [**MAP 3**], was captured by my camera traps for the first time. A sequence of photos on the night of October 31, 1993, taken near NGR 2.4 [**MAP 2, Point 24**], showed her two subadult cubs, a female NHT-111 and a male NHT-112, following her around. The male was never photographed again; he had either perished or dispersed out.

Over the years, Tigress NHT-105 was photo-captured fifteen times until February 1996. Thereafter, she was not detected by camera traps. I estimated her age at eight years and suspected she may have been evicted from her range by her own subadult daughter NHT-111, who at three years of age was still sharing her mother's range. Instead of being evicted by her mother, as is usually the case, NHT-111 had taken over her mother's range. As a resident tigress, NHT-111 was photo-captured nine times in the next six years, between October 31, 1993, and May 23, 1999.

Unfortunately, my research permit was denied between 2000 and 2003 by another misguided forest minister, who curiously was a cousin of BB who

Tigress NHT-105 and her daughter NHT-111 were camera trapped in 1993.

had stopped my work a decade earlier. I was unable to monitor the fate of NHT-111 in these crucial years in her life.

After getting my permit restored through one more court battle, I could resume camera-trapping only in October 2003. The following year, in February 2004, NHT-111 was photo-captured for the last time. However, by now, another resident female NHT-189 was occupying the central part of the range of NHT-111. I suspected NHT-111 would soon be evicted by her emergent rival.

The first record of a "man-eating" tiger in Nagarahole (in known memory) occurred two years later. On the night of January 10, 2006, a tribesman was killed and partially eaten by a tiger near Kodange [MAP 2, Point 25]. The forest officials left the human cadaver in place, hoping to tranquilize the killer tiger if it returned. However, when the tigress came at night, they were not on guard. She finished off what remained of the poor man.

After March 2006, several villagers working in farms and plantations on the fringes of the park reported seeing a tiger that killed several livestock and dogs. During the first week of April 2006, a forest ranger photographed an emaciated tigress in the Kolera coffee estate [MAP 2] during a failed attempt to dart her. From her photo, I identified the man-eater tigress as NHT-111. She was now over thirteen years old.

In the sixteen weeks that followed, within an arc of twenty-five kilometers along the western boundary of Nagarahole [MAP 2], the tigress attacked and killed nine cattle. She also attacked a man on July 27, 2006, who fortunately survived, despite his injuries. The next day, the man-eater killed and consumed her last victim, an old farmhand, near the Dalimbekolli settlement [MAP 2, Point 26]. The villagers erupted in angry swarms against local wildlife staff.

Finally, on September 23, 2006, the day after she had killed a pet German shepherd in the Raja coffee estate [MAP 2], the forest department veterinarian finally managed to tranquilize NHT-111. She was very emaciated and died under the sedation [MAP 2, Point 12]. In the thirty-six weeks between January and September 2006, NHT-111 had killed eleven livestock, mauled a man, and killed and consumed two human victims. Failing repeatedly to shoot and kill her and then misguidedly trying to tranquilize instead (which is far more difficult) had resulted in more attacks on humans and loss of livestock.

In the years that followed, there were increasing episodes of tiger predation on cattle and humans in the Nagarahole and Bandipur region [MAP 1]. Camera-trap surveys showed that these two parks together harbored a large

NHT-111, daughter of NHT-105, became a man-eater when she grew old.

tiger population that fluctuated between one hundred and two hundred tigers. Incidents of tiger attacks on humans have steadily risen around these and other parks in Malenad, as population densities of prey and tigers have rebounded. Between 2006 and 2016, there were thirty-two such incidents of tiger attacks across Malenad. Even though only a few tiger populations are at high densities, "problem tigers" would sporadically emerge, as we are now witnessing across India. This is inevitable given the high reproduction rates and territorial behavior of tigers.

How to Create a Man-Eater

From camera-trap surveys in Bhadra during 2012, I had identified a resident tigress BDT-115, who had a home range of about thirty square kilometers that spilled over the park boundary. However, her territory outside the park was also a good tiger habitat, covered by swathes of grasslands and forest patches adjacent to private coffee plantations on the inner slopes of the Baba-budan mountains [**MAP 1, Point A**]. Although not fully guarded by the forest department, these forest patches were also under government ownership.

Many private coffee plantations also hosted luxury resorts to which tourists thronged, attracted by the spectacular scenery.

In September 2014, tigress BDT-115 had two male cubs about six months of age when she was photographed. As these cubs grew up, I individually identified them as BDT-119 and BDT-146. A couple of months later, now much larger, they were accompanying her into the plantation landscapes. While the wild tigress remained wary and hid from prying human eyes, her cubs, which grew up in the security of the reserve, were often seen and photographed because of their boldness. Soon, videos of the juvenile tigers began circulating in the social media, attracting even more tourists. The two male tigers became habituated to vehicles and human presence.

The first warning sign came on November 11, 2014, when BDT-146 cantered after a car packed with noisy tourists, just as it would stalk any prey animal. The video went viral among thrill seekers who wanted more of the same. I was getting apprehensive about the fate of these young tigers, which had not yet acquired the skills of hunting wild ungulate prey under their mother's tutelage. They soon learned to kill cattle, which are easier to subdue, unlike the wary gaur and sambar, their natural prey in this montane habitat.

On November 15, 2014, a woman named Sumitra, a daily wage laborer on her way to work at a coffee plantation at Pandaravalli [**MAP 1, Point A**], was stalked and killed by one of the male tigers. Perhaps disturbed by people, he left without eating his victim. However, later that night the tiger raided a cattle shed nearby and killed two cows.

The entire village was now in an uproar, asking the forest department to immediately get rid of the dangerous predators. Quickly swinging into action, the forest staff and veterinarians staked out cattle as live bait to tranquilize and capture the tigers. On November 17, 2014, they darted and captured the male tiger BDT-146.

Although I was away on a visit to New York, I was very worried about what could follow. This tiger, having lost its instinctive fear of humans, was viewing them as legitimate prey. The animal was not yet of dispersal age and could adapt to life in a zoo. I e-mailed the chief of wildlife in Karnataka and the head of the National Tiger Conservation Authority in Delhi, strongly urging them not to release the tiger back into the wild. It was a potentially a dangerous man-eater that had to be either euthanized or sentenced to a lifetime in captivity.

Unfortunately, many enthusiastic urban warriors fighting the tiger's cause suffer from what I call the "Born Free" syndrome: they believe tigers are cute and cuddly animals that pose no danger to people and can therefore be "reha-bilitated" to roam freely. The pressure on the forest department from such tiger lovers was immense. This was a dangerous idea in a countryside packed with 340 men, women, and children per square kilometer. They would be in the path of a hungry tiger seeking a meal that could move twenty kilometers overnight.

Into this mess stepped in a half-baked, ill-trained biologist, GS. What he entirely lacked in terms of skills necessary to capture or radio-track big cats, he more than made up in the skills that ingratiated him to those in power. He was a former staffer under me, who had left because I felt he lacked the abilities neces-sary to be a big cat biologist, and advised him to stick to conservation advocacy.

GS may have simplemindedly viewed the freshly caught tiger BDT-146 as an opportunity for self-promotion, by rehabilitating a wild tiger back to a wonder-ful life in the jungle to prance around, presumably singing "Hakuna Matata." GS thought that by tracking this tiger he would join the ranks of the handful of tiger biologists who had gained recognition. He was backed by a powerful cabinet minister's son, who posed as a "tiger conservationist" in Bangalore's party circuits. Another backer was a senior bureaucrat who presumed he was a "tiger expert" because he had ridden in my car a quarter century earlier while I radio-tracked tigers in Nagarahole. A few forest officials trying to curry favor with them joined in. An order was issued to "rehabilitate" the problem tiger in Kali Tiger Reserve.

The truck bearing BDT-146 drove to Kali Reserve three hundred kilo-meters away [**MAP 1**]. However, having heard the unwelcome news, mobs of villagers gathered at Kali, barring its path. The stymied officials decided instead to surreptitiously sneak the tiger into the Bhimgad Reserve a hundred kilometers farther. Early in the morning of November 19, 2014, BDT-146 was fitted with a radio collar and released into the jungle in the Talewadi forest range of Bhimgad [**MAP 1, Point B**]. Before the tiger recovered from sedation and walked away into the jungle, GS, untrained in telemetry, failed to check whether the transmitter was fully functional.

As soon as villagers around Bhimgad learned of the man-eater in their midst, there was much anger and several forest staff were roughed up, although the biologist quietly escaped their wrath. To mollify the angry villagers, the officials rashly promised to recapture the tiger and take it away immediately.

Bhimgad was a newly established wildlife reserve in a forest area peppered with villages. Wild prey species were scarce because of poaching by villagers, as well as wealthy hunters from nearby towns. BDT-146 was a subadult male tiger unskilled at hunting wild prey, even where they had been abundant. Finding himself in an unfamiliar terrain, without his mother to show him around, the tiger started preying on livestock. Already habituated to people, he boldly hunted during the day, watched by terrified villagers.

Unsurprisingly, GS who fitted a dysfunctional radio collar on the tiger could not track its signals. Meanwhile, the villagers menaced by the tiger were piling pressure on forest officials to fulfill their promise to remove the rampaging predator from their midst.

Between November 21 and 27, 2014, BDT-146 wandered widely over an area of 160 square kilometers trying to find his way around. He attacked and killed at least twelve livestock, including cows, buffaloes, goats, sheep, and a tethered horse. The tiger even turned up in a photo in a camera trap set up by forest staff near the carcass of a cow it had killed. However, instead of making a serious attempt to shoot the tiger, officials persisted with their foolhardy attempts to catch this tiger alive to placate the vocal lobby of urban animal lovers.

Their capture tactics included hundreds of laborers noisily "combing" one forest patch after another, ignoring the fact that any tiger, unless it was stone-deaf, would have sneaked off and been miles away from all that racket. Having darted wary wild tigers in beats, where silence was the key, I could only marvel at the absurdity of these efforts.

Videos of the biologist waving an antenna around appeared regularly on television news to assure locals that he was on the job. Then, when GS's modern technology failed them, forest officials turned to ancient jungle craft. Half a dozen *Soliga* tribesmen (who possessed field skills comparable to that of the Jenu Kuruba in Nagarahole) were conscripted to find the tiger. As one newspaper reporter breathlessly announced, these men could track the tiger down using their acute scenting abilities, something which even the police tracking dogs deployed earlier failed to do.

The charade of trying to catch the problem tiger alive turned into a tragedy on the evening of December 24 at Mudgaivada village of Bhimgad. Anjana, a pregnant twenty-three-year-old woman, was attacked by the tiger just as she bent to collect water from a stream, in full view of her terrified companions. The villagers, and a posse of policemen and forest staff who arrived early next morning, finally dared to retrieve the victim's body. Having made a meal of the poor girl, the habituated tiger was calmly sitting near her remains.

In a classically Indian bureaucratic reaction, neither the armed police nor the forest staff shot the tiger. Their orders, on paper, were only to capture the man-eater alive. Killing the animal would need additional approvals from the state chief of wildlife in Bangalore as well as the National Tiger Conservation Authority in Delhi! Seeing the noisy crowd trying to retrieve the girl's remains, the tiger took off without waiting for his death warrant to reach those high officials.

After this tragedy, people of the entire district rose in revolt and rioted. They attacked the forest staff on sight and forced a general strike in the cities and towns, shaking up even the forest minister in Bangalore, a man who bore a remarkable resemblance to a beached whale, even while awake. Finally, a formal order to shoot the tiger at sight was issued.

Many hitherto covert poachers, quite skilled at hunting, suddenly emerged from the shadows. On the night of December 28, 2014, after hearing and tracking the tiger, a seasoned local hunter, TP, shot the animal as it glared back at his spotlight. Although the forest officials later claimed one of their own duly authorized guards had shot the tiger, this claim was suspect. Villagers of Kongla [MAP 1, Point C] had immediately celebrated the man-eater's death by garlanding and parading TP.

The entire incident, from the beginning to the end, illustrates how tiger conservation is hamstrung by such diverse pulls and pressures: glamorizing the tiger to tourists riding around in cars, and its emotional appeal to the animal lovers in cities, neither of whom were at risk from the marauding felid, and the surfeit of arrogance that often substitutes for genuine understanding of tiger behavior among many officials. I felt truly sad that even my own field of tiger science was getting infected. Unfortunately, tragic incidents like the one above, which took the lives of a tiger and two human beings, are now regularly reported from many high-tiger-density reserves in India.

The height of absurdity seen in the management of such crises was reached in another instance, in 2018, with a case of human-tiger conflict in Maharashtra state, which I was asked to study. It involved a tigress, rather cutely called "Avni" and celebrated by her fans in big cities far away, even as she rampaged, killing villagers in Yavatmal district. Finally, with the crisis exploding into public violence and litigation in the High Court at Nagpur, to placate the judge, the NTCA had issued an extraordinary order: it specified that each time the tigress was sighted, first an attempt had to be made by a qualified veterinarian to dart and tranquilize her. Only if that did not work, an attempt was to be made to shoot her! All this had to be done in daytime, when the crafty tigress hardly showed herself.

Soon after, a glory-seeking private hunter shot the tigress dead from a car as she crossed the road after dark. Then the official veterinarian, who was also in the car, appeared to have stuck a dart on to her rump, creatively ensuring the NTCA's ridiculous order had been followed to a tee!

To be fair to forest officials and administrators handling these man-eating crises, they are invariably between a rock and a hard place. They are attacked by local villagers, who want the marauding tiger killed immediately. Then, if tiger depredations continue, the local people take up arms or poison the tigers, as I witnessed several times around Nagarahole. Legitimately, such elimination should be quick and executed by park officials. However, the "tiger lovers" in cities are also a formidable lobby, particularly on social media. They file court cases to prevent officials from killing problem tigers. They insist the man-eater be captured safely and released back into the wild, "somewhere else." The judges in the courts are usually even more ignorant of tiger biology, the technical difficulties in capturing wild tigers alive, and the lack of safe spaces to release such dangerous beasts. The judges issue unimplementable orders in archaic English, trying to satisfy everyone, including their own craving for dense bombast.

Meanwhile, as tiger depredations continue, local hostility breaks into violence and rioting targeting park staff and officials. After the forest staff get too demoralized to effectively police their beats, local malcontents and ordinary villagers rachet up timber theft and poaching.

Very few officials clearly and honestly tell their political bosses, judges, or animal lovers the plain truth: a few individual tigers have to be killed, when necessary, to save the species and its habitats in the long run. Instead, everyone embraces the woolly "Born Free" doctrine of translocating problem tigers to new locations, repeatedly, until tragedy strikes again. Key problems, such as a lack of habitats rich in wild prey but devoid of wild tigers, are ignored.

If a new tiger is translocated into an already thriving population, either the introduced tiger will get killed, or it will kill and replace one that lives there. For instance, a three-year-old male tiger, BPT-241, camera-trapped in Bandipur on February 18, 2010, dispersed a linear distance of 280 kilometers to a rural landscape around Shikaripura to the North. On May 1, 2011, he was cornered by a mob, and while trying to escape, mauled a man who died later. However, BPT-241 was not a man-eater like BDT-146 who did not fear humans. After officials sedated BPT-241 for release, I suggested Bhadra reserve, where prey densities had already risen, while tigers had not attained commensurate densities. Although the young male tiger settled in and thrived in Bhadra, a more powerful male tiger killed him three months later [MAP 1]. In contrast, if tigers are translocated into landscapes deficient in wild prey but populated by humans and livestock, tragic consequences such as the ones witnessed in Bhimgad and Yavatmal will inevitably unfold.

Despite this, most translocated tigers (and leopards) in India are not radio-tagged. They are simply dumped in the jungle and forgotten. In known cases, most such relocations have led to new conflicts arising around the release site, with both local people and the big cats paying the price.

There is also a new factor coming into play after the massive inflation of tiger conservation budgets by the NTCA: catching and releasing problem tigers (and leopards) has turned into a lucrative source of funds, and thus become attractive to forest officials involved. Typically, about 1 or 2 million rupees ($10,000–$25,000) are shown as the expenditure for each big cat capture-and-release operation. That is a lot of money to play around with.

The issue of "problem tigers" needs to be faced squarely, remaining sensitive to the apprehensions of people compelled to live next to the cats. Total elimination of such conflicts is not feasible, given the natural population dynamics of the species and high human population densities in India. However, aggravation of such conflicts that result from professional incompetence, misguided sentiments, and ignorance of tiger science can indeed be remedied.

When the Saints Go Marching In

International funding agencies in the United States, Europe, and Japan are constantly on the lookout for "good green causes" to support. Since the 1990s, the cultural appeal of the tiger has attracted them to step beyond their usual agenda of uplifting humans to jump in and help the cause of the cat.

While the cause may be worthy, the rigid politically correct stances of such donors often lead to disastrous conservation outcomes. A toxic combination of self-interest among both the bureaucratic givers and recipients of such aid, and the deluge of money that follows, all but ensures such outcomes.

In 1995, when I examined the contours of the proposed India Ecodevelopment Project (IEDP) of the World Bank to support tiger reserves, including Nagarahole, I was taken aback. The funding earmarked for Nagarahole was a whopping 360 million rupees ($5 million), eight times the normal park budget! The project aimed to economically uplift poor people living in and around the park, naively hoping this would curb their negative impacts on the park. The flood of money was to be handled by a dozen park officials and consultants.

Along with Valmik Thapar, I made a vain attempt in Washington, DC, to convince the Bank officials to abandon the IEDP. I pointed out that opportunities to skim off such a huge budget would likely attract the most corrupt officials to Nagarahole, leading to the neglect of hard-core protection. The park staff would shift their attention away from the difficult task of law enforcement toward the more lucrative "village ecodevelopment" and "habitat improvements." Consultants enjoying the patronage of officials, without the necessary technical capabilities, would be hired. The critical need for incentive-driven village relocations would be the first casualty, because of the World Bank's explicit opposition to the idea. I concluded that the Nagarahole IEDP would only inflict damage on tiger habitats, without delivering the hoped-for upsurge of community support to tiger conservation. However, forest officials in India, as well as the bank's officials and ecologists, turned a deaf ear to my pleas. The IEDP juggernaut rolled into Nagarahole in 1997. To placate the World Bank, the voluntary relocation project, which was just gaining traction, was shelved indefinitely.

Unfortunately, my dire predictions soon started coming to true. The project began pumping vast sums of money into a network of forest officials, consultants, and ersatz "civil society" outfits that mushroomed overnight. The result was ecological mayhem.

In 2003, we decided to respond to this novel crisis. Thamoo filed a complaint before the *Lokayukta*, the Karnataka State's anticorruption ombudsman. The complaint highlighted the rises in official corruption and the consequent mismanagement of the park. It provided prima facie evidence of the negative impacts of the IEDP, such as penetration of the park by organized poachers, a resurgence of illegal logging, and extensive damage to natural habitats from unnecessary manipulation of vegetation and water flows. There was also proof of rising financial pilferage.

The Lokayukta, a tough retired judge of the Indian Supreme Court named NV, conducted a thorough investigation in the field, assisted by the complainants. The investigation showed park protection had virtually collapsed. A runaway forest fire had scorched nine thousand hectares in 2001, about 15 percent of the park. Not only had killings of elephants hit a new peak at fifty-two animals, but also professional tiger poachers from central India had boldly trapped tigers in the middle of the park. At least twelve thousand timber trees worth 51 million rupees ($660,000) had been illegally cut and smuggled. Natural habitats had been destructively manipulated—an example being 7 million rupees

($100,000) misspent to apply chemical fertilizers to wild bamboo culms. In the name of "village ecodevelopment," financial fraud had run riot. Project design and monitoring were reduced to a farce with the connivance of consultants.

The World Bank's staff responsible for project oversight, some of them known to me, jetted between Washington, DC, and luxury lodges in Nagarahole. They had no time to listen to anyone else except project officials and consultants.

Prashant Sen, a former director of Project Tiger, later estimated project consultancies and overhead expenses had consumed 45 percent of the funds spent under the IEDP. Ombudsman judge NV's scathing report on the project estimated the total financial losses at a staggering 60 million rupees ($830,000). Unable to ignore the stench of the scandal any longer, the World Bank prematurely terminated the Nagarahole project in 2004.

The Bank's apologists shrugged this off as a failure unique to Nagarahole. They insisted the IEDP functioned superbly at all other tiger reserves in India. The truth was, no one had aggressively tried to expose flaws of the project like we had done. A report of the Indian government's comptroller general for the year 2005–2006 castigated the project implementation across the country, citing a total financial swindle of 120 million rupees ($1.66 million).

What followed in Nagarahole, however, demonstrated the incredible adaptability of the Indian bureaucracy to creatively defend its self-interest. Multiple follow-up inquiries, triggered by Judge NV's indictment, cleverly relied on arcane rules to expand the list of the guilty from a handful of corrupt senior officials to more than a hundred lower-level forest staff. Ultimately, six years later, a forest department–sponsored follow-up inquiry by a district level judge dismissed the indictments as unproven or "partly proven." Senior civil servants thereafter cited a legal precedent to define "partly proven" as equivalent to "unproven," thereby letting every culprit go scot-free. Everyone except the complainants breathed a sigh of relief. A senior forest official even accused me of encouraging vigilantism to demoralize park staff.

Today, other than the stumps of illegally felled trees and bleached bones of slaughtered elephants in the forest, there is no evidence for World Bank's bespoke "community-based conservation" model unleashed against the tigers of Nagarahole a quarter century ago.

The message to nongovernmental organizations fighting the tiger's cause was clear and loud: if you see official corruption and mismanagement of tiger lands, look the other way. My carefully crafted conservation model of providing issue-based support to the government, while reserving the right to criticize wrongdoings, was beginning to crumble, driven by deeper changes transforming the Indian society.

Losing the Plot While Joining the Dots

In 2004, the official pugmark census reported that the Sariska Tiger Reserve, not too far from Delhi, harbored twenty-six tigers. This count was duly hailed as another success story. Unfortunately, the true number of tigers in Sariska was already zero! All the tigers in Sariska had been surreptitiously killed off by poachers. Local forest guards and villagers knew the truth, but kept conveniently silent.

Prashant Sen, active in conservation even after his retirement from Project Tiger, heard about this through his jungle grapevine. He tipped off an enterprising reporter who blew the lid off the scandal. The director of Project Tiger, RG, blew off the allegations, saying Sariska's tigers may have "temporarily migrated to the nearby hills." However, the public outcry forced the disinterested prime minister, Manmohan Singh, to empower a Tiger Task Force (TTF) with a mandate to reform the national tiger conservation strategy.

Around the same time, India's social activists and politicians had launched a campaign for granting land titles to tribal people and other "forest-dwellers" who were illegally occupying government forests. They were drafting a sweeping new law, titled the Forest Rights Act (FRA), that would override the existing conservation laws to grant new rights to claimants. Wildlife conservationists, a much weaker advocacy lobby, were pleading that at least wildlife reserves should be exempt from the FRA, and the option to relocate the forest-dwellers should also be provided.

The protagonists of the FRA were worried that the Tiger Task Force about to be set up would be used by tiger conservationists to sabotage the FRA's emancipatory goals. Their political clout ensured that nonofficial members appointed to the task force, including its chair, a feisty climate activist, possessed little knowledge of practical or scientific aspects of tiger conservation. These members also naively believed that "forest-dwellers" could "sustainably" live off the land, even the last refugia of tigers. Valmik Thapar, the only knowledgeable tiger conservationist on the panel, was outvoted on key issues.

There were also retired foresters serving on the panel. The member secretary of TTF was RG, the same director of Project Tiger under whose watch Sariska had lost its tigers. These seasoned bureaucrats had the skills to steer the Task Force's fuzzy do-gooder agenda to accomplish their own very clear goals. The first goal was to dodge any federal government responsibility for the Sariska debacle by blaming it entirely on the state officials of Rajasthan. The bureaucrats also loved the "ecodevelopment" model that had proven to be a such a cash cow earlier in the World Bank–aided projects.

At this juncture, Indira Gandhi's political inheritors, who ruled the country, watched mutely as the legal barriers she had put up to save tigers three decades earlier were pulled down through the populist Forest Rights Act. Their political calculus favored millions of self proclaimed forest-dwellers with votes over a mere three thousand tigers without any votes, come election time.

Although not sanguine about accomplishing anything useful, I decided to meet the task force members to make my case. Knowing their mindsets, I focused on pitching only two ideas.

One was to replace the flawed pugmark census used to audit tiger conservation. I made specific alternative proposals on how tiger and prey populations should be monitored, using more rigorous and cost-effective methods that I had developed in collaboration with Nichols, and successfully employed in Malenad. I also argued that "forest-dwellers" living inside tiger reserves who were willing to relocate should be assisted to move out.

When the task force submitted its final report, titled *Joining the Dots*, in July 2005—with a strong dissenting note by Valmik—I was surprised that my two submissions had not been ignored, as I expected. While the TTF report went on at great length about virtues of human–tiger coexistence, it did support relocation of willing people out of key tiger habitats. The TTF even suggested a budget of several million rupees be set aside for such relocations.

On the tiger monitoring issue, the TTF categorically ended the pugmark census, something I had been pleading for eighteen years. Unfortunately, on what should replace the pugmark census, the TTF was delightfully vague. It essentially suggested all good scientists should join hands and come up with suitable methods. None of the nonofficial TTF members had the necessary expertise to dig any deeper into this rather technical issue. While the officials had been forced to abandon their favored pugmark census, they were now free to come up with a replacement on their own.

The clear winners overall were the forest bureaucrats. The earlier compact steering committee of Project Tiger was replaced by a vastly expanded National

Tiger Conservation Authority (NTCA) with more than thirty members and invitees. This body was packed with even more bureaucrats, politicians, and social activists. Literally anyone could be a nonofficial member of the NTCA.

Quietly burying the ghost of the Sariska tiger extinction under his watch, Director RG was promoted to a higher level, reporting directly to the minister who chaired the NTCA.

Meanwhile, in the domain of wildlife conservation writ large in India, two conservation models had been jostling: the older "exclusive" model relying primarily on protected areas managed by the government, and the new "inclusive" model in which nebulously defined local communities would directly manage wildlife. These two models had been butting heads in academia since the 1970s.

The bureaucrats on TTF ensured the panel endorsed their own cocktail, mixing both these models. They labeled it the "core and buffer" strategy. The strategy recommended both an "exclusive" core zone and an "inclusive" buffer zone. The claim was that the "buffer" areas would benefit from ecodevelopment, while the "core" would remain inviolate. However, both zones would continue to be managed by the forest bureaucracy. The World Bank template that failed in Nagarahole became entrenched at the heart of the national tiger conservation strategy.

The nonofficial members of TTF had tried to join the dots but lost the plot. The officials were doing high fives—yet again.

In the two decades since, the NTCA has metastasized into a massive powerhouse of bureaucracy, bloated by funds for doling out extensive patronage and contracts. It has assumed sweeping powers to guide how tiger habitats should be manipulated, tiger populations managed, and conflict situations handled. The NTCA has also ensured park managers implement ecodevelopment projects in the buffer as well as take over tiger research and monitoring under its monopoly.

More recently, shedding its much-touted single-minded devotion to tigers, the NTCA has expanded its domain to include other big cat species, such as recovering populations of snow leopards in the icy Himalayas, and bringing back the long-extinct cheetah to the arid plains of India by importing them from Africa!

Whether the NTCA's largesse has commensurately benefited the tiger needs a closer examination. However, it has clearly succeeded in embedding its own hype deeply into the global media narrative about India's tiger conservation success.

The "Enron" of the Tiger World

As late as 2004, the director of Project Tiger, RG, had dug in his heels, claiming the pugmark census was an "Indigenous" scientific innovation, whereas the methods I—and, by then, other independent scientists—had been advocating were "fancy and foreign." He claimed 3,600 wild tigers still roamed in India based on the pugmark census of 2002.

Then came the shock of Sariska. The Tiger Task Force, of which RG was the member secretary, had to finally jettison the pugmark census. Without blushing a twinge, RG now did a breathtaking backflip in the full glare of TV cameras, deriding the pugmark census method as "trash." The government scientists at the Wildlife Institute of India who had endorsed this method for two decades took a bow, promising to come up with a brand-new method, to replace the "trash."

I expected this mea culpa would be followed by a serious revision of tiger monitoring methods. Without that, the efficacy of any tiger conservation strategy could not be judged. I fervently hoped qualified researchers outside the government system would be involved in developing the new methodology, at least in the future.

There were recent precedents for such radical "modernizations" within the Indian bureaucratic system. Norman Borlaug's agricultural research leading to the Green Revolution during the 1960s, the telecommunication reforms in the 1980s, and the economic liberalization in the 1990s—all had paid off *because* they broke free from the previous red-tape-bound stagnation.

I had recommended to the TTF that 90 percent of India's tigers, and their prey species, could be rigorously and cost-effectively monitored *every year* using camera-trap surveys and line transect surveys in the key tiger reserves. I had also practically demonstrated how this could be done at a cost of a mere 10 million rupees ($140,000) per year, in the Malenad landscape that harbored about 15 percent of India's tigers.

I argued that tiger densities in habitats outside such key reserves, which harbored only 10 percent of the tigers, were too low to be estimated accurately. I suggested only the presence or absence of tigers could be checked once every five years, to determine whether the tiger range was expanding or shrinking. In 2002 I had developed, jointly with Jim Nichols, an innovative method called "occupancy sampling" that required only low-cost surveys of tiger spoor by trackers, but with a robust statistical model. These "occupancy models" over-came a key problem with traditional tiger "presence" versus "absence" field survey methods, which underestimated areas occupied by tigers because of the surveyor's inability to distinguish "true absence" from chance "nondetection," despite their presence in some areas.

However, ignoring all these well-tested options, the NTCA and WII opted to reinvent the wheel. They developed a novel but fundamentally flawed national tiger estimation (NTE) method. Three "foreign experts," who were not specialists in animal population monitoring, were jetted in and out to quickly endorse the new method. This was like reputed heart surgeons from abroad being flown in to perform neurosurgery in India!

Four such "National Tiger Estimation" surveys have been conducted, in 2006, 2010, 2014, and 2018, at truly outrageous costs. Armies of poorly trained forest guards collected a bewildering array of observations to be crunched through creaky statistical models incapable of separating the signal from the noise in these mountains of messy data. The analyses are carried out under great secrecy to generate the much-hyped precise tiger numbers once every four years, like rabbits out of a hat.

Rigorous, proven methods were ignored, diluted, or replaced by seat-of-the-pants techniques. Before the adoption of the new methods, rigorous peer review that should have vetted them was ignored. Most egregiously, while the surveys routinely employed technical terms such as "occupancy sampling," "line transect sampling," and "closed model capture-recapture sampling," to misleadingly describe field practice and analyses that bore little resemblance to their original formulations.

There were serious flaws in the design of field surveys, collection of field data, and the final analyses. Consequently, for all the massive manpower and money invested in the four national tiger estimation efforts, their results are unreliable. Their results are of little use for knowing how India's tiger recovery efforts have fared.

When the results of the first national tiger estimation (NTE) survey came out in 2006, I noticed an audacious "confession" by the NTCA that tiger numbers in India had suddenly plunged from 3,642 in 2002 to 1,411 tigers! This drastic conclusion was entirely unwarranted. The older number came from "pugmark censuses," whereas the recent one was from the new "index-calibration" method.

It soon became clear that having dodged the bullet after the Sariska tiger extinction, NTCA officials were deliberately setting an unrealistically low benchmark of about 1,400 tigers. This trickery enabled them to gain media acceptance for their "new scientific tiger census method" in place of the "trash pugmark census," which they had sworn by for thirty-six long years.

Even more significantly, going forward from this absurdly low baseline, the NTCA could easily tailor future tiger numbers once every four years to suit their need for claiming success. The dense and opaque verbiage around new methodology ensured that media reporters, the public, or, for that matter, even scientists could not decipher details of how the surveys and analyses were conducted.

In retrospect, lowering the countrywide tiger numbers to a low of 1,400 in 2006 (lower even than the 1,870 tigers claimed by forest officials thirty-six years earlier) was a breathtakingly audacious trick. Officials had shrewdly guessed that media news cycles are spinning ever faster, and that public memory is short.

However, for this "national tiger estimation method" to deliver the results desired by the NTCA, there is one critical need: total secrecy about the raw data they gathered, as well as details of analyses performed. Anyone who understood such arcane technical issues in depth had to be denied access to the raw data or analyses, although the surveys were funded by Indian taxpayers.

Since 2006, the four NTCA tiger surveys have cost Indian taxpayers approximately 1 billion rupees ($13 million). A fifth survey is due in 2022. Each time they have involved 600,000 man-days. Yet the wider community of tiger monitoring experts are not provided access; the data are held in a crypt, appropriately named the "tiger cell," at the NTCA in Delhi.

In 2009, when a new federal environment minister took over, I got involved with the NTCA (at his request) to improve the protocols for monitoring tiger populations. The final set of protocols were prepared with assistance from my two most capable colleagues, Samba Kumar and Arjun Gopalaswamy. They both had PhDs in statistical ecology relevant to tiger-monitoring issues. The protocols covered the necessary details of data collection, storage, and analyses in a transparent manner, down to the finest-grained detail. These protocols had already delivered reliable results for us in Malenad, and been published in the top scientific journals and monographs.

However, the NTCA officials deftly rendered the entire effort futile by additionally offering lax alternative protocols to the reserve managers, under the pretext of gradually introducing our better methods to them later. The forest staff doing surveys simply ignored key elements of the rigorous protocols. Although the protocols we added remained for a few years on the NTCA's web portal, to my knowledge no one has employed them in the field.

During the discussions with the NTCA, I pointed out that my team of twenty-five technicians and a few dozen volunteers were implementing these rigorous protocols in Malenad at relatively low costs. I also proposed that a few larger conservation nonprofits and research institutions should join hands every year to implement the rigorous methods in all tiger reserves, as I was already doing in Malenad. Such a public–private partnership could not only save substantial public funds, but also eliminate the serious conflict of interest involved in the same forest bureaucrats managing tigers, while also judging their own performance through their monopoly over tiger counting and management evaluation.

However, there were no takers for my proposal. When I later critiqued the national tiger estimation survey results in 2010, the same federal minister who had invited me to contribute my expertise to the enterprise accused me of being impossible to collaborate with! He had arrived at this conclusion without ever discussing the issue with me.

Meanwhile, India's tiger monitoring under a government monopoly continues despite its glaring flaws, which have been highlighted in top scientific journals. In the field, the identification of individual tigers is often based on photos of a single flank, or even old images dug out from previous surveys, as lay citizens and journalists have pointed out. Ignoring strict protocols for the labeling of individual tigers has led to the same tigers being counted at multiple locations across boundaries of surveyed areas.

Instead of camera-trapping for short periods of forty-five to sixty days to ensure the tiger population remains closed to losses and gains, cameras are kept on for months on end, accumulating more and more new tigers, without deducting ones that have died or emigrated. This of course inflates the number of tigers that are on the ground at any given point in time. Analyses of such data using statistical models that assume the population was truly "closed" leads to further errors.

Estimates of tiger densities only once every four years, instead of every year, nullifies the ability to estimate key parameters like annual rates of survival and recruitment, which are vital to understand the impacts of poaching and other pressures. Knowing that even well-protected tiger populations lose about 20 percent of individuals each year, monitoring them once every four years entirely undermines the managers' ability to really know what is going on.

The monitoring of populations of the principal prey species, using strict line transect survey protocols, is not implemented in any tiger reserve. The effort and hard work involved has made officials simply ignore them. The prey densities and numbers being generated by NTCA, without employing robust line transect methods, are practically useless.

However, the national and international news media have, by and large, fully bought into the suspiciously precise "tiger numbers" and other statistics churned out once in four years by NTCA, accompanied by a self-serving narrative. The dubiously low baseline of 1,400 tigers established in 2006 has given ample room for creating flexible narratives well into the future. Perhaps the mainstream media is dazzled by the beautiful photos of tigers and high production values of these glossy NTCA reports. The media endorsements are amplified by even more gullible social media, and are finally swallowed by the public. Then everything is forgotten, and four years later the charade is repeated.

Since 2014, several scientists and conservationists specializing in various aspects of big cat monitoring methods have critiqued India's tiger survey methods and results in scientific journals. These critiques amply demonstrate their multiple ingrained flaws. The prestigious scientific journal *Nature* even published a report accompanied by an editorial advising the government to share the survey data with other scientists to refine the survey methods collaboratively. However, as far as any independent scrutiny is concerned, India's tiger data appear to be even more elusive than the secretive cat itself.

In 2017, Jim Nichols and I coedited a monograph titled "Methods for Monitoring Tiger and Prey Populations" in which thirty-one scientists presented cutting edge, cost-effective alternative approaches to tiger monitoring. However, India's ruling tiger oligarchy has simply chosen to ignore all these developments.

It all hit me clearly in 2017 during an official meeting in Bangalore. A senior forester—who had once served as the park director of Nagarahole without ever evincing any interest in my research—chose to admonish me. He had said, with a straight face, that questioning India's official tiger numbers endorsed by the honorable prime minister is an unpatriotic act! I realized tiger conservation was having its own "Enron moment." The auditors and executives were colluding to create a false narrative for the gullible investors. However, they were a step ahead of Enron; the auditors and the executives here were from the same company.

Tiger Conservation on Steroids

The two laws that enabled the early spectacular tiger recoveries in India were the Wildlife Protection Act of 1972 and the Forest Conservation Act of 1980. That recovery was achieved against overwhelming odds: the slow growth of the Indian economy, and a reliance on forest products to fill the government's coffers and meet people's needs. The rural poverty and the craving for wild animal protein that resulted in poaching and cattle grazing in tiger habitats had to be confronted. These challenges had been squarely faced by India's foresters of that generation. Astoundingly, tiger populations had recovered within a couple of decades, at least in a few reserves across the country.

However, around the year 2000, things began to change. At the top, genuine political commitment to wildlife conservation declined. The gradual transition of the field-oriented work culture of the forest department gave way to one that envied and imitated the multitasking Indian Administrative Service. This mission-drift occurred in the context of an upsurge in emancipatory politics. The political movements in support of loosely defined "forest-dwellers" led to the sweeping Forest Rights Act in 2006. The subsequent implementation of this law has turned it into an open-ended process for converting forests to farms and homesteads, even within tiger reserves.

The politically correct ideology and the fuzzy conservation science endorsed by the Tiger Task Force created a tiger management model that has mostly benefited a bloated forest bureaucracy. The United Progressive Alliance (UPA) government that came to power in 2004 began funding tiger reserves heavily, with ever larger park budgets, something the present National Democratic Alliance (NDA) government has faithfully followed after 2014, without even changing a comma.

A few tiger reserves where tigers had already recovered continue to be overfunded, while other areas with higher recovery potential remain neglected. New tiger reserves were created not relying on any scientific criteria, but simply based on the whims and fancies of individual officials and influential tiger conservationists.

The foresters who managed tiger reserves have been entirely seduced by the "ecodevelopment" paradigm sired by the World Bank and adopted by the

NTCA. These ecodevelopment activities merely duplicate what other government agencies and nongovernmental organizations do. The far more urgent need for voluntary village relocation has generally slowed down following the enactment of the FRA. Exceptions have been in the states of Madhya Pradesh and Maharashtra, where major relocation initiatives were executed because of the admirable focus and consensus among local officials and conservationists.

The worst was yet to come. Under the original mandate of Project Tiger, after tightening up protection, tiger habitats were supposed to be left alone to regenerate, letting tiger and prey densities reach levels natural to each habitat type. However, flush with funds and opportunities for corruption, many reserve managers came up with plans to further "improve" and "develop" the tiger's natural habitats. They hired their cronies, often retired forest officials, as consultants to prepare tiger conservation plans (TCPs) for reserves.

These TCPs have been expensive disasters. Often there is no justification for the prescriptions in the TCPs, which included massive civil works using earthmoving machinery, diversion and impounding of stream flows, formation of dense networks of redundant forest roads, wholesale removal of long-naturalized exotic plants, and artificial planting of trees, grasses, and shrubs to "provide food" for wildlife. There are even ancillary plans targeting individual species such as squirrels and birds, as though they were being managed in captivity. Any excuse to splurge is welcomed with open arms.

Unscientific management of tiger habitats has negative impacts on natural biodiversity.

Just the template for the preparation of a TCP ran into 150 pages; the TCP for a park like Nagarahole exceeded eight hundred pages of text and tables. All this verbiage has buried the simple dictum of doing nothing for tiger habitats unless the need is demonstrated by science.

The "consultants" who prepare the TCPs reap rich rewards, too. The Annual Plan of Operation (AOP) that allocates funds to activities identified by the TCP has gained sepulchral sanctity and priority over all else. These AOPs have become the stations where the gravy train stops every fiscal year to unload its largesse.

All these activities go against the very grain of the goal set at the beginning of tiger recovery in India in late 1960s: to maintain the natural densities of tigers, prey, and other forms of natural biodiversity, in as intact a condition as possible.

The previously low densities of prey species—and hence tigers—were consequences of excessive hunting and competition with livestock. After these pressures are eliminated, the densities of prey species typically rose to levels that are natural for a particular forest type, a process that may take a couple of decades. The tiger densities track the rising prey densities and eventually reach levels sustainable on the abundance of prey. In the entire process the management objective should be to maintain the vegetation and water resources in as natural a state as possible. Unnecessary interventions to "improve" forage, cover conditions, and water flows are contrary to the needs of maintaining the entire ecological community in as near a natural state as possible.

This is where the management of wildlife differs radically from that of domesticated livestock. However, the entire TCP-AOP exercise is predicated on misguided interventions to continually raise prey and tiger densities through artificial enrichments of habitat.

As far as the buffer areas of tiger reserves are concerned, the goal itself was set as "ecodevelopment." The template for such ecodevelopment had been set by the disastrous World Bank project in the 1990s. Under the NTCA dispensation it was more of the same, plus a plethora of other redundant rural development activities.

Clearly, the very motivation behind this "tiger conservation on steroids" is suspect. Its implementation is rife with both ecological ignorance and naked avarice. The consultants who created these tiger conservation plans, the officials who implemented them, and other consultants who evaluated their outcomes are all drawn from the same forest bureaucracy. This has ensured that deep conflicts of interest are endemic to the entire system of managing tigers in India.

The care and concern with which the Indian public had responded to the tiger crisis has been leveraged into a war on tiger ecology and nature itself, even within the few strongholds where tiger populations have recovered. While these tiger refuges were turned into tiger Disneylands, densities of common tiger prey species like chital and sambar often rose well above what they would be if the forest habitat had been left alone. Excessive densities of a few ungulate species have consequences: the plant communities that the animals forage on became less diverse, with plant species that withstand such pressures gradually dominating more fragile species.

Densities of some prey species, such as chital in Nagarahole and Bandipur, are now three to four times greater than those in a more natural forest. In the heavily manipulated tourism zones of Nagarahole and Bandipur, they now exceed eighty deer per square kilometer, in comparison to their "natural" levels of twenty to thirty animals.

In these over-enriched hotspots, tiger populations are at densities never seen in the past. Because of the improved survival of cubs and juveniles, their rebound has also quickened. But the downside of these unnaturally high tiger densities has been more intraspecific aggression, shorter male tiger tenures, and quicker turnover of territories. A further consequence of this intensified turnover is the higher number of "problem tigers" in the landscapes around tiger reserves.

My basic point is simple: if the same conservation investments had been deployed more evenly across a larger area of tiger habitats, by ratcheting up antipoaching operations instead of pumping resources into "habitat improvements," it is likely that prey and tiger densities would have been somewhat lower at these hotspots, but more evenly spread across a larger area. The way to having a larger tiger population overall should be through the expansion of tiger populations at reasonable natural densities. The present "tiger conservation on steroids" is a function of misplaced funding priorities, rather than any rational science-based, long-term vision for tiger recovery.

In a meeting of the National Tiger Conservation Authority in 2009, I had proposed that tiger reserves should be constrained by a "zero-based budgeting" policy. Except for basic antipoaching efforts, fire protection, and voluntary resettlements of families, any funding sought by park managers for the "development" of tiger habitats should be negated unless the need is evident from scientific research.

There was a brief aha moment when the minister showed momentary enthusiasm for my idea. Nothing changed in practice, however. There were too many stakeholders among officials who felt things were just fine as they were. In fact, the creation of the NTCA has greatly slackened the financial and audit processes in tiger reserves, making it far easier to splurge money on unwarranted schemes cooked up by officials writing the TCPs and AOPs.

In 1994, to make Prime Minister Rao, who was single-mindedly focused on economic and foreign policy issues, to pay some attention to India's tiger recovery, some of us led by Valmik had lobbied Minister Kamal Nath to establish a Global Tiger Forum (GTF). Gradually a clutch of south Asian countries under India's political influence—Bhutan, Nepal, Bangladesh, and Myanmar—joined the GTF. Some Southeast Asian countries in which tigers are extinct, such as Cambodia, Vietnam (a country whose wildlife trade drove tiger extinctions) and the United Kingdom as well as some nongovernmental organizations also became members.

Over the years, GTF has turned into a platform for holding one glitzy international celebratory tiger event or the other. Who wouldn't like to hang out partying for the cause of the cat in resorts like Nusa Dua in Bali, or Hua Hin in Thailand? At a side event of one such tiger conference, I was flabbergasted by the sight of voluptuous Indonesian models dressed in the most economical of bikinis, all painted up to look like tigers, standing around in the auditorium in varied postures imitating the big cat!

However, despite being lavishly wined and dined over the years, several major tiger nations have balked at joining the GTF. It is not hard to figure out why. The GTF has been entirely dominated by Indian bureaucrats. The original rules of the GTF have been conveniently twisted to maintain this Indian stranglehold. Although the powerful position of the secretary-general is supposed to rotate among member nations, for over a quarter century only Indian officials have occupied the chair, with the current incumbent clinging on like a barnacle for over two decades!

The headquarters of the GTF, supposed to rotate among member states, remains ensconced in a swanky office in Delhi. Even the mighty World Bank and the Global Environmental Facility have failed in their attempts to pry the GTF loose from India and move it to a location in Southeast Asia.

The tiger's plight, and its global cultural appeal, have convinced even Russian president Vladimir Putin and former president of the World Bank Robert

Zoellick to champion the animal's cause. There is already buzz about the next summit coming up in Vladivostok, Russia, although the freezing weather may prevent models in bikinis from attending.

It is amazing to see the extent to which spin has replaced substance in the narrative around India's tiger conservation efforts. On World Tiger Day, July 29, 2021, the Global Tiger Forum celebrated the increase in India's putative tiger numbers to about three thousand, apparently well before the targeted date. At the same time, the GTF's secretary-general timidly asked Indians not to aspire, ever, to seek more than thirty-five hundred wild tigers in their vast, beautiful country.

No one can dispute that India has done more for the cause of the tiger than any other range nation. I have personally witnessed the heroic efforts of forestry officials and staff in the first three decades of that effort. However, the fact remains that the tiger population has only nudged up from about two thousand animals in 1970 when these recovery efforts began to the current number of around three thousand. This implies an annual growth rate lower than 1 percent, 0.08 percent to be precise. India is a country with 3.2 million square kilometers of land, of which 380,000 square kilometers is potential tiger habitat. India also is the sixth-largest economy in the world, aspiring to hit a trillion dollars in size by 2030. Furthermore, the country is rapidly industrializing and urbanizing. Its huge educated population is rooting for the tiger. The state funding of tiger conservation, with substantial additional contributions from the nongovernmental sector, has also been massive. Yet astonishingly, India's blinkered tiger bureaucracy can only set a low bar of thirty-five hundred tigers as the recovery goal for India's national animal. Even back-of-the-envelope calculations can show that India has the potential to hold ten thousand to fifteen thousand wild tigers. What is lacking is the necessary vision, and a pragmatic plan to get to that goal in the next few decades.

In support of my claim, I have portrayed what I personally witnessed in the Malenad landscape of about twenty-five thousand square kilometers in the last five decades. My observations suggest there likely were only seventy to one hundred tigers in this landscape in late 1960s, when I had feared they would all soon be gone. The recovery of wild tigers that followed, against all odds, was the work of dedicated foresters and conservationists under the determined political leadership of Indira Gandhi. There are now about 350 to 400 wild tigers in Malenad, an increase of about 4 percent per year from those early days. Based on my research, Malenad forests can potentially harbor at least 1,300 wild tigers.

How we can attain this lofty yet attainable goal depends crucially on turning India's landscapes beyond the tiger reserves to be more friendly to the big cat.

Tiger Tourism: Discontents and Promise

By the late 1980s the tiger's popularity was attracting hordes of affluent and middle-class visitors to the reserves. Managing these undisciplined tourists was becoming an additional burden for India's tiger reserve managers. Outside my field camp in Nagarahole, busloads of noisy tourists arrived daily, took quick tours in the rickety green government vans, and departed as noisily as they had come. Some among them were picnickers who brought bottles of liquor, looking to party in the jungle. I once asked a teenager, who was busy chasing a herd of chital, what he thought he was doing. He smiled broadly and innocently, and replied, "I am just having a lot of fun!" Another time, a car full of obviously drunk youth screeched to a halt next to forest guard Subbayya, and asked where they could be sure of seeing "the most ferocious animals." Perfectly poker-faced, Subbayya had pointed them down the paved road to Kutta town, telling them to drive exactly twelve kilometers.

Although the tourism overload affects many species in varied ways, I will focus here on the specific kind of tiger-centric tourism in India, which has broad appeal across the world. By 2012, the tiger tourism pressure had escalated, and conservationists were filing court cases seeking tighter regulation, leading to legal battles with the tourism industry and park managers.

Lobbyists for tiger tourism make the following arguments in its favor: wild tiger populations in India have recovered *because* tourists and tour guides have been keeping a vigil around tigers; public support for tiger conservation will evaporate and nature education suffer if tiger-centric tourism is stopped; and tiger tourism provides significant economic benefits to local communities, thereby ensuring social support for tiger protection.

The conservation activists who oppose tiger tourism trot out their counterarguments with equal passion: wild tigers need peace and quiet, and tourists crowding the parks are a significant threat to their survival; it is unfair to curtail cattle grazing and forest exploitation by local villagers, but permit rich tourists from afar to come and watch tigers; and the ever-increasing numbers of tourist facilities are fragmenting and isolating tiger habitats and degrading them by sucking away water and woody biomass from the forests.

Then there is the omnipresent Indian bureaucracy, in this case officials dealing with the departments of forests and tourism at both the federal and state levels. Given a chance, they would like to take over all aspects of tiger tourism, all in the cat's cause, of course. My own state of Karnataka has already established such a government monopoly over tiger tourism.

The reality of the "tourists versus tigers" issue is more nuanced. It is simply not true that tiger tourism has led to recovery of wild tigers in India. The high-end tiger-centric tourism occupies less than 10 percent of the area out of the 70,000 square kilometers in tiger reserves. If we consider all of India's potential tiger habitats, some 380,000 square kilometers, the fraction affected by tiger tourism drops to a mere 1.3 percent.

Even more important, in the past decades, nowhere and at no time has tiger tourism been the causal driver of tiger population recoveries. Tiger recoveries have typically taken twenty to thirty years of hard struggle by the forest staff and conservationists, as well as sacrifices made by village communities coerced into giving up access to forest resources, or compensated to relocate. Tourists arrive after wildlife has rebounded. Clearly the claim that the tourism industry led these tiger recoveries does not have a leg to stand on.

The tourism lobby's second argument, that public support for tigers will be lost if high-end tiger-centric tourism ends, is also shaky, because most local people simply cannot afford this kind of tourism. However, the third argument, that high-end tiger tourism generates benefits to local communities around the reserves in the form of employment, and augments the local economy in many ways, is true, although the bulk of the revenues earned is commandeered by tour companies in faraway cities.

The biotic pressures driven by tourism on tiger habitats—both the high-end as well as the inexpensive type catering to local tourists—are becoming a serious problem. Despite this, the level of disturbance inflicted by tiger tourism is simply not on the same scale as the earlier damage from illegal hunting, livestock grazing, and forest extractions by local communities, which it has replaced.

Furthermore, the tigers at the center of tourist attention are only a few habituated individuals in some reserves. They form a tiny proportion of the tiger populations in most landscapes. Even these habituated tigers, if they feel harassed, can easily move out of sight of the tourists. The argument that tourists watching a few habituated tigers is an existential threat to tiger populations is an exaggeration.

However, for me personally, watching a bored-looking tiger surrounded by noisy, gawking tourists jammed into vans, is not a turn-on! It can never match the intense, near mystical feeling of anticipating a tiger while soaking up myriad other sounds, smells, and sensations of the jungle while I wait for the tiger. I worry that the rush to tick the box of having watched a tiger has desensitized the tourists to all other gifts of wild nature.

I find the proposal that the entire tiger tourism business should be owned and operated by government officials totally unconvincing. The truth is, just like scientific research, nature education, or wildlife moviemaking, tourism is also a part of the spectrum of activities that constitutes tiger conservation. All these activities would be managed far more creatively by domain experts, rather than forest official jacks-of-all-trades. Being out there with a gifted natural history guide itself is an experience that a bureaucratic system cannot deliver. Whether the management of tiger tourism should be under the domain of large companies, local private businesses, or other traditional authorities should depend on the site-specific economic and cultural setting.

Going beyond such details, I would argue, it is now incumbent on the tiger tourism industry in India to move beyond microscale "greenwashing," with token gestures like changing room linens less often, painting the lodges green, or recycling garbage better. It should begin to address how the tiger's magical appeal to affluent tourists can be harnessed as a new force to drive the expansion of tiger habitats and repopulate the cats on a scale never thought possible.

Toward this end, Krithi and I had proposed a Tiger Habitat Expansion Model (THEM, for short) as a tourism policy option in 2012. There are two key factors that might possibly make this model work by compelling the tourism industry to act.

Across India, political leaders wary of likely curbs on local farmers and enterprises are now resisting the creation of new tiger reserves or the expansion of old ones. Yet clearly, in a country with 3.2 million square kilometers of land, earmarking a mere 70,000 square kilometers for tiger reserves is not adequate to sustain viable tiger populations. Furthermore, many of the present tiger source populations are getting isolated from one another. Their insularity is being aggravated by intrusions of new linear infrastructure projects for railways, highways, and waterways.

The basic tiger habitat problems above can be resolved only if there is a major shift in the way the landscapes around and between tiger reserves are used. Such landscapes, which are now hostile to tigers, should be transformed to be friendlier to them.

Neither government fiats nor romantic illusions about harmonious coexistence between tigers and the rural poor have the power to drive land-use changes at the necessary spatial scale. How then can we induce voluntary shifts in land use favoring tigers? Individuals buying small patches of land with altruistic motives, as some people are now doing, while welcome, cannot expand tiger habitats at the required scale.

When I reflect on the scale of some voluntary land-use changes in Malenad that occurred during the nineteenth and twentieth centuries, I see large expanses of tiger habitats that were first deforested by farmers. No surprises there! More intriguing are some changes in cropping patterns that changed land use rapidly and at large scales. Among such episodes, the conversion of private woodlands for growing coffee, the conversion of rice fields to grow areca nut palms in the humid zones, and the shift from millet grains to hybrid corn, cotton, or tobacco in the drier zone stand out. In all these instances, the shift was driven by market forces. In each case, demand for the new crop by consumers far away was the incentive. These were the local consequences of globalization.

What caused farmers to give up traditional crops was pure economics. Individual households switched to new crops because they earned more money or enjoyed better markets. Sometimes the shortage of local labor or the impact of novel plant diseases swayed them.

Under the habitat expansion model we proposed, economic demand for more tiger tourism would trigger the necessary change: for more tigers to be watched by more rich tourists, more tiger habitats will be needed outside the tiny present-day reserves. While die-hard socialist opponents of commercial entrepreneurship of any kind may oppose this idea, undeniably the tourism industry does have a fundamental self-interest, beyond altruism, in expanding tiger habitats.

Here is the thing: except for rhetorical grandstanding, all serious political players in India—except the fringe elements on the left and the right—now support rapid industrialization and urbanization driven by private capital. Every other economic sector in India, including defense manufacturing, has embraced privatization. In this context, the argument that tiger tourism should remain an exceptional socialist island does not appear to be reasonable.

However, our model can work only if the owners of the lands converted to tiger habitats can earn higher profits, consistently, year after year, after they give up traditional crops. Only if that happens could tiger habitat expansion at the necessary spatial scale materialize.

The land acquisitions I had initiated with WCS funds in Kudremukh were small-scale examples of such outcomes. They did result in necessary ecological changes as the land turned fallow and the wildlife returned. However, high land prices in Malenad (and many parts of India), sometimes $50,000 to $75,000 for every hectare, make it harder for the economics to work at a large scale, as it does in parts of Africa, the American West, and Latin America where land is far cheaper. For example, when the economics worked, African beef ranchers first switched to game-hunting reserves and later to wildlife tourism, exploiting the presence of lions, rhinos, and other spectacular animals, which replaced the boring old cows.

In India, creating a private, for-profit conservancy of the right size—say twenty square kilometers, the size of a typical tourism zone in a tiger reserve—would require stitching together a land-quilt involving several dozen farming families. If the land is already being profitably farmed, the alternative profits from tiger tourism must be sufficiently higher to make the shift attractive. Much would depend on the specifics of economic feasibility. Even if the economics works, the social management necessary to assemble a cooperative of dozens of feisty farmers will be a formidable challenge.

Even a few decades ago I would have found this idea inconceivable. However, since those days, Indian society has been changing rapidly. Rapid economic growth has created a large, urbanized, affluent class of millions of people, with substantial disposable incomes. They are now thronging to tiger reserves in numbers impossible to imagine when tiger recovery efforts began half a century ago.

Unlike in Africa, where the luxury wildlife tourism depends on foreign tourists and is subject to vagaries of international travel—as amply demonstrated by the recent COVID-19 crisis—an overwhelming majority of Indian tiger tourists are local citizens, potentially ensuring the sustainability of income flows to the new tiger conservancies.

I would argue that tiger tourism should be reinvented so that its economic power can be harnessed to expand tiger habitats and augment tiger populations outside government-owned reserves. If such a radical shift does not happen, tiger tourism will largely continue to be a mere nuisance confined to tiger reserves, rather than a game changer for national tiger recovery, which it can be.

Given the tiger tourism industry's lack of foresight in the past, steering it in the right direction requires both a carrot and a stick. The carrot is to modify India's land laws to make it easier for wildlife tourism operators to gain access to privately owned farmland on long-term leases, or by coopting the farmers as shareholders. The stick should be to impose regulations that reduce, and eventually eliminate, the present ugly, unsustainable tiger tourism from government-owned reserves. These reserves should be primarily libraries and laboratories of nature, to fulfill the scientific and educational needs of India's citizens, youth, and students.

The present trend of promoting India's last tiger wildernesses as playgrounds for the rich, to meet their needs for entertainment, adventure sport, and "wellness," is not viable in the long run. There is no room in India's remnant wilds to create American-style national parks teeming with millions of citizens picnicking or driving around in cars, snowmobiles, and all-terrain vehicles.

Although farm holdings are smaller and land prices higher, India does enjoy some unique advantages over African countries in creating private wildlife conservancies: the demographic shift away from farming to the manufacturing and service sectors; the increasing unviability of small-scale agriculture, labor shortages, dependence on migrant labor, the reduction in cattle numbers, and grazing pressure; and rising rural wages and affordability of farm-raised protein to replace bushmeat consumption.

There are also cultural factors, such as higher tolerance of large wildlife species closer to human settlements; rising levels of education and technical skills in the rural populace; and the loosening of traditional ties to the land. While such factors vary across regions, the opportunities for private tiger conservancies do appear to exist in parts of India, including Malenad.

I am not suggesting this strategy would be easy to formulate or implement. However, there are durable examples of the Indian corporate sector's partnerships with farmers. Agribusinesses related to tobacco, coffee, tea, rubber, bamboo, quick-growing tree species, floriculture, and even horticulture have successfully induced land-use change at large scales across India. The social skills, patience, and institutional culture required are more often found in the agro-corporate sector than in the tourism industry, with its slick culture of instant gratification.

Whoever is going to be the agent for change in tiger tourism needs to be driven by profit and efficiency, rather than government diktats or unrealistic expectations of altruism. However, governmental policy changes that encourage—rather than discourage, as at present—necessary land-use changes can surely help.

9 | HOW THE TIGER CAN REGAIN ITS STRIPES

WE NEED TO SAVE TIGERS FOR OUR OWN GOOD. Their habitats shelter myriad other life-forms whose genes are imprinted with millions of lines of code. This unexplored library has immense potential to fulfill our growing need for novel medicines, foods, fuels, and fibers for the impending post-petroleum era. The same tiger habitats also protect precious soil and water resources on which millions depend. These practical reasons for recovering wild nature are at the core of the global consensus for sustainable development.

Moreover, saving tigers can be further justified based on aesthetic sensibilities, and our ingrained bond with animals—the "biophilia" of biologist Ed Wilson. I get Wilson: I am hardwired to love wild tigers for reasons I cannot explain.

Western religions expediently believe wild nature exists solely for the sake of humanity. The ancient Asian faiths, in contrast, recognize the intrinsic rights of other species to exist. This belief has been a factor—but not the only factor—in helping India's wildlife survive many past social turbulences. However, such beliefs did not prevent the extinction from India of the Javan and Sumatran rhinos, cheetah, banteng, and the pink-headed duck. Many other species—tiger, lion, one-horned rhino, and the great Indian bustard—have been evicted from most habitats.

Some advocates of animal rights argue each individual animal, domestic or wild, should enjoy the same rights as any human individual. Ethologist Marc Bekoff argues in favor of such "compassionate conservation." My own experience is that such a position has little utility for solving the all-too-real contradictions between wild tigers and people.

Professional wildlife conservationists tending to endangered species are, however, compelled to eradicate harmful pests and runaway exotic species. Occasionally they are compelled to kill individuals of threatened species. In other cases—fisheries for instance—they regulate the harvest of wild species. Within the framework of scientific wildlife conservation, conceding a right to survive to every individual animal becomes impossible. Even among endangered species, not all can enjoy equal rights. The degree of rarity and level of endangerment of species are weighed against their cultural appeal or economic value while setting conservation priorities.

What kind of moral compass can guide tiger conservation? Animal welfarists seem to argue that every individual animal should have a right to live. This is easy to preach, but impossible to practice. It leads to contradictions like the great Buddha's *Avatar* preaching kindness toward animals while also enjoying beefsteaks.

So, despite the precarious status of wild tigers, I cannot justify animal rights as the basis for pleading their cause. The moment I do, tigers will be democratically outvoted by the billions of dogs, cats, and cattle that can also claim such individual rights.

Going a step further, in theory every society accepts the equal right of each human being to live and be free. In practice, all societies constrain such rights for the common good. People struggling to protect their own individual right to life and liberty will not concede priority to the "rights" of every wild tiger.

Economic demographers predict the planet's human population will plateau at ten billion by the year 2050, and then begin to decline. For achieving this transient supremacy, during a mere 0.25 percent of the time after life evolved on Earth some 3.5 billion years ago, human *individuals* have ruthlessly stamped out thousands of animal *species*. The notion that same humans will enforce the right to life for every individual tiger, man-eaters included, is a kindly delusion.

During the last twelve thousand years of the Holocene, the rights of the individuals of our own species have clearly ridden roughshod over the rights of many other species. The advocates of human emancipation—emancipators for short—often assume wild animal species are not impacted by the rapid increases in human population density, life expectancy, and material consumption levels. The impact of the all-too-real human needs for space, water, energy, food, sanitation, and health care do not figure in the calculus of the emancipators. They also tend to ignore the positive conservation impacts of modernity—education, technologies, and culture—that result from behavioral changes among the same people whose cause they espouse. The blind promotion of the "traditionally harmonious" coexistence between tigers and human societies in transition to modernity will neither enhance human welfare nor bring back tigers.

I also worry that such faith among the emancipators sometimes arises from a feeling of personal guilt about the human deprivations they see in the society. Ironically, their promotion of human-tiger coexistence results in the persistence of the very same deprivations they feel guilty about. This moral feat only becomes possible by romanticizing such deprivation and hardships as some spiritually exalted state of existence. Of course, people compelled to live next to tigers will also sometimes echo such arguments, to gain an extra acre of land to plow or one more pound of bushmeat for the pot. However, when given the real chance to escape their forced coexistence with tigers to reach toward modernity, most people grab it.

Fifty years ago, when I began to plead the cause of the tiger with decision-makers, they did not respond with such academic sophistry about the assumed human-tiger harmony. Their answers were informed and honest: "The needs of poor people override that of tigers. Where there is no room for both, the tiger must go."

There are many other wild animal species that can coexist with certain traditional lifestyles when human population densities are low and cultural tolerance high. But this fact in no way negates the urgency for reducing negative human impacts on other threatened species like the tiger, which cannot do so.

Finally, I can only see a tentative moral arc: wild tigers should have the right to survive *as a species*. I believe the world will be a much poorer place for us without tigers. I can even say this is a matter of faith with me!

Who Should Save the Tiger?

Saving tigers has been one of the toughest challenges to conservationists. Millions of dollars have been sunk into the enterprise with relatively low returns. Can tiger conservation be made more effective as well as benefit people?

To create more habitats for tigers, people must occupy far less land for farming and energy production than they do now. These two land uses are our most expansive encroachments on tiger habitats. Each acre of land under human exploitation should be made to yield more farm produce and cleaner, denser energy. These efficiencies alone can ensure more land remains for tigers on this earth, even after Bezos, Musk, and Branson and their acolytes relocate to other places in the cosmos.

The technological and social transformations necessary to bring the tiger back require the right agents of change. Despite the admirable conservation investments made by governments so far, the bureaucracies that managed tigers have failed to dream big or act boldly. By their very self-serving nature they cannot. For all the official hype and hoopla, after half a century of effort, reproducing tiger populations now occupy barely 1 percent of their former range. Tigers have been wiped out from two-thirds of the countries they lived in two hundred years ago. Any number of glitzy international tiger summits where conservationists of all hues strut like peacocks does not change that grim reality.

Marxist economist Michal Kalecki had astutely foreseen that socialist bureaucracies established to promote egalitarianism would themselves turn into a powerful ruling class. This process has steadily advanced in the tiger-conservation world. Even the once independent and feisty nongovernmental conservationists and scientists have begun to genuflect before the socialist oligarchies that now run tiger conservation.

However, in the rest of society, by the end of the twentieth century, economic monopolies run by bureaucracies had been abandoned even in Russia and China. All former tiger range countries are now run under mixed economies driven by private enterprise. This choice has been made by countries that are electoral democracies as well as dictatorships under generals, commissars, or theocrats.

Tiger conservation must draw on this human entrepreneurial spirt, which has been so successful in other domains. Going forward, the omnibus role of the government in tiger conservation should shrink and be confined to law enforcement. This is a truly vital role, requiring a single-minded focus devoid of mission-drift.

The big, bureaucratic tent under which tiger conservation has been smothered has to be dismantled. The role of the forest bureaucracy should be only to protect the tiger from people and people from tigers. The present government monopoly over tiger research, monitoring, nature education, tourism, filmmaking, and voluntary village relocation should end. The vast untapped reservoir of talent, experience, and energy in these diverse domains that exists should be proactively applied to bring tigers back. Such talents do exist in abundance in the local communities, nongovernmental organizations, scientific institutions, and private enterprises.

After fifty years, India's much-touted tiger recovery model needs a total reboot. It must catch up with the nation's significant achievements and ambitions in other domains such as agriculture, technology, industry, commerce, education, and health care. A country of 3.2 million square kilometers, with the capacity to land a spacecraft on Mars, should set itself loftier conservation goals. It is absurd for some mid-level bureaucrat parked in GTF to decide that India can only aspire to harbor thirty-five hundred tigers. Such an overarching vision for India's national animal can be enabled only by the prime minister, wisely guided both by the success of Indira Gandhi and the failure of Manmohan Singh.

Setting Off with a Faulty Compass

The key to bringing back the tiger is to avoid distractions along the way. The tiger's charisma and popular appeal will ensure such distractions will proliferate. Everyone wants a piece of the tiger action by indulging in fuzzy thinking, misguided compassion, and inflated media hype. Hundreds of thousands of dollars evaporate into ill-thought-out "tiger initiatives," campaigns, and summits that are nothing more than fashion statements.

Over the years, both government bureaucracies and nongovernmental players have turned the fearsome big cat into a fecund cash cow. Among the tiger's newfound champions are also hordes of Luddites and ideologues who oppose economic development, modern agriculture, efficient energy production, and even the historical trends of demographic transition.

Tigers need far more extensive habitats to face the sporadic shocks delivered by the growing economies, trying to deliver what people need. This means less and less land must produce more and more food, raw materials, and energy to meet the rising human needs.

I am skeptical of ecologists' proposals that modern humans should voluntarily scale back to simpler and happier lives. Some of them suggest we go all the way back to live as hunter-gatherers; other prophets choose different intermediate stops for this reverse time travel. However, wherever we stop, for the average human being life would be far, far harder. Philosopher Thomas Hobbes had pointed out that life of the primitive man was "solitary, poor, nasty, brutish, and short." Probably even more so for the primitive woman. Psychologist Steven Pinker has demonstrated that, our impressions to the contrary, human society *has* progressively become less violent and strife-torn over time.

In this context, I find merit in the "ecomodernists'" view that we should rely on proven technologies with the least impact on natural wild areas. For instance, modern nuclear power generation and agricultural genetic engineering are such proven tools. I believe this approach has a better chance to make more room for tigers on earth than alternatives glibly offered by modern-day Luddites as well as the "petroleum forever" climate skeptics. I believe I am in good company: for instance, environmental scientist James Lovelock, the originator of the Gaia theory in 1969, and the icon of the old counterculture Stewart Brand, creator of *The Whole Earth Catalog* in 1968. While one can quibble with the ecomodernist's techno-optimistic framework for restoring wildlands, based on my own experience, it appears to be more practical than any other.

With each previous technological revolution, we Hominins (the apelike humans) have effectively escaped from the harsher and crueler life of our ancestors. Along the way, we developed better and better technologies: artificial fire, stone tools, language, cooperative hunting, domestication of plants and animals, metallurgy, and chemistry. Then came the game changer: production of mechanical energy by burning coal in the nineteenth century. Subsequent inventions led to electricity, telephony, wireless, nuclear energy, biotechnology, electronics, and the present information age. The invention of modern medicine prolonged the short life span of the "noble savage" by decades. I believe, rhetoric aside, no modern human society will choose to walk backward from all this progress.

There will be, of course, pretense in plenty around this aspiration for turning the clock back. However, such tokens—Mahatma Gandhi being a prime example—will not even remotely be on the massive scale necessary to achieve the reverse time travel desired by Luddites. I take this as a given; I think the path to recovering wild tigers cannot rely on that faulty compass.

My experiences buttress my submissions. In my own lifetime, I witnessed three major sociocultural upheavals led by charismatic leaders who tried to persuade their followers to voluntarily shun technological progress: Mahatma Gandhi during India's struggle for freedom; Chairman Mao through his cultural revolution in China; and the Western counterculture movement. Although the masses adored these prophets, in practice their ideas were abandoned whole-sale, except as faddish tokens. Gandhi's vision of a booming cottage industry based on handspun cloth has given way to a petroleum and polyester empire owned by Asia's richest man. The scientists, whom Mao banished to rural farms, have returned with a bang to land China's spacecrafts on Mars. The peacenik counterculture in the West has morphed into a crass entertainment industry worth trillions.

Conservationists often say tigers are a "conservation-dependent species." However, in my view, to be effective it is also a time for conservation itself to become a less ideology-dependent species.

An Optimist's View: Bringing the Tiger Back

According to the narrow definition of science favored by the practitioners of harder sciences like physics, chemistry, and laboratory biology, reliable knowledge can emerge only from rigorous controlled experiments. However, in other sciences, such as geology or paleontology, where such reductionist experimentation is impossible, scientific models arise from observations and induction. In economics and other "dismal sciences," because human whims also play a key role, the modeling of reality becomes even more uncertain.

I have come to realize that while my measurements and understanding of tiger ecology may be somewhat exact, their application to conservation is fraught with great uncertainties. Tiger conservation is also a "dismal science" needing much reflection at every step. Yet, when confronted by narratives inflated by nothing more than political correctness or Luddite hot air, many conservation scientists seem to be ducking the challenge. Increasingly, academic conservation science is becoming a parade of fashionable nonsense.

As I have muddled through my own career, wearing the hat of engineer, farmer, conservation advocate, and finally tiger ecologist, the results I have accumulated range from the relatively exact to the highly unpredictable. The former consists of carefully collected ecological data, whereas the latter are largely outcomes of human actions. Given this experience, I submit that two environmental proposals for recovering wild nature appear more likely to suc-ceed in the specific context of recovering tigers.

Neither proposal is new. Both emerged from accumulated empirical obser-vations, when their proponents realized conventional approaches to wildlife conservation were not making headway. On the other hand, traditional economic development on its own was not delivering conservation either. I will briefly examine these two proposals in the context of my own lived experience among the tigers of Malenad.

The mantra of sustainable development has been, for the past fifty or so years, the recommended medicine to overcome contradictions between the twin goals of human emancipation and nature conservation. No one can disagree with this noble goal.

Conservation thinker John Robinson has, however, robustly critiqued the underlying conflation of conservation (saving other species) with development (making life better for our own species), which is the fig leaf covering inherent contradictions in the sustainable development concept. His alternative proposal for "sustainable landscapes" offers a framework for resolving these contradictions. Robinson's scheme for "carving up tomorrow's world" purposefully segregates landscapes. Some are earmarked for the strict protection of nature and species that are threatened by human impacts. Others are reserved for some types of agriculture and land uses compatible with the ecologies of select wild species. In the third category are landscapes under intensive agriculture, industry, and urban settlements on which modern technologies can flourish.

Robinson's concept of sustainable landscapes stands on defensible science rather than the vague "sustainable development everywhere" model. It does not wish away social aspirations for techno-economic progress. I believe it can mediate better between the real contradictions that exist between tiger survival and human progress.

Undoubtedly, the application of the sustainable landscapes model to tiger recovery will present many scientific challenges. Success will also depend on evolving the necessary social and political consensuses at the right spatial scales. Nevertheless, I believe this approach is more likely to work than the alternative of perpetuating the conflation of conservation with human development: basket weaving does not save tigers.

I believe the sustainable landscapes approach and the "ecomodernist" framework for decoupling development from nature form a good mutual fit. Ted Nordhaus, Michel Shallenberger, Stewart Brand, and others have promoted ecomodernism as an alternative to the blind rejection of technology or mindless endorsement of economic development without concern for nature.

Sustaining Landscapes for Tigers

I will leave the details of dovetailing the proposals of Robinson and the ecomodernists to others and focus on their relevance to the Malenad tiger landscape.

As far as the present "tiger source populations" and areas earmarked for future tiger recovery are concerned, the decoupling of economic development and human extractive practices from nature reserves is inevitable and necessary. The key factor in such decoupling is the grain at which it is implemented. I believe the spatial scale for such decoupling should be an area capable of supporting a cluster of breeding tigers: to throw out an ambitious number, twenty-five breeding females, and a total of one hundred wild tigers.

In densely populated Asia, the decoupling of development from nature can take many forms. Some decoupling, in fact, has been underway in Malenad: the emigration of rural youth from remote tiger habitats to cities and smaller towns; the switch from wood fuel to hydrocarbons; the change from animal draft power to motorized, in both transportation and tilling; and the dietary switch from wild animal protein to farm-raised meat are examples that I witnessed. None of these quick shifts were ordained by any eco-prophet or dictated by any bureaucrat. They resulted from a combination of the carrot of economic development with the stick of wildlife law enforcement.

More opportunities for decoupling tiger habitats from development already exist or will arise soon in Malenad. A key one is the necessary switch in energy production from coal, hydroelectric, wind, and solar power projects to the compact and dense nuclear power, with its much smaller footprint on tiger habitats.

An excellent example is the 1,320-megawatt nuclear power plant at Kaiga near Kali Tiger Reserve commissioned in the year 2000. Its nuclear reactors occupy just 1.2 square kilometers of forest. It has worked flawlessly for twenty-one years so far. Had it not been built, forty million tons of coal would have already been burned to generate the same energy.

Two large hydro-projects in Malenad, with comparable capacities to the Kaiga plant, have drowned a total of 550 square kilometers of tiger habitats: these were as good as those in found in the Nagarahole, Bhadra, or Kali reserves.

A personal story: I had disagreed with my father, who was a truly inspirational figure, about the Kaiga power plant. He had written a well-informed popular book on the promise of nuclear energy in 1954, but was swayed by the doomsday prophesies of local Luddites when the Kaiga plant was being built. A quarter century after his death in 1997, I miss being able to prove him wrong about his anxieties.

Opportunities for decoupling also exist in building tiger-friendly infrastructure, such as modern tunnels and high-arch bridges instead of the multilane surface highways that are now ripping up fragile mountainous tiger habitats of Malenad. And, of course, most crucially, for incentivizing thousands of willing families to resettle to locations where roads, schools, hospitals, and jobs they desperately demand already exist. The present policy of delivering these services to the remotest corners of wilderness is a recipe for permanently fragmenting and degrading these last remaining tiger habitats.

Fifty years after I began roaming the forests of Malenad, there are now five times more tigers in these forests. In reserves like Nagarahole, where tigers boldly pose for photographers, their populations are ten times denser. There are also three times the number of people in Malenad. On average, these people are also ten times more economically better off.

Despite being densely populated by humans benefiting from rapid economic growth, Malenad and the surrounding Western Ghat areas now support over six hundred tigers. This is one of the largest wild tiger populations in the world. The process of economic development has not been only an enemy of the tiger, as I had feared in my youth. In strange and unpredictable ways, it has also helped tiger recovery before my very eyes.

Looking back, I see Malenad forests not as two-thirds empty of tigers, but as only one-third full. If the right lessons are learned, Malenad could harbor 1,300 tigers by 2050, when India's human population is predicted to plateau at 1.5 billion.

Even outside of Malenad, India has grown alongside its tiger population. Its economy is now ten times bigger, its human population three times larger, and its people five times more prosperous compared with half a century ago. Despite all this, it is clear to me that there is still room for more wild tigers in India.

This is all quite astonishing. While the future is far from secure for the Indian tiger, it is far brighter than it has been in decades. Densely populated by 1.3 billion people, India still has 380,000 square kilometers of potential tiger habitat. More encouraging still, if these forests can be nursed back to heath by employing proven means already at our disposal, they can provide enough habitat for fifteen thousand or more wild tigers. Finally, the promise of tiger recovery in India also offers a road map for recovering wild tigers across the world.

Tigers of the World

Tigers have fascinated us for millennia. Cave paintings of tigers in Bhimbhetka in central India are thought to be thirty thousand years old. An icon from India's Harappa civilization, one of the world's oldest at 3500 BCE, shows a woman fighting off two tigers. In local folklore and animistic traditions across Asia, the tiger has been worshipped as a spirit, a demigod, and an icon. Tigers also figure prominently in the Asian traditions that came after animism, such as Hinduism, Taoism, and Buddhism.

Three historical benchmarks illustrate the tiger's grip on human imagination. Around 350 BCE, Alexander's general, Selucus Nicator, displayed the first captive tiger to the Europeans. In 1200 CE, European globe-trotter Marco Polo recorded Mongol warriors on horseback spearing "striped lions." The tiger soon became established as a symbol of power and valor on the coats of arms of kings and generals across Asia and Europe. The Spanish discoverers of the New World, upon encountering another fearsome big cat, called the jaguar *el tigre*.

Soon the magnificent predator became a brand ambassador for modern political parties, sports teams, and universities, and for products ranging from automobiles to petroleum, beer, and breakfast cereals. The freakish tiger show of the Las Vegas entertainers Siegfried Fischbacher and Roy Horn enthralled its audiences for twelve long years, until one of its inbred white tigers attacked Horn, ending the show and, eventually, his life.

However, since then the tiger's popularity has only grown through an explosion of such entertainment shows, movies, natural history documentaries, and the all-pervasive social media. During 2020 an audience of thirty-four million people watched the Netflix hit show *Tiger King*, and in the first ten days over sixty-four million households sampled it. The outrageous cast of characters the show featured, and the shocking depiction of captive tigers in the "Land of the Free," had grabbed eyeballs like never before. Sadly, intent solely on entertaining its viewers, *Tiger King* missed a great opportunity to educate them about problems faced by wild tigers.

In the United States, China, and other countries, in addition to tigers in zoos, a thousand more are in ill-kept menageries, backyards, truck stops, and basements, compared with about five thousand wild tigers surviving across the 1.6 million square kilometers of remaining natural habitats.

Many among the swelling ranks of TV entertainers, movie stars, and social media influencers misleadingly promote themselves as saviors of tigers. They are becoming yet another major distraction from effective action necessary to bring back wild tigers. While exploiting the tiger's cultural appeal to line their own pockets, most of them distract the public from thinking seriously about real conservation needs of tigers.

Yet, in some way, even such distractions reassure me that the tiger will ultimately not be a lost cause. With so many people fascinated by tigers, I hope the odds of greater public support for tiger recovery will improve. If no one cared, as with that giant flightless pigeon, the Dodo of Mauritius (which was clubbed to extinction by Dutch sailors), the tiger could also go extinct. In my mind, the real challenge is to gently but firmly steer the millions of fans of the tiger away from such distractions toward informed actions.

Tigers, Burning Bright

Doomsday prophesies of the tiger's extinction have been around for a long time. In the 1930s the slayer of man-eating tigers, Jim Corbett, predicted its extinction in India by the 1950s, which came perilously close to reality. Even after the near miracle of their recovery in India after 1970, many of my tiger conservationist friends, the BBC, and *Time* magazine had all predicted the extinction of tigers by the year 2000. Now, two decades later, the tiger still hangs in there, albeit precariously.

Based on the evidence I have presented, bringing the tiger back will be difficult but not impossible. The willpower to save the tigers already exists, rooted deeply in our social psyche. That willpower must now be focused, laser-like, on actions that matter. Such focus can only come through a societal ability to separate the signal of science from the noisy hype around tigers.

That begins with facing the reality of the future: India, with 1.3 billion people, must cater to their desire for better lives in rapidly modernizing settings. Humans typically do not want to shun modernity to toil in remote forests, facing hostile elements and dangerous beasts. Their wannabe emancipators should stop pretending they do.

As I witness positive conservation transformations gaining traction in Thailand, Russia, Indonesia, or even China, I am convinced that we can make room for thousands more wild tigers elsewhere, too. Coupled with the ecological resilience of the tiger, this gives me hope the world could see the day when fifty thousand wild tigers would be roaming free.

Critics will scoff at this as a pipe dream. We're better off focusing on realistic goals, they would say. After all, fifty thousand tigers would be a tenfold increase over the current population guesstimate. However, a mere 150 years ago, trophy and bounty hunters were killing sixteen thousand tigers in India each year. This slaughter continued for a century before supplies ran out in the 1970s. Wherever the right tools were applied to their recovery, tigers have come roaring back.

To secure a bright future for wild tigers, in addition to protected reserves, new tools are needed. Economic development, urbanization, and modern technology, often perceived solely as enemies of the tiger, are in fact forging such tools. A deeper understanding of tigers is leading to new ideas at the intersection of conservation and development. While there are places where conservation and development can overlap, they must remain separate at other places to bring back tigers on the scale that is possible.

Tiger recovery is not a zero-sum game. We do not always have to choose between people and tigers, between concrete jungles and real wild places. It is true that people and tigers cannot live cheek by jowl inside small reserves, because that does not end well for either species. But both can still thrive if the vast and diverse landscapes of Asia can be sustainably managed using the full range of tools we already have at our command.

Across Asia, habitats where tigers once lived extend over twenty-three million square kilometers, more than the area of the United States and Canada combined. They can reoccupy a significant part of that expanse again, if abundant, dense, noncarbon energy and advanced agricultural biotechnology help us to rewild some of today's farms and pastures. Meanwhile, sensibly managed industrialization and urbanization can provide the necessary habitats for the humanity that is rapidly gravitating toward them.

I am hopeful that people's compassion for the tiger *as a species* will lead us to a world where fifty thousand *individual* wild tigers can roam free.

ACKNOWLEDGMENTS

I OWE DEBTS OF GRATITUDE to two broad categories of people:
First, those who assisted with the writing and production of this book.

Geoffrey Ward, for the warm, informative foreword, and the following colleagues and friends who contributed endorsements: George Schaller, Jeffrey Sachs, John Robinson, David Western, Mel Sunquist, Jim Nichols, Dale Miquelle, John Terborgh, Douglas Chadwick, Sy Montgomery, Ruth Padel, Thomas Kaplan, Valmik Thapar, Ruth De Fries, Stuart Pimm, David Quammen, and Bill deBuys.

For help in formulating the early versions of this manuscript, thanks to Jonathan Cobb, Jonathan Adams, Lisa Adams, and Rachel Nuwer. For technical support in the preparation of maps and help with some of the scientific information used, fact-checking and proofing, I am grateful to N. Samba Kumar and Chandan Pandey.

To Fiona Sunquist, Giri Cavale, Diinesh Kumble, Phillip Ross, Pranav Vajapeyam, Aditya Singh, and Niren Jain for generous permissions for the use of their splendid photographs.

I am grateful to my agent Jane Dystel and her team at Dystel, Goderich & Bourret and to my publisher, Chicago Review Press, including Jerome Pohlen, Benjamin Krapohl, Preston Pisellini, and their support teams.
Second, my deepest gratitude to those who are a part of the longer story.

Several individuals, some of whom are no more, including family members, friends, fellow scientists and conservationists, government officials, political functionaries, donors, conservation institutions, and governmental and nongovernmental agencies have played key roles in the events narrated here. Prominent among them are:

My father Kota Shivarama Karanth, wife Prathibha Karanth, and daughter Krithi Karanth.

Indian Forestry officials: Someshwar Shyam Sunder, D. K. Deshmukh, Sanjay Debroy, H. S. Panwar, S. Parameshwarappa, U. Taranath Alva, M. K. Appayya, A. C. Lakshmana, N. Sampangi, Prashant Kumar Sen, R. M. Palanna, M. G. Gogate,

C. Srinivasan, D. Yatish Kumar, P. J. Dilip Kumar, Deepak Sarmah, B. K. Singh, G. S. Prabhu, K. M. Chinnappa, S. N. Devaraju, and A.T. Poovaiah.

Other officials and political functionaries: M. K. Ranjithsinh, H. Y. Sharadaprasad, Gopalakrishne Gowda, M. Veerappa Moily, Ramakrishna Hegde, Kamal Nath, Suresh Prabhu, Jairam Ramesh, and Maneka Gandhi.

Colleagues associated with the Wildlife Conservation Society and the Centre for Wildlife Studies: George Schaller, John Robinson, William Conway, Alan Rabinowitz, Joshua Ginsberg, Liz Bennet, Tim O'Brien, Margaret Kinnaird, Dale Miquelle, Anak Pattanavibool, Cristian Samper, John Calvelli, Joe Walston, Kent Redford, Samba Kumar, Arjun Gopalaswamy, Devcharan Jathanna, G. Vishwanatha Reddy, Srinivas Vaidyanathan, Ajith Kumar, Avinash Sosale, Krithi Karanth, Chandan Pandey, Amarnath Javaji, Karthikeyan Srinivasan, Shridhar Bhat, and K. V. Phaniraj.

Scientist collaborators from external institutions: Mel Sunquist, Jim Nichols, John Seidensticker, R. Rudran, Brad Stith, J. Andrew Royle, Bob Dorazio, Jim Hines, Mohan Delampady, R. Sukumar, Uma Ramakrishnan, K. VijayRaghavan, Mahesh Rangarajan, Shiv Someshwar, and Satyajit Mayor.

Partners in conservation actions: Valmik Thapar, Brijendra Singh, Udaya Holla, Pandira Muthanna, Krishna Prasad Vajapeyam, H. N. A. Prasad, Praveen Bhargav, Niren Jain, D. V. Girish, Nachaiya Chittiappa, Thamoo Poovaiah, Satish Appachu, Palekanda Aiyanna, Shekar Dattatri, Bittu Sahgal, Mewa Singh, Manju Barua, Harsh and Poonam Dhanwatey, and Ramki Sreenivasan.

Long-term donors who have supported my work: Art Ortenberg, Irene Geary, Muneer Satter, J. Michael Cline, Indra and Raj Nooyi, Sumati Prabhu, Jayaram Bhat, Nina Rao, Vikram Nagaraj, Sunil Somalwar, and Udayan Das Roy.

Institutional support: Staff of Wildlife Conservation Society (WCS), Centre for Wildlife Studies (CWS), Department of Wildlife Ecology and Conservation, University of Florida, United States Fish and Wildlife Service, US Geological Survey–Patuxent Wildlife Research Center, Liz Claiborne–Art Ortenberg Foundation, World Wildlife Fund, Robertson Foundation, Exxon Save the Tiger Fund, Global Tiger Patrol, Ranthambore Foundation, Wildlife Conservation Trust, National Centre for Biological Sciences—Tata Institute of Fundamental Sciences (NCBS-TIFR), Manipal University, and the departments and agencies dealing with forests and wildlife, science and technology, and biotechnology in the Government of India and the Government of Karnataka.

There are far too many others who have assisted my work on and off the field at various stages, whom I am not able to individually acknowledge here because of constraints of space. I am grateful to them all.

BIBLIOGRAPHY

Brand, Stewart. *Whole Earth Discipline: An Ecopragmatist Manifesto*. New York: Viking Press, 2009.

Champion, Fredrick W. *With a Camera in Tiger-Land*. London: Chatto & Windus, 1928.

Gee, Edward P. *The Wild Life of India*. Glasgow, Scotland: Collins, 1964.

Joseph, Tony. *Early Indians: The Story of Our Ancestors and Where We Came From*. New Delhi: Juggernaut Books, 2018.

Karanth, K. Ullas, Malavika Kapur, and Kshama Rau. *Growing Up Karanth*. Chennai, India: Westland Books, 2021.

Karanth, Ullas, and James Nichols, eds. *Methods for Monitoring Tiger and Prey Populations*. Singapore: Springer, 2017.

Karanth, K. Ullas. *The Way of the Tiger: Natural History and Conservation of the Endangered Big Cat*. Beverly, Massachusetts: Voyageur Press, 2001.

Lovelock, James. *A Rough Ride to the Future*. New York: Abrams Press, 2016.

Nasser, Sylvia. *Grand Pursuit: The Story of Economic Genius*. New York: Simon & Schuster, 2011.

Sachs, Jeffrey. Common Wealth: Economics for a Crowded Planet. London: Penguin Books, 2009.

Schaller, George. B. *The Deer and the Tiger: A Study of Predator Prey Relations in India*. Chicago: University of Chicago Press, 1967.

Sunder, S. Shyam, and S. Parameswarappa. *Forest Conservation Concerns in India*. Uttarakhand, India: Bishen Singh Mahendra Pal Singh, 2014.

Sunquist, Fiona, and Melvin Sunquist. *Tiger Moon: Tracking the Great Cats in Nepal*. Chicago: University of Chicago Press, 1988.

Ward, Geoffrey C., and Diane R. Ward. *Tiger-Wallahs: Encounters with the Men Who Tried to Save the Greatest of the Great Cats*. New York: HarperCollins, 2000.

INDEX

Page numbers in *italics* refer to photographs.